I0756285

Memoirs of Marshal Oudinot
Duc de Reggio

Marshal Oudinot

Memoirs of Marshal Oudinot Duc de Reggio

Marshal of Napoleon During the Revolutionary Wars, the Consulate and First Empire

Eugénie de Coucy
Maréchale Oudinot, Duchesse de Reggio
and
Gaston Stiegler

Memoirs of Marshal Oudinot Duc de Reggio
Marshal of Napoleon During the Revolutionary Wars, the Consulate and First Empire
by Eugénie de Coucy
Maréchale Oudinot, Duchesse de Reggio
and
Gaston Stiegler

First published under the title
Memoirs of Marshal Oudinot Duc de Reggio

Leonaur is an imprint of Oakpast Ltd

ISBN: 978-0-85706-691-6 (hardcover)
ISBN: 978-0-85706-692-3 (softcover)

http://www.leonaur.com

Publisher's Notes

The opinions of the authors represent a view of events in which he was a participant related from his own perspective, as such the text is relevant as an historical document.

The views expressed in this book are not necessarily those of the publisher.

Contents

Chapter 1

Oudinot's Family

Nicolas Charles Oudinot sprang from the country of the Meuse, contiguous to Champagne and Lorraine, which the proximity of the foreigner and the constant threat of invasion keep in a perpetual fervour of patriotism. He was the son of a respectable brewer, and his uncle on the mother's side was M. Adam, Mayor of Bar-le-Duc, his native town. The house in which he was born, on the 25th of April 1767, is a dwelling of gloomy appearance, situated in the lower town, which contains the business quarters. The back of the house is washed by a canal which supplies the adjacent factories; the front opens upon the foot of a steep slope on which are perched houses which, at the summit, spread out and form the aristocratic streets of the upper town. Before the door, commences a tough and difficult ascent, in which large steps have been cut: this is known as the Road of the Eighty Stairs.

Young Charles's childhood was boisterous and undisciplined. He was kind-hearted, affectionate, and *sensible* (in the phrase of those times); but even then he displayed signs of the fiery and commanding character which he retained through life. His iron will, which gave him so invaluable a power of endurance and tenacity, was never ready to accept opposition or contradiction.

Later, he himself used to relate, in his familiar conversation, a comic anecdote showing the impetuousness of his nature. I repeat it in the words in which he told it; it goes back to the spring of 1794. Hebert, the substitute of the Public Prosecutor of the Commune, had ascended the scaffold on the 24th of March. His ideas found little favour in the eyes of Oudinot, who, although in the service of the Republic, held moderate opinions.

It was after my wound at Haguenau, (said the marshal). I returned from the army with a broken head, kept together only by the bandages, which almost blinded me. I was then colonel of the 4th Demi-Brigade, and was home on sick-leave, which I was spending with my father. One day there sat down to table with us a sort of relation. He came from Paris, where, I believe, he was something in business. He straightway began to talk politics. I did not say a word, but ate as one eats when he has been shattered.

Our Parisian went on exalting the revolutionary Commune, and telling a thousand horrors, until he began to boast of preserving as a relic a portion of Hebert's slipper. I continued silent, munching the bit of my indignation, but feeling my patience growing exhausted little by little. At last they put upon the table a great deep dish full of steaming haricot beans. It was as though I had received an inspiration: I put out my hand, took up the dish, and *whoosh!* sent the platterful of beans flying into the face of the friend of Hebert. I leave you to imagine what my father, most hospitable of men, must have thought! As for the Parisian, he got up and went out to wash his face.

This warmth of temper was not to decrease with advancing years. Eleven years later, in July 1805, at the camp at Boulogne, the Emperor was reviewing the Grenadiers, commanded by Oudinot. When the manoeuvres were completed, the general wished to march past Napoleon at the head of his troops. But his charger kicked under the spur, and refused to go forward. After a short struggle, Oudinot, in his exasperation, pierced its neck so violently with his sword that the restive brute fell in a heap to the ground. At dinner that night, at the Imperial table:

"Is that the way you treat your horses?" asked Napoleon.

"Sire, that is my way when I am not obeyed."

A nature so impetuous was incapable of enduring the sedentary existence which the young man's mother would have wished to see him lead by her side, a desire the more easily understood since Charles was the last survivor of her many children. He was intended for trade. But he had scarcely reached his seventeenth year when his irresistible call came, and in 1784 he enlisted in the regiment of Méedoc-Infantry, then garrisoned at Perpignan. He was fond of describing how he had mounted his first guard at the door of Marshal de Mailly. But after this separation, so painful to those who loved him, his affectionate deference to the solicitations of his mother brought him home again.

Oudinot was twenty when, for a time, he laid aside his uniform. His parents, still cherishing their dream of honest trade for him, sent him to Nancy in the hope that he would get used to business. But, unable to adapt himself to unsympathetic work, he returned to Bar, where the first advent of the Revolution soon gave him an opportunity of distinguishing himself. A company of paid troops, raised in that town in 1789, placed the former private in the Médoc Regiment at its head, with the rank of captain (14 July), and the new officer proved within a few days, by his decision and energy, how worthy he was of the choice.

Long privations, caused by two successive bad harvests, had cruelly harassed the population of Bar: the workshops were closed for want of work; there was a lack of provisions; food was hard to obtain at any price. A rich corn merchant called Pélissier, who was regarded as a monopolist, was held responsible for all the evil, and soon became the object of popular vengeance. Crossing the square in the upper town amid an excited and discontented crowd, he was suddenly threatened, assailed, and dragged off by a thousand arms. The clamours reached Oudinot, who was sitting quietly in his father's house in the lower town, far removed from and ignorant of the fray.

In a moment he was in the saddle; spurring his horse, and at the risk of breaking his neck, he climbed at a gallop the Road of the Eighty Stairs facing his house and leading to the upper town, where there was a danger to encounter and a human life to save. Although taking the shortest road, he came too late to prevent the murder of Pélissier; but he silenced the ringleaders by the firmness of his attitude and language, and appeased the crowd; and his intervention, by stopping the riot, doubtless prevented greater misfortunes (27 July).

Two months later, with that firm confidence which he had in the future, Captain Oudinot, although scarcely twenty-two years old, not rich, and far from foreseeing his dazzling future, married Mlle. Charlotte Derlin, who, possessed of no fortune, displayed a disinterestedness equal to his own, gave him twenty years of happiness, and became the mother of many children. We shall see later how the sons distinguished themselves in their father's career.

Each year brought Oudinot a fresh mark of the growing esteem in which he was held by his fellow-citizens. On the 6th of November 1790, he was made *chef de legion*, commanding the National Guard of the department. Later, when patriots sprang from every side to respond to the foreign threats against France, it was to him again that eyes were turned. Elected to the command of the 3rd Battalion of the Volunteers of the Meuse (6 September 1791), he soon won the affection of his men by his respect for justice and his kindly rule. Living in their midst, teaching them by his example, he succeeded in disciplining their courage, in animating them with the soldierly spirit with which he was impregnated, and in thoroughly preparing them for the gigantic combats that were to follow.

1792! The hour struck when the fruits of this care and foresight were to be garnered. The old world swooped down to crush the world that was springing into existence: the Prussians and Austrians, the vanguard and delegates of the rest of Europe, fell upon France: every patriot was on foot to resist them. The 3rd Battalion of the Meuse was sent to one of the most threatened points, the north-east frontier. Then commenced for Oudinot the intoxicating and terrible life that he adored, a life of abnegation, of cruel anguish and of exquisite joys, wherein he spent the exuberance of his activity.

For three years on end, winter and summer, he waged war between the Moselle and the Rhine, in the plains of Alsace or the wild region of the Vosges, wherever the fight was, thickest, tossed from danger to danger, disputing the ground foot by foot, advancing or retreating through precipitous mountain passes, victor and vanquished turn by turn, seizing Luxemburg and the Palatinate only to lose them again, alas! But only losing them to recapture them, and to recapture them once more, always keeping his men in hand and bringing them up to time, despising the party-cries that divide politicians, forgetting everything so that he might keep before his mind the great image of his country, and only returning to embrace his wife and his first-born in its cradle at rare intervals, when too serious a wound had made the sword drop from his crippled hand. And as he was in this his apprenticeship in war, so was he to remain throughout the course of his stormy career.

It is difficult to follow our hero step by step during the early part of these campaigns; nevertheless, we can mention the most important combats, gleaned from the records of the 3rd Battalion of the Meuse in the archives of the Ministry of War.

On the 25th of December 1792, the 3rd Battalion was under fire at Vaverenne, near Trèves. On the 9th of June 1793, it entered victorious into Arlon. On the 20th of September, it masked the town of Bitche, pursued the enemy, and harassed their retreat. On that day began for Oudinot the long series of wounds which were to stamp his sturdy frame with a network of scars: he received a sword-wound in the head. A month later, he revenged himself by a success at Saverne and encamped himself the next day in front of that town, at the foot of the hills, at Saint-Jean-des-Choux.

Conduct so valiant could not fail to draw attention to the young officer. A fortnight after, he was appointed colonel and placed in command of the 4th Demi-Brigade, which had just been enrolled out of one of the most brilliant factors of the old army, the Picardy Regiment. His companions in arms of the 3rd Battalion of the Meuse took leave of him with keen regret, of which valuable evidence remains in the shape of twelve addresses, all spontaneous, and drawn up by the soldiers in the ingenuous, turgid style of the period. With an inversion very characteristic of democracy, it was the subordinates who gave certificates to their superior officer. Here is a specimen which is touching in its undeniable accents of sincerity:

> Army of the Rhine, 3rd Battalion, 4th Demi-brigade.
>
> If to combine the courage of a soldier with the talents of a leader, the love of one's country and one's duty with an inveterate hatred of kings and tyranny, a constant profession of the purest principles with the practice of re-publican virtues, constitutes a claim to the gratitude of all good Republicans, the Grenadiers of the 3rd Battalion of the 4th Demi-Brigade of infantry bear witness that no one has a greater title to the regrets of his brothers-in-arms and the esteem of his fellow-citizens than Citizen Oudinot, their chief; that during the twenty-seven months he has been at their head, he has justified their choice and the expectations of the country; and that, while reigning over their hearts, the authority confided to him by the law has grown daily in his hands through the ascendancy which he derived from his proved intrepidity, his calm valour in the midst of danger, and all the qualities which endear an officer to his soldiers and make him precious in the eyes of the Republic.
>
> At the bivouac, on the heights of Saint-Jean-des-Choux, the 5th of November, Year II of the One and Indivisible Republic.

But very different was the spirit which animated the new officers subordinate to Oudinot, those of the Picardy Regiment, noblemen by birth and strongly attached to their recollections of former times.

They felt aggrieved at serving under a colonel of modest parentage, a leader whose merits they had not yet learned to appreciate. A dull feeling of discontent spread among them, and a number threatened to emigrate, as so many of their friends had already done. Warned of this hostility to his person, Oudinot sent for all the officers, and addressed them in these concise and manly terms:

> Gentlemen, is it because I do not bear an old name that you propose to desert me and to return to your former titled chiefs? Or do you think that I am too young to command you? Wait till the next engagement, and you shall judge for yourselves. If you then think that I bear myself badly under fire, I promise to hand over my command to the worthiest among you.

Need we say that, after the fight, none thought of repudiating a colonel so brave and already so experienced, in spite of his six and twenty years?

One day, in his old age, when he was relating this anecdote, someone remarked how he must have loved these brave men, who had been able so quickly to stifle their prejudices, and who had so fully given him their hearts. "Ah, you asked me if I loved them!" he exclaimed, eagerly. "I should think I did love them! I got them all killed!" To his mind the most enviable ending for a true soldier was a glorious death on the battlefield.

On the 27th of November, in the course of an offensive movement on the part of the Army of the Rhine, with the object of recapturing the lines of Wissembourg, a hot engagement took place in the woods surrounding Haguenau. Oudinot, who was fulfilling *ad interim* the functions of general, received a bullet in the head. The wound was so serious that three months later it had not yet healed, and Colonel Oudinot was compelled to go home to his family at Bar-le-Duc on sick-leave (24 February 1794).

He returned a little later, in time to save a division of the army of the Vosges, which, under the orders of General Ambert, was encamped at Kaiserslautern and connected our lines on the Moselle with those on the Rhine. It had been found necessary to weaken Kaiserslautern in order to reinforce the army of Sambre-et-Meuse; and Field-Marshal Möllendorf, taking advantage of this weakness, attacked this point with a superior force. We were obliged to give way. But Oudinot, who occupied the centre of the position at Morlautern, conducted the retreat so energetically, and led the rear-guard so surely through woods, gorges and defiles, that our soldiers were able to fall back in good order upon Pirmasens, where they established themselves firmly (2 June). It was there that the representatives of the people, a few days later, appointed him brigadier-general, in reward for this signal service. He was twenty-seven years of age.

Meanwhile, our armies were victorious in Holland and Luxemburg, and the honourable check encountered at Kaiserslautern was not enough to reduce us to the defensive. The corps to which Oudinot was attached was directed upon Trèves. But hardly had they come upon that place, when the young general fell from his horse, while leading a victorious charge against the enemy (11 August). The fall was so heavy as to break his leg. The fracture was very serious; the surgeons doubted whether it could ever be quite cured; and he beheld himself, in despair, removed, perhaps forever, from active service. So soon as he was able to stand up, he was appointed governor of the city he had helped to conquer. But his enfeebled condition did not even permit him to fulfil this sedentary office. In January 1795, he was obliged, as in the preceding-year, to apply for sick leave. The following hand-some certificate was handed him by one who was a good judge of men, General Moreau:

> A brave soldier, has great firmness, is possessed of a pure and well-proved patriotism, and fulfils the duties of his grade with zeal, intelligence, and distinction.
>
> Moreau,
>
> General commanding the Army of the Moselle.
>
> 25 *Nivose*, Year III (January 1795).

When Oudinot returned, after six months of wearying inaction, he had the satisfaction to find our troops victorious on every hand and masters of the left bank of the Rhine. He took up his post with Pichegru, who was preparing to cross the river. This operation took place on the 20th of September, before Manheim, which surrendered. But the absence of harmony in the movements of the different armies impeded our progress in that direction. The enemy attacked us to their advantage, on the night of the 18th of October, at Neckerau, where General Oudinot received five sword-strokes and was left lying on the field. The Austrians raised his blood-covered body with respect.

After a captivity of three months, which he underwent at Ulm, Oudinot was exchanged against Major-General Zainiau, who had been taken prisoner at Heidelberg. The treatment of his wounds compelled him to seek several months of repose, and when he returned to active service he was so weak that they would only give him the command of the fortified place of Phalsbourg (2 June 1796). But his talents were not made to remain hidden in this obscure post. Never satiated nor discouraged, his ardour thirsted for the fight, for danger, for glory. The occasion was favourable to him.

Our armies had invaded Germany. He begged permission to hasten to the battlefields, and early in July he received leave to join Moreau, who had crossed the Rhine and was marching up the valley of the Necker. The army had entered Bavaria. Oudinot, after occupying Nordlingen, Donauwert and Neuburg, was instructed to invest Ingolstadt, on the Danube. Attacked during the investment by General Latour, and obliged to replace his chief Delmas, who was wounded at the commencement of the action, he withstood the attack at Neuburg for more than six hours with unflinching resolution: a bullet in the thigh, three sword-cuts in the neck and a fourth on the arm were scarcely able to tear him from the field (14 September).

After a month's nursing, and still covered with contusions, he returned in time to assist Moreau in his glorious retreat, which is celebrated as equal to a victory. At Ettenheim, men wondered to see him charge the enemy with his arm in a sling, and force them to fall back. Then, after again passing, at Brissach, that deceptive line of the Rhine which we were always crossing without ever remaining masters of both banks, he crossed Alsace with crushing speed, masked Landau, recaptured the defences of Queich and Spirebach, reconquered the Palatinate, in which he had already so greatly distinguished himself in former years, and pushed on to Oggersheim, opposite Manheim. There he completely defeated the Austrians in the battle of the 7th of November, which permitted him to winter at Grunstadt, in the heart of the country, where he remained during the year 1797.

Surely a marvellous military career! One can picture nothing finer than this commander always in the front rank, risking his life in the *mêlée*, never intimidated, flying to wherever the danger was thickest, venturing into hand-to-hand conflicts at the sword's point, and purchasing his steps with the blood from his wounds. And yet these wounds, which placed him so high in the general estimation, were bound on the other hand to delay his advancement. They removed him for long periods from his command; he seemed, so to speak, to appear only to vanish again from the battlefield, and the army was too often deprived of his services. Had he been less unlucky under fire, and able to lead his men continuously, he would perhaps more speedily, if not with more brilliancy, have attained the supreme rank which he was only to receive very late and in times of disaster.

At last, the Italian campaign and the Treaty of Campo-Formio put a stop, at least temporarily, to the war; but a secret convention of the Congress of Rastadt having granted us Mayence and the head of the Bridge of Manheim, on condition that we should seize it by force, Oudinot was charged with the execution of this stroke upon ground so familiar to him, a commission of which he satisfactorily acquitted himself (25 January 1798).

It seems as though such success through six years of fighting should have earned us peace, under the shelter of that belt of the Rhine now become inviolable; but British jealousy refused to recognize our extension of territory, and the Directory, in order to strike a blow at a constantly hostile influence, prepared to invade Great Britain. Oudinot was sent to the army which was being organised in Normandy, and arrived at Coutances in March. His stay was as short as the dream, no sooner imagined than effaced, of that famous descent. He soon returned to Mayence, and remained on the lookout before our questionable neighbours.

The truce did not last long, and this time there marched against us, from the depths of Europe, enemies hitherto unknown. At the end of 1798, Oudinot was ordered to proceed, under Masséna's command, to Switzerland, where, in the course of the following spring, the greater part of this gigantic campaign was to be enacted. The Army of Helvetia, which had boldly advanced to the eastern shore of Lake Constance, attempted to join hands with Jourdan, who was engaged on the Danube. In order to effect this junction, it was necessary to open up a passage straight through the Vorarlberg, past Feldkirch, a sort of narrow, marshy and almost impracticable gorge, sunk in the breast of the most rugged mountains on either side of the current of the Ill. It was to Oudinot's imperturbable devotion that this thankless task was confided.

On the 6th of March 1799, he attacked, made six hundred prisoners, and all but passed. On the 15th, he again delivered a fruitless assault. On the 23rd, he succeeded in fording the Ill, advanced over that frightful ground, in spite of a hail-storm of bullets, grape, and round shot, in spite of the rocks which the peasants rolled like avalanches from the mountain-tops; but he lost three thousand men before his obstinacy could make any impression upon those impregnable rocks.

Masséna saw all the advantage to be gained from a man of this extraordinary energy; he made him a general of division, and soon after appointed him chief of staff.

But it was not possible to keep the offensive, at least for the time. The army entrenched itself in a strong position behind the River Limmat, which issues from the Lake of Zurich, and showed that it did not mean to allow itself to be easily dislodged from this line of defence. This was proved by the engagements of the 24th of May and 4th of June, in which General Oudinot took a glorious part. In the latter he was struck by a ball in the chest.

It was at this time that the Army of Helvetia was enforced by the arrival of an unexpected recruit. Oudinot had a son, quite a young child, who was always in his thoughts. In order to inure him to the hardships of war, and to train him to the service of his country, he thought he could not do better than give him his own example and that of his soldiers, and allow him to mingle in the camp duties and the fortunes of the battlefield. Young Victor, destined himself one day to become General Oudinot, to capture Rome and re-establish the Papal power, was noted for the Corps of Guides in June 1799-although he had not yet completed his eighth year. Mounted on a pony, he gravely went through his duties, with a droll and attractive rigidity; and though occasionally interrupting this severe schooling in order to play at marbles with bullets, he hardened his little body and tempered his spirit in these terrific combats, to the echo of the cannon reverberating through the Alps.

On the 14th of August, at Schwitz, Oudinot stopped the Austrians and their peasant levies, who were threatening to turn our rear while we were making head to the Russians; and on charging at the head of a regiment of Dragoons, he received a bullet in the shoulder.

Meanwhile, the position of the army became daily more critical. Inferior in numbers, threatened on the north by the Russians under Korsakoff, on the east by the Austrians under Hotze, and on the south by the Russians under Souwaroff, it became necessary to burst through this iron girdle, which every day drew closer around it. Masséna first attacked Korsakoff, who was on the right bank of the Limmat, and occupied Zurich. He entrusted to Oudinot, who was in command of a corps of fifteen thousand men, the task of crossing the river, swarming up the right bank, and surrounding the town. So well did Oudinot take his measures, so prompt and secret were his movements, that he broke up the camp at Houg, forestalled the Russians on the road to Winterthur, which was ardently disputed, and succeeded in cutting off their retreat. Then, next day, he returned on his steps, and after a terrible combat, although receiving a bullet in his chest, he took Zurich by storm, and there rejoined his general-in-chief. Korsakoff was crushed (26 September).

A fortnight later Oudinot made himself master of Constance, which was defended not only by the Austrians, but also by the French emigrants, the last remnants of Condé's army. This event gave him an opportunity to display that greatness of heart and that spirit of moderation and clemency which so happily tempered his hot-headed character.

The emigrants, who had been taken prisoners to the number of about two hundred, expected to be shot as traitors to their country, as others had been before them, especially in the early days of the Revolution. So little hope had they of mercy, that one of them, addressing Urbain, one of the *aides-de-camp*, said:

"Before I am put to death, I should like to make a request of the Prince de Condé."

Urbain, who knew his chief, flew into a rage:

"For what do you take my general, *monsieur?*" he cried. "Do you think it is his custom to massacre his prisoners?"

Certainly, it was impossible for a patriot like Oudinot to love Frenchmen who had taken up arms against France, and he had shown his feelings some years before when he kept back the officers of the Picardy Regiment. Nevertheless, he was not contented on this occasion to spare the lives of the offenders: he had the further generosity to wish to save them from the punishments in store for them if they returned to their country. It was impossible to release them openly. He determined to wink at their escape, and sent them to Masséna under an inadequate escort. Almost all availed themselves of this chance, straggled on the road, and found means to escape. The general-in-chief employed the same artifice in sending those who reached him to Besançon, and when the soldiers arrived at their destination, they came empty-handed.

This Swiss campaign, which saved France from an invasion, is the most memorable of those in which Oudinot had taken part to the time which this narrative has reached. Masséna wrote in his report to the Directory:

> I owe the greatest praise to General Oudinot, my chief of staff, who knows how to apply his fiery energy to clerical labour,

> but whom I am always glad to have back on the battlefield. He has followed me in everything, and has made a perfect second in command.

He also wrote Oudinot the following letter:

> Headquarters, Zurich, 9 *Brumaire*, Year VIII.
> (31 October 1799).
>
> The Executive of the Directory has expressed to the Army of the Danube, in its letter of the 22nd of *Vendemiaire* last, the recognition of the public, and its private satisfaction, at the Army's glorious achievements from the 3rd to the 18th of the same month. The Directory has also been pleased to extend its notice to those who have so bravely contributed to them.
>
> How eagerly I seize this opportunity, my dear general, to refer once more to the energy, bravery and intelligence with which you have seconded me, not on one occasion only: you were everywhere. Accept at once the assurance of the public recognition, of the satisfaction of the Government, and of my personal esteem and attachment. I feel sure that you will consider this the most gratifying reward for your invaluable services.
>
> With friendly greetings,
>
> Masséna.

After a leave of five months, necessary for the cure of his numerous wounds, Oudinot rejoined the Army of Liguria under the orders of Masséna, who wished again to make sure of his "invaluable services" as chief of staff. This time the task set him was a very difficult one, and unattended by much hope of victory. He was to immure himself in Genoa, so as to keep idle around him a proportion of the Austrian forces, and thus enable the young master of France, Bonaparte, now First Consul, to hurl the thunderbolt of Marengo. It was a work of sheer self-sacrifice.

The small French division was bottled up in the fortress on the 6th of April 1800, between the Austrian troops, who crowned the mountains, and the British squadron, which blockaded the port. It would not be possible to describe here in detail this famous siege, with its sorties, its incessant combats, the sufferings of the inhabitants, the riots of women, the endurance of the soldiers, the famine, the necessity of eating uneatable things, herbs, unclean beasts, and, under the illusive name of bread, a mysterious compound of starch, linseed and cocoa.

Oudinot distinguished himself among the most indefatigable. He even risked leaving the city, under the most venturesome conditions, to go him-self in search of news of General Suchet, who was engaged on the Var, and to carry him his orders. On the 16th of May, a *bark*, commanded by a *corsair* called Bavastro, bore him boldly through the English fleet, risking, a hundred times, capture or destruction. In spite of all, he got ashore at Finale, accomplished his errand, and returned to Genoa to resume, amid his companions, his post of want and famine.

An episode related by Oudinot himself describes the horrible situation of the city:

> We made three thousand prisoners at the time when the famine was raging at its worst. I took the orders of the general-in-chief, and wrote to General Ott, who commanded the hostile army, describing the condition in which his men would be in consequence of our own predicament. The Austrian replied that, as the town was shortly about to be captured, the prisoners would not have time to starve.
>
> The famine grew more and more oppressive. I wrote again, and during six weeks, each of my renewed messages received the same reply. At the end of that time, not a single prisoner was left alive: the poor wretches, imprisoned in a ship at anchor, had begun by eating the rigging and their shirts, and ended by eating one another.
>
> We ourselves were reduced to such a state of distress that our soldiers were glad to eat the straw of the hospitals. Soon this last resource gave out, and we were only able to keep up our strength by drinking the generous wines which we discovered in quantities in the cellars of the town. One saw sentinels, unable to hold themselves erect, mounting guard seated in gilt armchairs, and drinking claret in their misery.
>
> In 1815, when I met the Emperor of Austria, I learnt from his lips that the disaster of these three thousand men had been turned against me. I then informed him of the truth, and offered to let him verify the facts from my letter-books. The emperor refused to examine them and accepted my word.

In the end, lest he should undergo the same fate, Masséna had to resolve to evacuate the town. Famished, reduced by half, but still terrible, the soldiers, or rather their ghosts, issued proudly forth, and retained their freedom. They made use of this to rejoin Suchet's army.

Ten days later, the victory of Marengo having led to an armistice,

Oudinot went to Bar-le-Duc to restore his health shattered by so many trials, returning to his post in Italy, under the orders of Brune, in November, at the commencement of hostilities.

The army advanced eastwards across Lombardy, driving the Austrians before them, who entrenched themselves on the left bank of the Mincio in order to dispute its passage. The attack was delivered upon two points, first at Pozzolo, and the next day at Monzembano (26 December). It was there that Oudinot, seeing one of the enemy's batteries crushing our troops from the top of an eminence and paralyzing the movement, collected some Chasseurs of the 14th Regiment, rushed with them upon the bridge, crossed it, leapt upon the Austrians, overturned them, drove them to flight, himself took possession of a gun, and by this bold exploit enabled Boudet's division to come up, thus assuring the success of a manoeuvre the issue of which had till then remained uncertain.

On the 30th of December, Brune wrote to the First Consul:

> General Oudinot has sabred the enemy's gunners at their pieces. Would you not think it right to bestow some honourable distinction on him?

In the sequel, Oudinot, when sent to Paris with the text of the armistice signed by the belligerents on the 16th of January 1801, was received in the most flattering manner by Bonaparte, who presented him with a sword of honour and with the piece of ordnance which he had so nobly carried off.

During the years that followed, France, satiated with battle and military glory, hoped to enjoy a lasting peace. Oudinot was appointed inspector of infantry, and then inspector of cavalry, and was able at intervals to seek rest at home, without being driven to do so by the care of his wounds. In 1802 he lost his mother, and in the same year he began his political career, and was elected by his fellow-citizens to the presidency of the electoral college of the Meuse.

The formation of the camp at Boulogne gave him the command of a corps, under the orders of his old friend General Davout. He assisted for the second time in the preparations for that chimerical descent upon England, the idea of which carried away Napoleon as it had before seduced Hoche and the Directory. Two years of hard work were spent in the organization of infinite details, to which his versatile intellect lent itself as readily as to the leading of men under fire.

It is here that we first meet with a person of modest condition,

Oudinot's *valet-de-chambre*, who deserves mention because of his extraordinary devotion to his master, the fidelity with which he followed him through all his campaigns, and the memoirs which he left behind him, memoirs of no literary value, but sincere and refreshing in their very simplicity. This worthy man, Pils by name, was an Alsacian. Oudinot met the lad in camp, took an interest in him, and attached him to his person. He followed the general wherever he went, even under fire; and as he had no business there, he concealed himself as much as possible, slipping in among the officers of the staff, for fear of a scolding.

One day, Pils, who had ventured out as usual, in spite of his master's orders, had his horse killed under him. Oudinot saw in this circumstance the occasion for a peremptory argument which would for good prevent his servant from exposing himself.

"You see you are killing my horses," he said, with apparent roughness. "I forbid you positively to return."

In the next battle, the incorrigible Pils was behind his master.

"I thought I had forbidden you to come back!"

"Oh, general, I don't deserve any reproaches; the horse belongs to me: I bought it out of my savings!"

Pils, for that matter, had a mission in life: he knew that "the Governor," [1] as Oudinot was affectionately called by his officers, was almost regularly wounded in every engagement, and Pils made it his business to carry a case of instruments, so as to be able to apply the first dressings at once. On the other hand, as he had a great natural taste for drawing, he liked to plant himself in a corner of the battlefield, take from his pocket a note-book and pencil, and calmly sketch the scene of action and the action itself with ingenuous awkwardness but striking precision. When peace was made, Pils endeavoured to commence his artistic education; he was admitted to Horace Vernets studio, but was never able to learn the first elements of art, or to achieve correctness of drawing.

However, he transmitted more easily cultivated natural gifts to his son—Isidore Pils—whose well-known picture, "Rouget de l'Isle for the first time declaiming the *Marseillaise*," has been so often reproduced. Isidore papered the walls of his studio with his father's daubs, and either in comparison of their quick spontaneity with his own somewhat frigid art, or from respectful piety, used to say:

"My father was more of a painter than I."

---

1. *Le Patron*.—A.T. de M.

Chapter 2

The First Austrian Campaign

Time passed by at the camp of Boulogne, the bad season approached, and the descent upon England became more and more perilous. Suddenly Napoleon abandoned the idea, changed his plans, and hurled upon Central Europe the whole of the formidable machinery which he had been building up so laboriously during the past two years. Oudinot set out for Germany at brief notice (16 August 1805), proud at commanding the finest, most warlike and most famous troops in the army. He had been placed at the head of the Grenadiers whom Junot had formed at Arras the year before. These consisted of carefully chosen veterans, proved in numerous campaigns, of tall stature, thoroughly disciplined, irreproachable in their drill, and embodying in their own persons the summit of the military spirit. They could be told at a distance by their imposing appearance as well as their new uniform: they had replaced the old-fashioned busby by the sober *shako*, and the long, powdered pig-tail by close-cropped hair. They reached Strasburg in September with their commander.

The army advanced into Germany with such rapidity, mystery and suddenness that they were well into Bavaria before the Austrians suspected the direction they had taken. On the 7th of October, the advance corps, and Oudinot with them, were on the right bank of the Danube, ascending the stream in order to cut off Mack's retreat and imprison him in Ulm. On the 8th, they encountered the Austrian advance posts at Wertigen; the shock was an ardent one; the enemy was pursued by our Dragoons, but retired in fighting order and concentred upon a plateau in a solid mass, which our cavalry could not succeed in breaking through. Finally Murat attacked the front square, while the Grenadiers charged impetuously upon the flank. Everything yielded before them: two thousand prisoners, two flags and eleven guns were the result of the day's fighting. The campaign opened with a success in which Oudinot played a prominent part. The Grenadiers, in their enthusiasm, nicknamed him "their father."

Ten days later, Mack was reduced to capitulating in Ulm, whence the Archduke Ferdinand escaped with difficulty with twenty thousand men. Murat and Oudinot, rushing in pursuit, harassed him incessantly to Nordlingen, and took twelve thousand prisoners.

The Russians, who had not arrived in time to support Mack, hastily retired towards Vienna, pressed by Murat, Lannes and Oudinot, who joined their rear-guard upon the right bank of the Danube at Amstetten, on the border of Upper and Lower Austria (4 November). Thus Oudinot found himself once more confronting the Russians, for the first time since the Battle of Zurich, where he had crushed them six years previously. They were astride the Vienna road, their wings overrunning on either side into the forest.

The following details of the operations are taken from a manuscript of Oudinot's:

The division of the grenadiers, unsupported by artillery and preceded by its light cavalry and two hundred *carabineers*, bore down upon Furnbach, where was a corps consisting of three Russian and Austrian battalions, who were forthwith attacked by the two hundred *carabineers* alone, pending the arrival of the column. French pluck made up for deficiency in numbers. In spite of his obstinate resistance, the enemy was dislodged from this important position and retreated toward Strenberg. There the ground was disputed foot by foot and carried after three *mêlées* with the Russian Hussars, who were forced to yield once again before the valour of the grenadiers. The hostile troops fell back upon the main Russian army, consisting of some twenty battalions drawn up under Bukaufen. This junction induced the enemy to take the offensive, and he began to manoeuvre upon our flanks.

Soon General Dupas arrived with his brigade, and the engagement spread to all the troops. The enemy's artillery, which had not yet come into sight, began to make itself heard, and Dupas was charged by several masses of Russians. They were calmly received by his brigade, which withstood the shock and kept up a well-sustained fire. As night drew near, Oudinot felt the necessity for a fresh attack, and determined to move forward General Ruffin's brigade, which, together with that commanded by Dupas, charged the enemy, overthrew him, and compelled him to leave the field in our possession. In this engagement the position was taken and retaken three times at the point of the bayonet.

The enemy received our several attacks with great resolution; its own were pluckily delivered, but the courage of the grenadiers prevailed.

The fight at Amstetten was of great importance, not on account of the numbers engaged on either side, but because it cleared the road to Vienna, the enemy having abandoned the right bank of the Danube. Entrenched behind the powerful protection of this mighty river, the Austro-Russians thought themselves in safety, and, in order completely to separate themselves from us, had only to destroy the last bridge standing before the gates of the capital. This bridge, the Thabor-Brücke, was built of wood, and spanned the principal arm of the river, on the further side of a group of small islands. It had been covered with fascines and powder-barrels, so that it might easily be set on fire at the slightest signal. Moreover, it was defended by some thousands of men, and by cannon on the left bank.

Murat, Lannes and Oudinot, always in the van, were the first to enter Vienna. They very soon understood that neither strength nor courage would suffice to take this precious means of passage intact. Nevertheless, at about 11 o'clock in the morning of the 13th of November, the column of the grenadiers, preceded by Murat and Lannes, noiselessly entered upon the labyrinth of islands, and easily reached the Thabor Bridge, which stretched its length before them. Lannes crossed it, accompanied by a few officers, reached the other side, asked to speak to Count von Auersberg, the commander of the Austrian forces, and endeavoured to persuade him that we were no longer at war with the Austrians, but only with the Russians, an assertion which the armistice demanded by Giulay rendered fairly probable.

While the enemy's attention was diverted by these parleys, Oudinot and his grenadiers advanced briskly upon the bridge, flinging into the water as they went all the inflammable material heaped up under the arches. The passage had already been three parts effected when the command to "Fire!" rang out from the Austrian side. A moment more, and the guns would have been discharged and the grenadiers drowned beneath the sunken bridge. Lannes darted towards the gunners, argued with them, persuaded them, and stopped them. Oudinot and his men completed their crossing at the charge, sprang upon the left bank, and snatched the matches from the hands of the men who had been about to fire.

The Thabor Bridge was saved, and the French themselves were the most surprised to find themselves masters of it without having fired a shot, thanks to this sudden and perilous artifice, which served to display once more the imperturbable coolness of the grenadiers and their leader.

This obstacle overcome, the army marched northwards, and came up with the Russians under Prince Bagration at Hollabrünn. Though it was winter, the battle commenced towards the close of daylight, at three o'clock in the afternoon. The shock was one of extraordinary severity, thanks to the tenacity displayed by both sides, the prolongation of the fighting into the closest darkness and the consequent confusion.

A regiment of grenadiers posted in front of the village of Schöngraben, at three hundred paces from the Russians, hurled itself upon the latter after a heavy fire; the Russians very coolly held their ground, and bayonets were crossed around the village, which was soon in flames, set on fire by the shells. A second regiment hastened up to support the first, and overturned the enemy, who seemed to contemplate a turning movement on their right. In order to prevent this movement, and to endeavour to block the road to Znaïm in the rear, two brigades groped forward in the darkness; they got lost in a ground intersected with ravines, streamlets and marshes, and were forced to take an oblique direction. Sebastiani's Dragoons, who led the way, struck upon a mass of infantry, without knowing if they were friends or foes. It was only by the light of a musket volley that they were seen to be Russians.

The French charged, made way through the enemy, and continued their march, without perceiving that they had left behind them a troop of the enemy, which revealed its presence with volleys of grapeshot. A fresh charge destroyed it, and robbed it of its cannon; while the grenadiers continued to advance, but without meeting any adversaries, and ventured into a village with dark, deserted and silent streets. This silence, which astonished them, caused them to scent an ambuscade; they drew back and then returned, while the Russians, who had been lurking in the houses, suddenly rushed out, roaring like wild beasts, and striking furiously.

It was impossible to fire in the scrimmage. The men knocked against shadowy forms, recognizable only when they spoke, through the difference in language; they threw themselves upon one another with their side-arms; they cut each other's throats without seeing one another, and the carnage did not cease until eleven at night. The ground remained with the grenadiers, and the next morning, at daybreak, they counted six thousand nine hundred Russians killed, wounded or prisoners. Oudinot, who received a bullet in his thigh during the action, continued nevertheless to give his orders until the end (16 November).

He had to return to Vienna, by Napoleon's orders, to nurse his wound; but two weeks later, knowing that a great decisive battle was imminent, he hastened to Moravia to resume his post. It was two days before Austerlitz.

"Your courage is beyond your strength," said the emperor to him. "I shall give your grenadiers to Duroc, and you can stay with me."

In spite of these instructions, Oudinot was unable to leave his dear *troupe d'élite.* Towards the close of the action, the grenadiers vigorously supported the attack upon the village of Kobelnitz and captured an important column of the enemy.

A victory so complete necessarily entailed the conclusion of peace: a treaty was signed at Schönbrunn on the 15th of December, and the French army, which had crossed the huge territory situated between the German ocean and the confines of Hungary, without stopping except to fight, was at length able to breathe and to return home. It was a triumphant and yet painful march, in the middle of winter, across frozen plains and mountains covered with snow. Oudinot, though still in the convalescent stage, endured the journey with as much good-humour as energy, and arrived at Strasburg uncertain what his next command would be. He was not left long in doubt. After no more than a fortnight's respite, the emperor entrusted him with a very novel mission, half military and half civil, requiring tact and prudence, and a great sense of justice and conciliation.

By a clause of the treaty of Schönbrunn, Prussia ceded the Principality of Neuchâtel to the emperor, who presented it to his chief of staff, Alexandre Berthier. Oudinot was ordered to occupy the country in the name of the latter. He set out with his grenadiers at the end of winter, and crossed the Jura by roads so bad that it was necessary to clear them expressly for the artillery, and that sometimes as many as twelve horses were not sufficient to draw his carriage. At the last halting-place the latter broke down: he had to mount his horse, and the train did not reach the Chaux de Fonds until two o'clock in the morning.

The next day, the 18th of March 1806, Oudinot made his state entry into the city of Neuchâtel.

The population of the country, attached to their former princes by long custom, were hostile to the newcomers. The authorities observed a frigid and dignified attitude, but the townsfolk, alarmed at this military display, dreading the exactions too common among soldiers, and jealous of their customs, laws and liberties, showed their mistrust by staying at home.

The general had sufficient penetration to grasp this difficult situation, and sufficient nobility of heart to respect such natural sentiments. He reassured the citizens as to their rights, and guaranteed them against any arbitrary demands or taxes; he left the administration of the police and of justice in their hands; and he succeeded so well in respecting their lawful susceptibilities that their minds were, in a very short time, won over in favour of the French. One fortunate measure of tolerance assured the entire sympathy of their dispositions. Napoleon, in his eternal duel with England, had formally prohibited the purchase of English merchandise: wherever any British goods were introduced, they were confiscated and ruthlessly burnt, and this meant ruin to the trade of the people of Neuchâtel, who carried on a considerable commerce with Great Britain. Oudinot listened to their complaints with kindness, examined them, forwarded them to the court of the Tuileries through the intermediary of Hutin, his *aide-de-camp*, and his credit was great enough to move his master's will and to obtain a modification of the Imperial rigour, which saved a number of fortunes.

The gratitude of the inhabitants showed itself in his election to the honorary freedom of the city of Neuchâtel, a privilege the more noteworthy inasmuch as it involved the abrogation of a clause in the municipal constitution which formally denied all rights of citizenship to members of the Roman Catholic religion, to which Oudinot belonged.

He left Neuchâtel on the 18th of July, loaded with the blessings of the people. His stay in France was a short one. Napoleon recalled the grenadiers, who had been dispersed, restored to them the chief under whom they had so greatly distinguished themselves, and joined these picked troops to his own Guards. They went through the Prussian campaign and were present as reserves at the Battle of Jena, but without taking part in the action.

The end of the year was employed in the boldest march that had yet been attempted. We had no longer the Prussians only against us, but also the Russians, who had entered into an alliance with them. At the commencement of 1807 we were occupying Poland, and Oudinot was placed beyond Warsaw, at Ostrolenka, on the bank of the Narew, in the midst of an inhospitable country bristling with forests and swamped in marshes. Napoleon had given him this dangerous post so that he might cover his right wing while he himself went north and attacked Eastern Prussia and endeavoured to force the enemy into the Baltic, a result which the sanguinary Battle of Eylau was far from producing.

Almost at the same time, Oudinot was warned of an approaching attack of the Russians, who were threatening Warsaw from both banks of the Narew. His constant, restless vigilance saved him from a surprise; for, on going his rounds of inspection, he found his sentries grown torpid with the cold and slumbering under the Russian muskets. The action began the next morning (15 February) at daybreak with a very lively discharge of artillery, followed by an engagement between the enemy's infantry, which wanted to enter Ostrolenka, and a brigade of grenadiers commanded by General Ruffin, who was entrenched behind the churchyard firing grape-shot. Campana's brigade, which was on the other bank of the Narew, crossed the bridge to lend assistance, when its chief was cut in two by a cannon-ball. In spite of this loss, the two brigades were able to join forces and to drive out the Russians, who were already penetrating into the streets of Ostrolenka. Oudinot and Suchet arrived in person; the first at the head of the cavalry led a most brilliant charge, which completed the victory: two thousand five hundred Russians were left on the field of battle, and we took two flags and seven guns.

This long and arduous Polish campaign seems, when one remembers the distance of its basis of operations, the nature of the ground, the resistance of the enemy and the difficulties of every kind, to have been as it were a prelude to the fatal Russian war.

Meanwhile, the emperor, annoyed at not having yet put an end to the war, felt the need of reducing the extent of his lines and of better assuring the safety of his rear, while retaining his hold upon Warsaw. He concentrated his army upon the Lower Vistula, recalled Oudinot to Ostorode, in Eastern Prussia, and ordered Marshal Lefebvre to lay siege to Dantzig. The place was strongly fortified and well defended; the work of the besiegers proceeded slowly; the French were few in number. After more than one arduous conflict, which led to no immediate result, Lefebvre asked for reinforcements, and Oudinot was sent to his assistance with the grenadiers. He arrived on the 3rd of May and set up his headquarters at Langfurt.

On the 14th the Russians attempted a sortie; it was little more than an alarm. But Oudinot, always disdainful of danger, once more played the common soldier: he pushed forward with his officers, and on entering a little wood, he suddenly saw a Russian non-commissioned officer spring from behind a tree, and, with a thrust of his bayonet, pierce the breast of Colonel Magnac: the general ran up to him, and killed him with his own hand.

The next day he had the singular good fortune to capture a ship with his foot-soldiers. The sloop *Dauntless*, belonging to the British squadron which was cruising in the Baltic, was trying to revictual Dantzig, and under cover of a thick morning fog, which rendered her utterly invisible, she imprudently sailed up the canal which joins the fortress to the sea. But the sun soon scattered the fog, the presence of the vessel was revealed to all, and as the wind had fallen, she stopped short, spreading her useless sails, incapable of stirring, and as easy a prey to our soldiers as a stranded whale is to the fishermen. After a few volleys of musketry, the *Dauntless* hauled down her flag.

Meanwhile, the Russians received by sea the succour which they had so long been awaiting, and the moment had come for them to make a supreme effort. One night, at three o'clock, they issued from the fort of Weichslemunde, to the number of eight thousand, in four columns, to attempt to destroy our works and pierce our lines. They attacked them with extraordinary vigour: driven back with grapeshot, and pursued at the point of the bayonet, they returned stubbornly to the redoubts, only to be driven back again. Their obstinacy was such, and so great their need to break through the circle which hemmed them in, that they formed themselves again for a last effort in mass, and once more hurled themselves upon us.

Lannes and Oudinot saw that this affair was to decide whether the city of Dantzig was to be taken or delivered: they hurried into the thick of the fighting, and the irresistible Oudinot, charging at the head of a battalion of grenadiers, forced his way into the enemy's squares like a wedge. A scrimmage ensued; he pushed forward; his horse was killed under him by a bullet; his soldiers, seeing him fall, took alarm; but he sprang up again, all shouted, "Hurrah for the General!" while he, never disconcerted, continued to lead them on foot. They gained ground little by little. The Russians, astonished, gave way, and finally retreated, pricked on by our bayonets, to the walls of the fort of Weichslemunde, where they enclosed themselves, and capitulated a few days later. On the 26th of May, the French army was mistress of Dantzig.

Oudinot waited for a fortnight at Marienburg, and then received orders to march rapidly eastwards, in order to catch up the Russians, who, after a lively attack and an unforeseen resistance, were retreating in good order with a view to saving Königsberg. The advance-guard, consisting of ten thousand men, was commanded by Marshal Lannes and himself. On the 13th of June, in the evening, they arrived at Donnau and perceived that they were almost in contact with the whole of the hostile army, whose bivouac fires could be seen three leagues away in the direction of the village of Friedland on the River Alle. Oudinot made all the arrangements to place his men to advantage, did not return to his quarters until eleven o'clock, ordered his horse for two o'clock in the morning, and threw himself in full uniform on his bed.

At two o'clock he was in the saddle, under a sky as bright as it usually is in countries of high latitude, and recognized the enemy's strong position. To set a handful of men against the whole Russian army with any hope of victory was not to be thought of; but it was possible to occupy the village of Posthenen, the little wood of Sortlack, and the heights commanding the Alle, in such a way as to bar the road to Königsberg. They would thus compel the Russians to await the arrival of the French army, and then to give battle with a river at their backs, a very disadvantageous position.

The firing began at three o'clock in the morning, and was vigorously kept up until seven. The advance-guard was exhausting itself in this unequal conflict, when at that moment Marshal Mortier appeared with the divisions commanded by Nansouty, Dupas and Verdier, bringing up the total of the French to twenty-six thousand men: not many to oppose to seventy-five thousand! But the ground was favourable, and it was defended by heroes. They held firm until noon, when Napoleon appeared with the main body of his army. His officers hastened to him. Oudinot, his uniform riddled with bullets and his horse dripping with blood, was eager to complete what he had so brilliantly undertaken:

"Quick, Sire," he said; "my grenadiers can hold out no longer: but give me reinforcements, and I'll pitch all the Russians into the water."

They were in full force. Napoleon wished the troops to have a moment's respite, of which they stood in great need after a forced march and nine hours' fighting; and at four o'clock in the afternoon the battle recommenced. At six o'clock the village of Friedland was carried, all in flames; the bridges over the Alle were destroyed, and the Russians drowned in attempting to cross the river at the fords or in spots filled up with accumulations of carriages, waggons, men and horses. The last shot was fired at midnight.

Oudinot was not able to take a direct part in this second half of the battle, in spite of his expressed desire. The emperor ordered that his grenadiers, who were half destroyed, should remain in the second line: they had done enough for one day, inasmuch as their invincible tenacity and courage had kept the Russians at bay and made the great decisive action possible. None the less, even in the second line, they were very much exposed and suffered severely from the effects of the artillery. Oudinot's horse had its leg broken, and his *aide-de-camp* Hutin, by his side, had his face grazed so closely by a cannon-ball that he lost his breath, choked, and fell down dead.

Peace was signed at Tilsit on the 7th of July, and Oudinot went to take up his quarters at Dantzig. He divided his time between the cares of his army and the society of his fellow-officers, and led a quiet and often festive existence, giving and attending very gay parties. These included Marshals Soult, Mortier and others, like the grave Davout; and together, satiated with combats of ever-increasing grandeur and horror, they forgot the spectacles of death that they had lately witnessed, and relaxed their minds with youthful follies and subalterns' diversions; in the evenings they would amuse themselves, in the magnificent apartments in which they gave their receptions, in putting out the candles with pistol-bullets. Fortunately the damage done was always paid for with magnificent generosity.

But fate, which seemed to bear a grudge against Oudinot's body, prevented him from enjoying a long repose. On the 12th of December, as he returned from inspecting one of the forts, he set his horse to jump a ravine that barred the way; but the beast missed its footing and fell upon its side, crushing its rider and breaking his right leg. The general was carried home on a litter, and said to the surgeon, thinking of the similar accident which had interfered with his career at Trèves twelve years before:

"Get it over quickly: this is not the first time this has happened to me."

He was not able to leave until March 1808, and, even then, he was not fully restored to health. The journey home to Bar-le-Duc was no easy one for a cripple unable to move without crutches. But it was on his return that he first made the acquaintance of a girl of sixteen, Mlle. Eugénie de Coucy, who was destined, four years later, Oudinot being then a widower, to become his wife. Very many years after, when she in her turn had become a widow, she occupied her old age in collecting for her children the interesting souvenirs from which this work is mainly drawn. The following extract contains a sketch of country life at the time of the Revolution and the Empire, and tells us of Mlle, de Coucy and of her family, and of her first meeting with Oudinot.

******

My children, you urge me to write down my life, although I have often told you the details of it, and what I have not revealed to you has been the secret of others.

To begin at the beginning, I will remind you that my father was a captain in the Artois Regiment and a Knight of St. Louis. He was the eldest of ten children: two of his brothers served in the same regiment as himself; a third was grand vicar to the Bishop of Agde; and as to his sisters, one was a canoness, one a nun, and four others lived together under the paternal roof. None of them was married.

My grandfather de Coucy and his wife, who was Mlle, de Conyngham, of a Scotch family, were still alive at the time at which I commence my narrative. They were assisted in the cares and expenses resulting from so large a family by the Mlles, de Coucy, my grandfather's elder sisters, who lived at Hancourt, two leagues from the manor house at Lentilles.

This patriarchal family lived in perfect harmony. The greater part of the year was spent both at Lentilles and Hancourt in a life of agriculture and retirement; but when the time of furlough came, and the three young officers and the *abbé*, who was perhaps the noisiest of the four brothers, came home, everything grew lively and assumed its most festive air. Then our country neighbours, who all led a more or less similar existence, met together in joyful and crowded gatherings: for in those days families were immense; one saw ten or a dozen children at every table; and if all did not succeed in attaining an equally splendid position, at least they were all able to live, and neither they nor their parents possessed that distrust of Providence, that dread of the future, which nowadays so frequently embitters all family happiness.

Among the poor nobility of the country, the girls thought it quite natural that they should remain unmarried, in order not to encroach for their dowries upon the fortune which it was preferred to save for the eldest of the boys.

My father was the handsomest of the four brothers. His education was stopped at thirteen, the age at which he entered the service under the patronage of the three Conynghams, his uncles, who were all officers in the Artois Regiment. His studies naturally suffered from this interruption; but he continued to work of his own accord, and without attaining the pitch to which a classical education might have brought him, he nevertheless achieved a facility of style in speaking and writing which in those days was a rare accomplishment.

When he was thirty years old, my father met my mother, then Mlle. de Merçuay and eighteen years of age, at Luxeuil, where he had gone to take the waters. She was pale and fair, and graceful and sweet as an angel; and she was there with her father, in mourning for Mme. de Merçuay. The little estate from which they took their name lay at three leagues from Luxeuil, and the rumour soon spread that the handsome officer had offered his hand to the charming orphan. The arrangements were promptly made, the marriage took place shortly after, and my father took up his residence with his wife and father-in-law at the latter's estate of Merçuay in Franche-Comté. They received visits from the brothers and sisters, visits which they returned each year in Champagne. The peace seemed lasting, and my father retired from the army three years after his marriage.

The birth of my sister was followed in a few years by that of my elder brother, Maximilien, a charming child, who died at the age of seven. This was their first deep sorrow. My grandparents in Champagne died next, and soon the first rumblings of the thunder of the Revolution were heard. My father foresaw the storm which was about to burst forth; but he made up his mind at once to face it on the spot, and refused to emigrate. I was born in the meanwhile. They had hoped for a boy and I was badly received, although idolized later, whether to atone for this first bad welcome, or from any other reason, I know not.

Before long my father was denounced as a suspect by the villagers whom he had loaded with kindness, and together with my mother and sister, who was then fourteen, he was taken on foot, between four fusiliers, to Faverney, a neighbouring market town, where all three were locked up in an old convent that did duty for a prison. Soon, however, it was considered that the company of his family was too pleasant for him, and he was sent alone to Gray, while my mother and sister were transferred to Vesoul.

I was two years and a half old, and was also imprisoned. An order was issued for the arrest of my small person, and I was locked up with my mother, who was in despair at seeing me thus deprived of the air which is the life of children. Suddenly we learnt that Robespierre the Younger was in our part of the country, in his quality as people's representative. With great difficulty leave was obtained from the warders for me to go out for one morning.

My nurse Rosalie, who, from devotion to the family, had joined the popular side, had been left her liberty; she watched over our interests outside the prison, and came to take me from the arms of the horrible men who boasted in the title of *sans-cullotes*. I remember they wore caps made of foxes' skins. He who handed me to my nurse had left the beast's long bush hanging to his, and it swung to and fro, following all his movements, a sight which filled me with frightful terror. I cried, but Rosalie, who had made all her plans, lectured me on what I was to do; and placing a paper in my hand, she took me to Robespierre.

I see him now. It was morning, and he was not yet up, and was giving audience to a host of people in bed. My little look of fright caught his attention.

"Who is that child?" he asked.

My nurse stepped forward:

"Citizen representative, she is the daughter of Citizen Coucy; her parents—"

"Ah, I see, nobles. Put the child down there," pointing to his bed.

I clung to Rosalie, uttering terrible screams, while the people's representative ran his eyes over my petition. He then sent for some sweets and kissed me.

"Your beard hurts," I exclaimed, struggling to get away.

This made him laugh, and he said, "You tell me she is only two years and six months, and they issued a warrant for her arrest? Absurd! It is enough to make the Government ridiculous! Make out an order," turning to his secretary, "for her to be set at liberty at once."

"And her parents?" asked Rosalie.

"Ah, that is beyond my power."

Nevertheless he uttered his refusal kindly. My nurse, seeing there was no more to be done, took me back to my mother, who had not hoped for any great result from this step for herself or my father, but who felt at least some relief at seeing me leave the dark, damp walls of the prison, in which her health and my sister's were already undergoing a visible change. Rosalie took me to Merçuay, where I found my grandfather, who, too old to be moved from home, was watched night and day by twenty volunteers fed and lodged at his expense.

At last, thanks to the efforts of my father's youngest brother, married to a daughter of the Comte d'Allegrin, the Aunt Clotilde whose memory I cherish and revere with a sort of worship, my father obtained his release from prison in 1794, on the 9 *Thermidor*, together with my mother and sister.

It was high time for my father: his moral agony had become intolerable, and he never completely recovered from the trial. Nor, for that matter, was this the end of it, for many sad years followed upon the terror itself. Not long after my parents' return to Merçuay, my grandfather, the good ex-lord of the manor, died. He was very old, but until the Revolution he was wonderfully hale. Having served in the Hussars, he had retained in his old age the habits peculiar, they say, to that branch of the service. He loved noise, movement, gaiety; he sang at table, and composed joyous couplets which lingered long in the memory of my relations in Champagne. I still have a clear remembrance of his tall figure and his dress, which was always green.

The birth of my brother Gustave was an immense consolation to my parents; but it was followed, alas! in less than ten months by the death of my dear, noble father. He set out one morning for Vesoul. I see him now, dressed in a coat of dark cloth, with a pale blue satin waistcoat, embroidered with white stars. He was going to the elections to try and carry the return of Pichegru for the Haute-Saone. I never saw him again! Four days after his departure, my mother was sent for, then Rosalie, and at last my sister: it was to nurse him in an inflammatory fever which carried him off in eight days, at the age of fifty-three.

It was decided to let Merçuay, where my mother could not bear to remain, and we went to Champagne to join my father's family. Our departure took place in the spring of 1799. My mother was never to see her birthplace again.

Before describing Lentilles to you, where we made our first stay, let me tell you who were awaiting us there.

My Aunt de Coucy was plain-featured; but her stature, which was tall and well-shaped, and her wont of governing all around her since her fifteenth year, had combined to give her the grand air. She had a generous and devoted heart, a playful humour, and a great love of amusement. Having voluntarily spent her youth in caring for her mother and the long array of brothers and sisters who came after her (there were twelve of them, for two of whom I have not spoken died in their cradles), the result of this life of self-abnegation was that, in her maturer years, my aunt, relieved of the duties which she had so conscientiously fulfilled, was taken with the desire to enjoy herself; but the modesty of her fortune, not to mention the Revolution, constantly stood in her way. What was the upshot of it all? She was content to witness the joys of her fellow-creatures, and to make them her own.

My uncle the *abbé* was by nature lively, hot-headed, and brave to temerity: he had only become a priest because he was the youngest of the family. Nevertheless, while recognizing the difficulties of his task, my uncle had nobly fulfilled them, first from a sense of honour, and later from an enlightened and sincere feeling of religion.

Mlles, de Louvrigny and de Velly were weak and delicate, and slightly deformed. You will be less surprised at the unfortunate malformation of the two sisters, when I tell you that at that time it was the custom to swathe newborn children as tightly as mummies.

My uncle the *abbé* was my godfather and Louvrigny my godmother. This title, which is nowadays accepted so lightly that its obligations are never fulfilled, was in the old days taken in its true acceptance, and was considered what it really is, a religious engagement. Brother and sister had therefore vowed beforehand to take a special interest in me, without permitting this to diminish that which they bore to the other children of their dear brother.

Louvrigny and Velly, who were known among the family as the two inseparables, both because of their mutual sympathy and the similarity of their figures, seemed to have united themselves in a common destiny. To attend to their department in the inner working of the house, to love and work for their family, was the employment of their lives. As the youngest, they were generally left at home, where their delicate health would in any case have frequently retained them. Louvrigny had that sparkling natural wit and that piquant pertinency which became the charm of the fireside by the manner in which she availed herself of the gift, always pleasing, never wounding any. Velly, gentle and calm, was every one's *refugium peccatorum*; her angelic character carried peace wherever she went. She had a charming head; when I knew her, the remains of her beauty were her almond-shaped eyes, of a velvety gray, whose soft expression still haunts me.

The old family house occupied one side of a great square courtyard, formed on the three other sides by rural buildings. Two breaks in the masonry gave a glimpse of a fine orchard. So much space was there in the grass-carpeted courtyard, so green was it, and so animated by the presence of an enormous number of birds and poultry of all kinds, that its appearance was never gloomy.

As in almost all the houses of that time and of that part of the country, a long covered verandah ran before the house, where we often sat. One had to descend a step in order to enter the ground-floor, which was paved with tiles; this will give you an idea of the dampness of the place. I feel cold when I think of it now; but then all seemed delightful to me, not excluding the branch of the climbing rose-tree, which one day audaciously pierced the wall of my bedroom and went on growing finely inside. Do not think that this suggested to any one the idea of repairs. No, nothing was ever changed: what had held out last year would last the next, they said. People did not then spend money on house-comfort. Nevertheless, the table was always well and amply supplied: it was shared with friends, relations and neighbours, who in their turn reciprocated the hospitality received.

My uncle the *abbé* loved the smaller comforts of life. He had kept good cheer upon the twelve thousand *francs* of his grand-vicariate, and my aunts were a little afraid of the daintiness of his palate. Whenever they felt uncertain of a dish, they would avoid his look, especially my Aunt de Coucy, who was responsible, since the kitchen was her special charge. On those occasions her brother would look at her fixedly, without saying a word. Vainly she turned her head, talked to her neighbours on the left and the right: that fixed eye fascinated her. Willy-nilly, she was bound to meet it; and then, driven to bay, she would pluck up courage and haughtily ask him why he stared at her so. Sometimes the matter ended in jest; sometimes there would be a few words: but these little clouds soon passed away.

To come to my aunt the canoness: after her chapter had been broken up, she had gone to live at Vitry-le-François. It was in that town that my mother, when coming to Champagne, had resolved to take up her abode.

To complete the picture of the family, I will mention the inmates of Hancourt. Of my uncle and my Aunt Clotilde I have already spoken: three children had since come to add to their happiness. Our dear Enguerrand was the eldest. Hancourt was a charming little English farm, a model of care and cleanliness. We stayed there a few weeks before finally installing ourselves at Vitry, where we had a small house near that of my aunt. Our days were spent in retirement, in household cares, reading, lessons and work, and in the evenings we would walk out to take the air. There was perhaps no place in the world where so little politics was talked as at Vitry. My mother, sister and aunt, who all held definite opinions, contented themselves with meeting their intimates from time to time in order to deplore the criminal days of the Revolution, or to celebrate behind closed doors the old solemnities of the Monarchy; but all happened without noise or bravado in this little circle of friends, who were none the less welcome in the other drawing-rooms which they visited.

Thus passed sweetly the first few years of our residence in Champagne. Meantime, General Bonaparte had returned from Egypt to take up the command of the army of Italy. Domestic tranquillity was being gradually re-established in France; the churches were reopened for public worship; the priests were allowed to show themselves once more, and religion was freely practised; the emigrants were returning; and there were signs on every side that a strong hand had seized the reins of public affairs. This general improvement was especially appreciated by those who had been the most severely tried by the Terror. Nevertheless, the misfortunes were still too recent, the wounds too fresh, for it to be possible to live without hatred of the past and distrust of the future.

I have not yet mentioned one who is well known to you and who unwittingly played a part in my destiny: I mean M. Eugène de Villers. His father was killed at the Tuileries on the 10th of August; his mother, an aunt of my Aunt Clotilde's, was sent to prison at Bar-le-Duc, where the family lived. The poor young man, on the point of becoming an orphan and but little endowed with fortune, was welcomed at Hancourt and treated as a son. His natural good qualities and his misfortunes interested all my relations, who received him with affection. Eventually his mother escaped the scaffold, and, when order was re-established, she wished her son to take service in the army, whose constantly increasing glory attracted even those who had most suffered. Mme. de Villers presented her son to the natural patron of her native town, General Oudinot; and after a campaign in which he bore himself bravely, the young man returned with his epaulets. Thenceforward he applied himself with heart and soul to his profession, and always remained an enthusiastic supporter of the man who had assisted him to enter it.

I think I have told you enough to give you a definite idea of the political opinions which my family at that time entertained. Bonaparte had deceived the hopes which a few Royalists (notwithstanding the 13 *Vendémiaire*) had formed of him. A fraction of the party had persisted in regarding him as the restorer of the Royal Family of the

Bourbons; and this may have been one of the reasons which prompted the murder of which M. le Duc d'Enghien was the victim, since this act could leave no more doubts as to the feelings of the First Consul towards the Bourbons. Thenceforth the fraction of which I speak remained in opposition to him; it was a very small minority, but my family formed part of it, and invariably kept up its remembrances and its regrets.

We had just lost my Aunt de Louvrigny, and were living in greater seclusion than ever, less interested than at any time in outside matters, when M. de Villers returned from his first campaign. He was full of the name of Oudinot, representing its owner as a model of bravery in battle and generosity after victory; and he succeeded in arousing the interest of my relatives, who had heard speak of the magnanimity of this commander, admired by all. As for me, my children, I was then a little girl of eight or ten years of age, and I felt my heart beat at the tale of all the battles of those times. Strange contrast! I was born a timid creature, as you know, and I loved to hear of fighting. I had always liked bustle! In history, as in my story-books, what I most loved was military subjects, and I listened with all my ears to our excellent M. de Villers; so that you see he had something to do with the determination which ten years later decided my fate. When I told him this one day, he was delighted. But for the present no idea of glory, you can well believe, came to trouble the peace of my days.

On the 5th of June 1805, my sister was married to the Vicomte de la Guérivière, younger son of an old Poitou family, who, on attaining the requisite age, had been received into the Order of Malta. Under M. d'Estaings he went through the War of Independence of the United States. He was subsequently appointed Colonel of the Chasseurs of the Order of Malta, and was on that island during the French Revolution. He defended the fort of Rohan against General Dessaix, and with his small force was still resisting while the Grand Master, prompted either by weakness or treachery, was signing a pitiful capitulation on board the *Orient*. It was not until after receiving this official news that M. de la Guérivière capitulated in his turn; but he marched out from the fort with the full honours of war, at the head of his garrison, which consisted of only eighty men.

He understood that thenceforth all was over for Malta, and returned broken-hearted to France at the age of thirty-six, and possessed of no fortune. He obtained from the Pope a release from his vows, and resolved to enter the Department of Finance, in which determination he was assisted by his friend M. Buffault, at that time receiver-general at Bar-le-Duc.

My mother and I stayed a month at Bar-le-Duc after the marriage. The wedding-repasts succeeded one another without interruption; they seemed long to me, but nothing ever wearied me. At that time it was the habit to sing at table, each in the place where he sat, without accompaniment.

One of the most solemn entertainments was a dinner given by M. Leclerc, the *Prefect* of the Meuse. His honest reputation and appearance and his distinguished manners had won my mother's sympathy. He was the first important functionary with whom she had come into contact since the Empire. We kept up pleasant relations with him both before and after my marriage. Although he had been created a count of the Empire, the *Prefect* of the Meuse was nevertheless regarded at Bar as a third-class personage, and kept in a sort of disgrace. He was brother to the Princesse d'Eckmühl and brother-in-law to the Princesse Borghèse, the widow of General Leclerc, and consequently was closely connected with the court; but he was not in the least ambitious, and asked nothing better than to live on the same level as his neighbours. Nevertheless he remained on friendly terms with the emperor's charming sister.

He used to entertain us by relating a proof of her remembrance which she had recently given him. She was travelling to Germany, and one fine morning a courier in her livery came knocking at the *prefect's* house. He had come to announce the arrival, he said, of Her Imperial Highness, who would ask him to give her some breakfast; nothing simpler so far; but the messenger was instructed moreover to order that, when she stepped out of her carriage, a milk bath should be in readiness for her, to be followed by a shower-bath of the same liquid.

It was not an easy thing to do, in a small town; nevertheless, means must be found. The *prefect* despatched to the neighbouring villages the whole force of his Departmental Guard. Each soldier brought back his can of milk, and they were beginning to heat it when the fair traveller arrived.

"Carry me as you used to do, dear little brother," said she; and the *prefect* resumed his former functions, and set the princess down in the handsomest room in the house.

"And my bath?" she asked, in a wheedling voice.

"It is ready for you."

"And my shower-bath?"

"Ah, that was more difficult, we have no apparatus for it."

"Have some holes pierced in the ceiling just over the place where my bath will stand when it is brought in. Forgive the trouble, dear little brother, but it is necessary for my health."

They did the best they could, and the result was that the *prefect* received many gracious *adieux*, the furniture was splashed with milk-stains, and the room long smelt of a badly-kept dairy.

When the emperor came to Bar, he always preferred to stay at General Oudinot's. The *prefect* generally waited until he sent for him. The last time he was a little late; it was in the evening, and the Emperor, when he saw him, said, "You like to sleep, *monsieur le prefet*." That was all, and it was not until some years later that this modest and worthy administrator was rewarded by being created a Senator, only shortly before the fall of the Empire. During his residence at Bar, he continued on terms of intimate friendship with my brother-in-law.

On the occasion of this our first visit, we saw none of the Oudinot family. Mme. la Comtesse Oudinot, your father's first wife, had just taken up her abode with her children in the house I now live in, which was scarcely finished, and they were still laying out and beginning to plant our beautiful gardens. The emperor was expected the very next day; the town was all excitement, and I heard with delight that he was to pass under our windows in the Rue du Bourg. I got ready to behold with my own eyes the man who till then had played so fantastic a part in my imagination. He was preceded by a number of couriers.

About mid-day his carriage drove slowly past; but, alas! I was only able to catch sight of the edge of his cloak, thrown carelessly over his knee. Towards the end of the winter of 1807-8, my sister first told us of her acquaintance with Mme. la Comtesse Oudinot. Her praise was in every mouth, and that which came from my sister increased my desire to meet her. My sister, being the wife of a State functionary, obtained for me, with my mother's permission, an invitation to a fete given to commemorate some solemnity or other.

The reception took place in the theatre; it was crowded; all the boxes were filled, and one particularly attracted my attention: it was the Comtesse Oudinot's. They whispered that the person on her right was one of the empress's ladies. It was, in fact, the Comtesse de Marescot, and three of the emperor's pages, in their rich and brilliant uniform, completed the party. At last I saw the wife of General Oudinot; her beautiful, gentle blue eyes met mine; they seemed to glance at me with a look of kindness, while I, on my side, felt drawn towards her by a subtle sympathy. What a reminiscence!

Mme. Oudinot was thirty-eight or forty years of age: I cannot give you a better idea of her face than by asking you to look at that of Charles, her grandson. She was short and very stout. Victor, her eldest son, one of the three Imperial pages, resembled the portrait in my *boudoir* at Jeand'heurs. He was then fifteen or sixteen years old; he came and asked me for a country-dance, and soon I was dazzled by his talent in this art, which at that time was an object of great interest. Not only was one taught to put an infinitude of lightness and grace into his steps, but the men paid great attention to their manners with their partners; at least this was the habit of well-bred people, and the son of General Oudinot was known to have received a perfect education, and to have turned it to the best advantage.

They had introduced at Bar a foreign dance which replaced that known as the "Grandfather," which generally ended the balls. I have never seen it danced anywhere else; it was a general hopping-match. Every one took part in it, to the sound of a tambourine, which singularly reminded one of the music of the performing bears. Somewhat surprised at this novelty, the page began to burst with laughter. I felt greatly inclined to do as much.

"Well," said he, "we must join in this motion," and we soon followed the general impulse with the enthusiasm of the two children that we were. But the orchestra stopped, and M. Oudinot, bringing me back to my seat, made me a gay and smiling bow, which I returned. Those were my first relations with the Oudinot family: you see they opened under happy auspices.

After the Peace of Tilsit, the grenadiers occupied Dantzig; and it was during his stay there that their general-in-chief broke his leg while galloping on the execrable pavements of that city. It was a serious and complicated fracture, and so soon as the invalid was able to bear transporting, he applied for sick leave to come and take the waters in France, and to be present at the wedding of his eldest daughter with General Pajol.

We ourselves were at Bar in the summer of 1808. During the short visits which the general had paid to Bar since my sister had come to live there, he had often been to her house. Christine's relations with the Comtesse Oudinot had drawn closer; both of them, as they grew to know one another better, learnt to appreciate each other more. And this was the time for redoubling one's proofs of sympathy, since the general, still suffering from his accident, made it none the less his habit to receive every evening all those who called upon his wife.

Meanwhile our visit was being protracted amid a round of various amusements, when a lady of our acquaintance, Mme. Oudot by name, arranged with my sister a day upon which to call at the general's house, and both joined in begging my mother to permit me to accompany them. "It is a very new and very brilliant world for the child to enter," she replied (I was then about sixteen years old). My sister insisted until my mother gave her consent, and I was delighted; for my interest and curiosity had long been excited about this general of whom we had heard speak so constantly since our arrival.

Perhaps I had better tell you what sort of idea I had formed of the commander-in-chief of the massed grenadiers, a formidable troop which was nicknamed, as you know, "the infernal column." I pictured him as enormously tall and stout, with a voice of thunder, speaking with the gestures and tone of command; I saw him armed to the teeth and dragging a huge sword behind him. In all this I resembled a little the children who often take the drum-major for the colonel of the regiment on account of his great height, his position at the head of the regiment, his ferocious air, and his authoritative gestures.

Filled with this picture of my imagination, I followed my sister with an agitation which increased as we approached the house. It was between seven and eight o'clock in the evening; the weather was warm and splendid, and after dinner the inmates had dispersed through the garden. The countess received us with kindness. She was accompanied by several ladies and young girls, and we soon saw coming from behind all the bushes a number of men of different ages, among whom I noticed many in uniform.

Mme. Oudinot despatched some of her husband's *aides-de-camp* to fetch us bouquets, and meantime resumed her stroll in our company. "My husband," she said to my sister, "has gone to see my father in the upper town. I fear it is a rather long distance for him to walk with his broken leg." She had hardly finished speaking, when she exclaimed, "Ah, here he is! "We were close to the bridge over the canal and in sight of the great stables, from which we saw a man come out who walked slowly and with difficulty, leaning on the arm of an officer. He was dressed in a brown frock, and wore nothing by way of uniform except a forage cap embroidered with the lace denoting his rank.

At the first glance, he dissipated all the ideas I had formed concerning him. His slender and supple figure displayed the gracefulness peculiar to those who habitually wear uniform; his complexion was very pale, and he wore a slight moustache of the same brown shade as his hair and whiskers. His open forehead, adorned with fine and distinctly-marked eyebrows, was really admirable; his smile, a little haughty, rare and fleeting, was nevertheless perfectly gracious; his piercing glance never stared, and in the whole of his physiognomy there was something deep and dreamy that preoccupied one.

The general took his place by my sister's side at the head of the procession, and I mechanically followed. Soon we entered the drawing-room on the ground-floor, which was brilliantly lighted. The general, who was fatigued, sat down at once on the sofa before the fireplace, begging permission to put up his leg, which was not yet cured, and persuaded his wife to go to the piano and form some *quadrilles*, which she did with her usual kindness.

M. de Bourcet, whom I expect you remember, was our only orchestra, and his merry companions, who had been joined by a few young men of the town, kept us dancing till eleven o'clock. The moon had risen over Mount Farémont; the weather was so warm that the three doors leading to the garden had been left open and admitted the delicious perfume of the flowers. It was a delightful evening and I enjoyed myself thoroughly. I loved dancing, and did nothing else. Yet I seemed to perceive, during a momentary interval of repose, that I was the object of the kindly observation of the general and his wife; but this fleeting thought left no trace in my memory and only returned to me in later years.

★★★★★★

On the 25th of July 1808, Oudinot had received the title of Count of the Empire, together with the gift of the domain of Inoclavo, which represented a value of a million *francs*. He purchased, in the neighbourhood of Bar-le-Duc, the immense estate of Jeand'heurs, which had been sold under the Revolution as national property. The old abbey, founded in the middle ages by the Order of Premonstrants, rose in the midst of a huge park surrounded by walls, with gardens, woodland, pieces of water, hot-houses, an orangery. Each year Oudinot took greater pleasure in beautifying this property, in filling it with his triumphs, decorating it with his trophies, his swords of honour, and the celebrated cannon of Monsembano, whose deep voice boomed out on days of festival.

Later, the little River Saulx, which crosses the park, was used to work an industrial establishment—a paper-mill—which was of great service to the municipality of Lisle en Rigaud, and employed a number of hands.

CHAPTER 3

Oudinot's Mission to Holland

After Tilsit, Napoleon went to Germany, to the meeting at Erfurt, where, in conjunction with his fickle friend, the Czar Alexander, he hoped to be able to settle definitively the fate of Europe. All the kinglets and princes of the Confederation of the Rhine were there; and to his mind there was no pomp sumptuous enough to give them an idea of his might. He wanted a man with a glorious name to govern this little town for a few weeks under these imposing conditions, and he selected Oudinot.

The Duchesse de Reggio supplies some curious details concerning the incidents at Erfurt:

★★★★★★

The general had left Bar when, a few days later, my sister and I went to leave cards. We ourselves soon returned to Vitry and went on to Hancourt, where we spent the autumn.

At this period I used to listen with exceptional interest when the newspapers were read out aloud. They were filled with details on the famous Congress of Erfurt General Oudinot had been appointed governor of this town, where all the sovereigns of the North were assembled; but the emperors of France and Russia attracted the principal attention, and naturally threw into the shade the mass of crowned heads, who, in fact, were only grouped there by the will of one man.

The political objects and results of this Congress are not in my domain. As to the details of the magnificence of this assemblage, they have been described at length. Who has not heard, for instance, how, at the performances of the Théâtre Français, brought bodily from Paris, all the boxes were occupied by more or less powerful monarchs, while the pit was filled with officers of high rank? An unique spectacle in history!

Unfortunately, few generals thought of taking a personal note of these remarkable events, and your father less than any of them. Nevertheless, I will narrate here two anecdotes which he has told me, although I cannot hope to give an idea of his inimitable manner of relating them.

It fell to the general who, as governor, commanded all the troops massed at Erfurt and neighbourhood, to supply guards, escorts, and so forth, to all the kings and princes, in proportion to each highness's importance; and this brought him into daily contact with them all.

One day, on going his rounds, he was surprised, on passing the door of the Grand-Duke Constantine, not to see the sentry to whom that prince was entitled; and as he observed on this to one of the officers accompanying him, he heard from within a loud voice conducting the drill in the drawing-room, the windows of which were open to the street. The general without hesitation sprang from his horse and presented himself to the grand-duke, whom he discovered in the strangest *négligé* face to face with his sentry, whom he was putting through his drill. At the moment when the general opened the door, the prince cried, "Fire!" The musket, naturally, discharged its bullet.

"Ah, Sir, what are you doing?" asked the general in amazement.

"I am amusing myself," replied the prince.

"Yes; but apart from the fact that you are exposing the sentry to being court-martialled, have you not reflected that his musket is loaded, and that you have a neighbour opposite you?"

"Pooh! my Uncle Wurtemberg," replied the grand-duke; "it will wake him up."

The last-named monarch was so well roused by the bullet which had just traversed his bedroom that, furious and, it must be allowed, not without reason, he sent at once to know where the shot had been fired from; and as his messenger found the prince, my husband and the sentry still together, he went back and told his master that it appeared to be the grand-duke who, together with the governor, was amusing himself by firing at His Majesty. This might have turned out seriously, but fortunately explanations were given in good time, and the thing went no further.

The other anecdote also relates to that brother of Alexander's, a typical Cossack, morally and physically. He was the constant exception amid the civilization that distinguished Erfurt.

One morning he asked the governor to allow him to be present at a review of the grenadiers of the Old Guard. Constantine, always enthusiastic about anything military, examined these picked troops, who pulled a grimace under their *mustachios* on seeing a Russian come to inspect them.

Your father, who perceived this, and who was anxious that everything should go off well, followed him closely. Suddenly, as he passed behind a rank, and thinking he had to do with a soldier of his own army, he touched one of the *grognards*, to illustrate some remark. You should have heard your father imitate the Grenadier, who exclaimed in a voice of thunder:

"Who touched me?"

"I did," said General Oudinot, quickly placing himself between the prince and the soldier.

"That's all right," replied the latter, on recognizing the well-known voice, which instantly calmed him.

★★★★★★

Napoleon had occasional moments of forgetfulness which prevented him from displaying in his relations with the sovereigns all the forethought expected in a host.

"One day," related Oudinot, "we were riding into the country, the two Emperors riding side by side. At a given moment ours, carried away by his thoughts, took the lead, whistling, and seeming to forget about those he was leaving behind. I shall always remember Alexander, turning stiffly towards his neighbour, and asking, "Are we to follow?"

"Yes, Sire."

I rejoined Napoleon and told him of this little scene. He fell back, offered an explanation, and that was the end of it."

And that was the end of it! Who knows? Autocrats have singularly sensitive minds. And for that matter, the friendship of the two emperors was not so firm as they would have the world believe, and Alexander retained the instinctive distrust natural to a man accustomed to the catastrophes of his country. An instance of this is given by Victor Oudinot, whom we have seen as a Guide at Zurich, and who was at this time one of the emperor's pages:

> One day, he says, the emperors, when out riding, were suddenly stopped by a ditch which their horses refused to jump. I put mine to the gallop, leapt the ditch, and dismounted; then, taking Napoleon's horse by the bridle, I persuaded it to cross the obstacle. Alexander, spurring his horse, also reached the other

side; but the effect of the shock was that his sword-belt broke and his sword fell to the ground. I picked it up; and Napoleon, seeing what I was doing, said, "Keep that sword and bring it to me later." Then looking at Alexander, "You have no objection, Sire?" he added.

Quick as thought, an expression of surprise and of vague apprehension came into the *czar's* eyes. But soon, resuming his calm and confident attitude, he in few words gave his assent.

On dismounting from his horse, Napoleon said to Constant, his valet, "Keep this sword of Alexander's, and give Oudinot one of mine." Then, to me, "Take this sword to my brother of Russia, and beg him in my name to consent to this exchange of arms." I hurried with it to the *czar*, who, on hearing my errand, ordered me to tell Napoleon that in a few moments he would express to him personally his very sincere gratitude. The Grand-Duke Constantine, who was with Alexander, let fall these words, "I say, Monsieur Oudinot, if your august master were to give me one of his swords, I should take it to bed with me!" I repeated these words to Napoleon, who made me go back at once to the grand-duke with a sword which was received with transports of joy, although it was not quite the same as that which the emperor usually carried.

At the breaking up of the Congress, Oudinot received marks of esteem from all the sovereigns, with the exception of the King of Wurtemberg. Alexander gave the governor a gold snuff-box, enriched with diamonds of great value. Constantine heard of this present, and determined to make one himself which should be original, if not very costly.

"Faith, my dear general," he said, "I am only a younger son; I am very sorry to have nothing better to offer you than my plume."

With that he unfastened the old bunch of cock's feathers from his hat and presented it gracefully to Oudinot, expecting him to hoist it on the spot for love of him. It was difficult to make him understand that a French uniform did not lend itself at all well to this feathered decoration.

These demonstrations of friendship were vain, as events soon showed. After Erfurt, Napoleon hastened to Spain, where the bad condition of our affairs required his presence; and no sooner did Austria feel that he was inextricably engaged in the heart of the Peninsula, in all the turmoil of that disastrous expedition, than she began to think of taking advantage of these difficulties to revenge herself for the campaign of 1805. The emperor had to be everywhere at once. He reappeared suddenly in Paris in January 1809, m order to hurry on the preparations for a new campaign against the Monarchy of the Hapsburgs.

Oudinot, who was in cantonment at Hanau, near Frankfort-on-Main, received orders to enter the Kingdom of Bavaria, whose sovereign was then our ally, and to march along the right bank of the Danube as far as Augsburg, the extreme end of our lines on that side. He was there joined by his old friend and leader, Masséna, who assumed the command of the army corps. They stayed there some time before the commencement of hostilities; but when the Archduke Charles unexpectedly opened the campaign and endeavoured to cut them off from Davout, who was at Ratisbon, they marched forward eagerly in order to effect their junction with the Marshal. After a sharp encounter with the Austrians at Pfaffenhofen, they reached the Isar in time to make sure of winning the Battle of Landshut (12 April).

The victory of Ratisbon drove back the Archduke Charles upon the left bank of the Danube, while the Archduke Louis was held in check upon the right. The whole French army now descended the river along the right bank, striving to prevent the junction of the Archdukes. Oudinot was in the advance-guard with Masséna, and to them fell the laborious task. They crossed the Inn and entered Upper Austria. On the 1st of May, Oudinot had a brisk and successful encounter with the enemy at Ried.

On the 4th, a tremendous combat took place at the crossing of the Traun, with the object of carrying the town of Ebersberg and its castle, perched upon a height. The contest was exceptionally fierce. The shells set fire to the town; it was taken, lost, and taken again; or rather, all that was captured was a heap of smoking ruins, where the air was so stifling that it was impossible to penetrate into what remained of the streets. The wounded were left to die. The next day, Napoleon himself, used as he was to massacre, was unable to refrain from manifesting his horror.

On the 9th, Oudinot was encamped within musket-shot of the walls of Vienna. The capital, although in a weak state of defence and badly garrisoned, prepared to resist, so greatly was the patriotism of the inhabitants excited against the French. After vainly demanding a capitulation, the general forced the suburb of Maria-Hilf. As he passed through the streets, a cannon-ball struck the angle of a house at two steps from him; the grenadiers received stones and boiling water poured down from the windows. But the shells set fire to the theatre and to different parts of the town; it was unable to sustain a siege and was soon reduced to open its gates.

The French now found themselves in the same situation from which a subterfuge had released them four years earlier: although masters of Vienna and of the right bank of the Danube, they were obliged to go and put down the enemy on the left bank. But this time, instead of the remnants of an army, the Archduke Charles had at his disposal one hundred and fifty thousand men, and so great a mass would not allow itself to be surprised either by Masséna's artifice or Oudinot's dash. After a prolonged examination, Napoleon resolved to cross the stream below Vienna, at the spot where it divides into two arms containing between them the large island of Lobau.

The action commenced on the 21st, at Essling, and remained undecided. Oudinot crossed the river on the night of the 21st and occupied the centre, having on one side the village of Aspern, held by Masséna, and on the other that of Essling, held by Lannes. He pushed forward, drove in the Austrian centre, and was on the point of separating the two wings, when suddenly he learnt that the bridge of boats joining the island of Lobau to the right bank had broken down. The emperor, fearing that the ammunition, which was already running short, would give out entirely in the thick of the fray, gave the order to fall back. Lannes and Oudinot saw the victory, which seemed within their grasp, snatched from them. They retreated step by step, making head to the enemy; the grenadiers suffered terrible losses, but without discouragement, thanks to the gallant bearing of their chief, who was himself wounded in the arm.

Upon the death of Lannes, who was slain during this retreat, Oudinot was thought worthy of the very great honour of replacing him at the head of the 2nd Corps.

"The Emperor," said the tenth *Bulletin de la Grande Armée*, "has given the command of the 2nd Corps to the Comte Oudinot, a general tried in a hundred fights, in which he has displayed equal courage and judgement" (2 May 1809).

Unable to mount his horse because of his wound, Oudinot returned in his carriage to the island of Lobau, where the army took up a strong position while awaiting the construction of bridges strong enough to ensure a solid base to the operations. Six weeks were necessary to complete these great works. At last, on the 4th of June, at 9 o'clock in the evening, Oudinot received the order once more to commence the passage, a truly wonderful exploit, considering the number of troops engaged (150,000 men on either side) and the difficult position of the French army in having to fight with its back to a great river, into which it could be flung in case of defeat.

Oudinot's soldiers, crossing in great barges, surprised the enemies' sentries, and speedily captured a redoubt known as the White House, despite a terrible storm which suddenly burst upon them. In order to facilitate the passage of Masséna and Davout, Oudinot pressed forward between the White House and the hamlet of Muhleiten, shelling on his right the castle of Sachsengang, held by an Austrian battalion; at daybreak the little garrison surrendered.

By seven o'clock the advance-guard was mounting the lower slopes of the plain, and at nine the army was drawn up in line before the heights of Neusiedel and Wagram, occupied by the Archduke Charles. Having Masséna on his left and Davout on his right, Oudinot was in the evening at Grosshofen, in presence of the corps of Hohenzollern, from which he was separated by a stream called the Russbach. Napoleon wishing to finish the business by the evening of the 5th, he flung himself upon the village of Baumersdorf, but at the same moment a portion of Macdonald's troops fired by mistake upon our Allies the Saxons, and the latter, seized with panic, gave way on all sides. This incident compelled us to abandon the attack.

The next morning, Oudinot received orders not to attack, at least so long as the Archduke Ferdinand did not advance; but this eventuality was doubtful. In any case, when he saw that Davout had succeeded in occupying the heights of Neusiedel, which were easily captured owing to the gentleness of their slope, he understood that the possession of these ridges by our troops would make the heights of Wagram more accessible. The latter were very steep and formed the key of the position. In spite of his instructions, he crossed the Russbach, attacked Baumersdorf a second time, carried it, and continued his march forward, notwithstanding the opposition of the Austrians, who sheltered themselves in the clefts in the soil in order to fire at their ease.

But nothing could check his impetuosity, although his left ear was pierced by a bullet and his horse killed beneath him. Massing his battalions, he drove in the enemy's squares, and forced his way to Wagram, where he received a bullet in his thigh. Nevertheless, he held out until the victory was assured. By three o'clock in the evening the enemy was retreating at every point.

The next day Napoleon said to Oudinot:

"Do you know what you did yesterday?"

"I trust, Sire, I did not too badly do my duty."

"What you did was —— you deserved to be shot!"

Some days later, in a letter to the Minister for War, dated Schönbrunn, 29th July 1809, the emperor expressly says:

> It was General Oudinot who took Wagram on the 6th, at midday.

And in the order of the day of the 5th of August, he confirms the fact:

> His Majesty owes the success of his arms to the Duc de Rivoli and Oudinot, who pierced the centre of the enemy at the same time that the Duc d'Auerstadt turned their left.

The French pursued the Austrians as far as Znaïm, where the last battle took place, and where a truce was signed on the 12th of July. On the morrow, Oudinot, exhausted with fatigue, was camping amid his men on that road to Moravia which had twice been watered with his blood. He was simply stretched on a truss of straw, when Colonel de Flahaut entered his tent and handed him a sealed missive from the emperor: it was Oudinot's promotion to the rank of Marshal, a worthy recompense to a career so well fulfilled.

A month later he received the domain of Reggio, in Calabria, with the title of duke, and a grant of eighty thousand *francs per annum.*

******

It was just at the time when the news of these well-deserved rewards reached Bar, says the Duchesse de Reggio, that we arrived there to spend the remainder of the summer at my sister's. She prepared to go and offer her congratulations to the Duchesse de Reggio, and remembering her gracious reception of me in the preceding year, I asked and readily obtained leave to accompany Christine. I therefore went with all my heart to offer my sympathy to her upon whose head were accumulating all the titles and honours which were later to revert to me. How strange a thing is destiny!

In the midst of her happiness and her legitimate triumph, the new *maréchale* remained as kind and as single-hearted as in the past.

Among the numberless letters of congratulation received at this period was the following from the Emperor of Russia:

> *Monsieur le maréchal*, I take too lively a part in all that interests yourself not to express to you the pleasure with which I heard of your promotion to the rank of Marshal. It is as sincere as the esteem in which I hold you. It is always a matter of satisfaction to me to recall the day upon which I made your acquaintance, and I beg you to believe in the sentiments with which I am always yours,
>
> (Signed) Alexander.
>
> *Reply of Marshal Oudinot, Duc de Reggio, to the Emperor Alexander.*
>
> Sire,
> I did not think it would be possible for me to experience twice in my life a feeling of satisfaction and, if I may say so, of enthusiasm equal to that with which I was seized at Erfurt, when Your Majesty completed the favours with which you had deigned to honour me, during the too short moments I had the happiness of spending with you, by making me the inestimable gift of your portrait; but, Sire, the letter which I have just received from Your Majesty has, if that be possible, moved me still more deeply.
> The recollection of a prince who is as good as he is great and powerful swells my heart with noble pride, while at the same time it fills it with the liveliest and most respectful gratitude; and I have ventured, Sire, to think that, having obtained the most brilliant proofs of the favour of my sovereign, nothing is so glorious as not to be judged unworthy of them by so enlightened an appreciator as Alexander.
>
> (Signed) Marshal Oudinot, Duc de Reggio.

This was not the only mark of sympathy which the marshal received from sovereigns of foreign countries. And yet he had attained his position by fighting against them! Your hearts and your intelligence can draw their own conclusions from these facts.

Towards the end of that winter one began to hear of the emperor's divorce, and soon after of his marriage with an Austrian archduchess. These pieces of news seemed so extraordinary that they woke Vitry-le-Francois from its habitual indifference to all that went on outside its little ramparts.

The wedding had been celebrated in Austria by procuration, as is usual in the case of crowned heads. The Prince of Neuchâtel (also Prince de Wagram) had represented the emperor at the ceremony. He brought back the princess, who was eighteen years of age.

The recollection of what I then saw in our little town was perhaps of some use to me later, when in different times and under another princess I had to make many a country journey with her.

One of our friends put her windows at our disposal near the hotel where Marie Louise alighted. Each moment the scene assumed a more varied and animated aspect. There arrived servants in the imperial livery, swaggering insolently about, puffed up with the effect produced upon the crowd by their brilliant trappings. Then came the *maréchaux des logis*, hurrying to and fro with an air of importance, to take account of every one's lodging; civic authorities panting; a general unusual movement.

The cannon thundered: couriers, covered in dust, cracking their whips, followed each other at short intervals, crying, "The Empress is at your gates!" The carriage arrived, drawn by eight horses. It was followed by several others, all filled with the officers and ladies who had gone to receive the young princess in Germany.

We only caught a glimpse of Marie Louise. With her were her sister-in-law Murat, then Queen of Naples, and the Duchesse de Montebello, her Mistress of the Robes. All were dressed in purple, embroidered with gold—only the Empress's gown was richer than the others.

Soon one of the emperor's pages was seen riding up from Compiègne, smothered in dust. He had covered the whole distance at full speed, and he came to lay at his empress's feet his master's bag, a brace of partridges shot by him the day before.

It was at that time that the destiny of my two Paulines was decided, my best friends at Vitry. Pauline de Cloys married M. Brandon du Thil. Pauline de Montendre left that part of the country to live at Abbeville with her relations.

As the latter and I strolled sadly along, bidding each other farewell beneath the trees of la Doutre, where we had been so happy, we made guesses at our futures.

"It will be long before you return," I said to her. "They will marry you down there."

"And you here?" she replied.

A pause followed these words. We continued to walk along arm-in-arm. Lost in the endless unknown that opens up before youth, Pauline, suddenly stopping, said:

"Promise me to let me know of your marriage, as I will inform you of mine, by simply sending me a gold ring: the details will follow."

Struck by the originality of this idea, I agreed, and added, "Yes, but if your betrothed or mine is decorated with the Legion of Honour, we must add a stone to the ring."

"Very well," she replied, "but two stones if he is a baron."

"Then three if he is a count," I cried.

"And if he is a duke?" asked Pauline.

"Ah! in that case the news must be announced by a cluster of diamonds," I replied, laughing heartily.

We returned enlivened by this novel discussion. Soon after, we parted, and two years later it was I who despatched the cluster of diamonds.

★★★★★★

Oudinot was recalled to France at the end of December, in order to preside over the electoral college at Versailles, and was only able to stop a week at Bar-le-Duc. In February 1810, he was sent to Holland, in command of the Army of the North, upon a very delicate mission. The emperor, jealous of his authority, considered that his brother Louis, whom he had placed upon the Dutch Throne to act as the docile proxy of the Imperial will, did not show himself a sufficiently supple instrument, and that he was assuming airs of independent sovereignty. Anxious for the interests of which he had accepted the control, the king closed his eyes to the trade which his subjects drove with England, and nothing was more calculated to wound Napoleon's pride. The arrival of our army therefore partook in itself of the nature of an ultimatum: either Louis and his people must submit, or the country would be annexed to the Empire.

Though the order was a brutal one, the agent selected to put it in force was the man most capable of minimizing its cruelty. Although Holland had for a moment thought of burying itself beneath its waters to save its existence, as in the days of Louis XIV., Oudinot realized that his would be a peaceful rather than a military role; it was not the hero of Friedland and Wagram, but the organizer of the Principality of Neuchâtel, who was now called upon to show his talents.

He did not at first penetrate into the heart of Holland, but stopped at this side of the Waal, at Bois-le-Duc, awaiting events and applying himself to maintaining the discipline of his troops, respecting customs, sparing individuals. His tact, his moderation, the wisdom of his conduct caused the always humiliating presence of a foreign army to be accepted without collision, and when, affairs refusing to be arranged, he advanced beyond the Waal as far as Utrecht, the population took no umbrage at this progress.

It was at Utrecht that the marshal received the news of the death of the Duchesse de Reggio. His son Victor and M. Pierre, Mayor of Bar-le-Duc, who, from a feeling of respect for the illustrious native of Bar, had accompanied the young man, travelled to Holland to bring the painful tidings.

I resume the narrative of Mme. la Duchesse de Reggio:

★★★★★★

In the spring of the same year, 1810, died at Bar Mme. la Maréchale Oudinot. In spite of certain sufferings which preceded the catastrophe, it came much earlier than was foreseen. The marshal was in Holland, charged with an important mission at once military and diplomatic, to which I shall have occasion to return. His eldest son Victor, a lieutenant in the mounted *chasseurs* of the Imperial Guard, was scarcely in time to give his last caress to his mother. He himself undertook the sad task of carrying the melancholy news to his father.

As I have already said, Élise, the marshal's eldest daughter, had been married two years earlier to General Pajol. Next came Nicolette, the second daughter; although she was not yet fifteen, her hand was promised to General Lorencez, who was then in Spain. Then came Auguste, a charming child of ten or eleven; he was at the College at Bar, where he carried off all the prizes without an effort. He was followed by Elisa, who was then about eight years old. Last came dear little Stéphanie, who was eighteen months.

Apart from the well-earned regrets which followed the Duchesse de Reggio to the grave, who could remain indifferent to the terrible loss endured by all her family? Who can witness unmoved the departure from this earth of the mother of six children?

★★★★★★

Meantime Louis grew more stubborn in his policy of resistance, and rather than allow himself to be reduced to being his brothers lieutenant, he resolved to abdicate (1 July 1810). Oudinot forthwith made his entry into Amsterdam. During the past six months he had succeeded so well in making the French name beloved, that the army on its arrival met with a sympathetic reception on which it had far from reckoned: the people came out to meet it; the dykes and trees were crowded with sightseers; in the town itself numerous flags floated from the windows; the Dutch soldiers fraternized with ours in the barrack-rooms. But Cambier, the minister whose duty it was to hand over the capital to the French authorities, was unable to conceal his sorrow at the disappearance of this proud little nation, which had fought for its liberty so bravely during centuries; and he wept as he addressed the marshal. Oudinot felt all the natural bitterness which must needs fill that wounded heart, and he confessed his emotion by the brusque tones in which he tried to dissimulate it:

"Come, come, Monsieur Cambier," he said, "don't cry like that, for, upon my word, I am ready to do the same, and what fools we should both look."

The Duc de Reggio spent the following months in superintending the cantonments of his troops, in visiting the country, and in commencing its assimilation to France.

In 1811 he divided his time between Holland, where he served as guide to Napoleon and Marie-Louise on the occasion of their visit, and Bar-le-Duc. But here I must allow the author of these *Memoirs* herself to narrate events with which she was so intimately connected:

******

After my sister's recovery, we left Bar, where Marshal Oudinot was expected. A year had elapsed since his wife's death; a thousand interests called to him in vain; his military and political mission in Holland had set an absolute obstacle to his return home before the time of which I speak.

Nothing could be more interesting, my children, than the documents relating to this great piece of business. It was even more diplomatic than military. Your father was able to achieve a really unhoped-for result, since he at once satisfied the highest wishes of the emperor, acquired a right to the gratitude of the sovereign he had dethroned, thanks to the carefulness of his procedure, and lastly was able to obtain the esteem and sympathy of the state he had invaded; all this in the face of unspeakable difficulties and obstacles.

All that refers to this fine page in your father's life is to be found in the archives of our house. I have already spoken of the homage paid him by the city of Amsterdam in 1811. Why should I not mention now the remarkable souvenir which came, some years later, to prove that, in spite of revolutions, and conflicting interests, what is just and fine always remains?

When the House of Orange, after the Peace, resumed its reign in Holland, the king of that country sent the grand cross of his orders to the Duc de Reggio, whom he had never seen, but whom he had learnt to know by the memories of justice, disinterestedness and loyalty which he had left behind him.

But let us return to my mother at Vitry, who had finally taken her resolution, so constantly postponed, to realize her property in Franche-Comté. As this kept her very busy, she often sent me to my aunt the canoness, an excellent, sensible woman, who always began by allowing me to paint the future in the bright colours which are pleasing to youth, and little by little, with her power of reasoning and her experience, brought me back to the realities of life.

At last my mother fixed the date for her departure and mine on the long-planned journey to Franche-Comté. We intended at first to go by Saint-Dizier and Langres, picking up on our way our man of business, M. Paillot, a notary of Bar, when my brother-in-law wrote to my mother urging her to fetch the lawyer at Bar itself. She decided to do so, and we were making our preparations when a second and more explicit letter arrived, which informed my mother of an urgent personal invitation from Marshal Oudinot to an evening party at which his daughter, the Comtesse Pajol, was to do the honours. "The marshal's insistence," wrote my brother-in-law, "seems to us to point to a preconceived plan; his repeated enquiries after my sister-in-law incline us to believe that he wishes to ask you for her hand in marriage."

This overture gave my mother food for deep reflection, with the result that she sent a messenger forthwith to fetch my uncle at Hancourt. He arrived without delay, and encouraged my mother to decide in favour of the road by Bar over that by Langres.

"Why should you hesitate," said he, "to select the road which naturally takes you to your children? Are you alarmed at the distinguished attention paid you by such a man as the Duc de Reggio? To accept it in no case commits you any further than all the others invited; and supposing, what is still very uncertain, that there is some idea of marriage for Eugénie beneath it, would you be justified in going out of the way of it, without first calculating the chances? "

This argument settled the question, and two days later we set out. Gustave was at school, and my mother, my nurse Rosalie and I travelled in my sister's carriage, which she had sent us from Bar. The weather was sultry and we were all asleep, when a sudden shock aroused us; we had tumbled down the steep slope of Saudrupt, at the foot of which our carriage was violently upset. The windows were broken; the glass wounded my left eye and cut a muscle in my mother's right hand, while my nurse, still more unfortunate than ourselves, was thrown off the box to the ground, where she lay insensible, with her head cut open.

My sister's house was soon transformed into a kind of hospital. Dr. Moreau, a friend of my brother-in-law's, hastened to give my mother and me the benefit of his zeal and intelligence. He saved my eye by applying leeches, and set us on our feet in a very short time; while his colleague Champion restored Rosalie to us in ten or twelve days after the catastrophe.

The marshal was dining at the same house as Dr. Moreau when the latter was hurriedly sent for, with the exaggerated report that Mme. and Mlle, de Coucy had been carried to Mme. de la Guérivière's more dead than alive. The marshal was thunderstruck; and soon returning home, he begged his daughter, the Comtesse Pajol, and Mlle. Oudinot, since Comtesse de Lorencez, to call and make enquiries.

Meantime, the whole town was set in a ferment by our accident. Apart from the interest that people were kind enough to take in us and in M. and Mme. de la Guérivière, who were very popular, a fact had occurred which mightily stirred public curiosity. The marshal had countermanded his reception, giving frankly as his reason the distress inspired by our condition.

A few days elapsed, when suddenly the marshal sent to ask my mother on what day and at what time he might call and personally assure himself of our progress.

He arrived, accompanied by his son Auguste in a collegian's uniform. I attentively examined the child and the father. The latter had shaved his mustachios; his figure and his step, which were impeded by his wound when I first saw him, had resumed their normal state, and his whole appearance seemed to me as attractive as it was distinguished. I had just arrived at this opinion when the marshal turned to me and put a question specially directed to my condition. So much interest was displayed in his words that my brother-in-law, impelled by a movement for which he was quite unable to account to himself, raised my veil, and said, "See, *monsieur le maréchal*, what has happened to that poor young face." The keen, rapid glance which the marshal threw upon me will never leave my memory. It was one of curiosity mingled with lively interest. We exchanged monosyllables, and he soon took his leave and withdrew, leaving a most favourable impression upon my mother.

We had also seen Mme. Pajol, who was in very weak health at the time, and who had left for Plombières, where her father was to join her. He continued to send to enquire; and a few days before his departure, he returned in person, and found us well and cheerful. This time the ice was broken. The conversation was easier on both sides. Your father was charming, and told us many curious anecdotes of his interesting career.

The day after the marshal's second visit, we were just going out for a walk, about eight in the evening, when Pils, the marshal's valet, came up with a note for M. de la Guérivière, and stopped him as he was about to accompany us. We had already taken a few steps.

"Go on without me," he said; "the marshal wishes to see me; I will go round to him."

With a common accord, and without exchanging a word, we returned at once to the house, and sitting down in the drawing-room, awaited my brother-in-law's return. He was away a long time. Evening fell, and the daylight gave way to a fine moonlight night. All the sounds of the town had ceased one by one. Thus, in complete silence, and without any light but that of the moon, we waited till eleven o'clock. At last steps were heard in the distance, and soon M. de la Guérivière's tall figure appeared before us.

Throwing his hat on a chair, he came up to me, and said:

"Sister, would you like to marry Marshal Oudinot?"

We all three gave a single cry. It was one of delight, not of surprise; for without confessing it to one another, we had for some hours guessed the real reason for this interview.

None of us spoke; and my brother-in-law, striding to and fro, sought to gather the necessary calmness to fulfil his errand conscientiously. At last, turning to my mother, he told it her more or less in these words:

"I found the marshal awaiting me impatiently. When he saw me, he familiarly and confidently took my arm, led me to his room, and said, 'I can no longer remain in the position into which my bereavement has thrown me. I want to marry a woman young enough to be able to mould herself, without effort, to my character and habits. Both for my children's sake and my own, I wish to find guarantees of security in her family, her education and her principles; instead of a fortune, I hope to find simple and modest tastes. As soon as I began to entertain the idea of contracting a new union, my memory went back to your young sister-in-law. I considered that she must unite in her own person all the conditions I have named. Will you undertake to put before her and her mother the wishes I entertain?' Without giving me time to reply, the marshal continued, 'She knows that I have six children; but they are good children, who will only look at my happiness in the step I am contemplating. Tell Mlle, de Coucy also that I am forty-four years old, and that I have five hundred thousand *francs* a year. My social position is well known, and I shall be happy to share it with her.'

"That," resumed my brother-in-law, "is the purport of the first and most important part of our conversation. The marshal leaves for Plombières tomorrow, and he has asked me to despatch an express to him in a few days to bring him your reply."

Thereupon all three turned to me, and I saw that I should have to give my decision; but, before all, I wished to know the opinion of my mother, who said, "No, I will not direct you in this. The position offered you is too well known; the person who offers it is too celebrated; you yourself understand the question too well for me to seek to influence you. This important decision rests with you alone."

"Well, then," said I, "I accept!"

The confidence with which the marshal asked of me his own happiness and that of his family, which included some very young children, placed this mission before me in such touching, such honourable colours, that I put on one side all that was perilous in it: I seemed not to have the right to refuse. Why should I not add that the glory of that name placed a great weight in the balance?

I shall not relate here all the details of my first private interview with the marshal, in which were laid, so to speak, the foundations of our future. Your father was at once frank, communicative, and full of compassion for me, under-standing my agitation and embarrassment, and when, after half an hour, my mother and sister returned, they found me reassured and full of gratitude. Thenceforward the marshal came to visit us quite simply. He also invited us to a great ceremonial dinner at his house, at which Mme. Poriquet, the sister of the marshal's first wife, received his guests. I there met again, for the first time for about four years, the marshal's eldest son. The lapse of time, his change of uniform, his graver and more serious air would have prevented me from recognizing him elsewhere than at his father's.

We also spent a couple of days at Jeand'heurs. The entertainments were to last a week longer, but my mother resisted all persuasion to prolong our visit, and it was then that she had a serious interview with the marshal.

"I am going to Vitry, and from there to the country," said my mother.

"And I," replied the marshal, "before returning to Holland, where the emperor has ordered me once more, will first go to Paris to take him into our confidence. I will send you my news; permit me also to write direct to Mlle, de Coucy."

On the day of our departure from Bar, the marshal came to say goodbye. I was much affected, and talked little. He accused me of coldness, and complained to my sister, who wrote and told me of it; but the cloud soon passed away.

The marshal wrote that he had seen the emperor at Rambouillet, who, after receiving the confidence of his projected marriage, told him that before all he must return to Holland to complete his work there and prepare the country to receive the emperor himself as its new sovereign. He added that he would be accompanied by Marie Louise, and that he would rely entirely upon the marshal to see that they were well received. This was so difficult an undertaking that we at once understood how much time and care would be required for the task.

Meantime the marshal had gone straightway to Holland, whence he wrote to us frequently, but briefly, and we were unable to find in his letter any reference to an approaching solution. As a matter of fact, he did not yet know the date of the Imperial journey, and on the other hand he had hard work before him, as I have said, to persuade the country, all bruised with the last measures of which it was the victim, to put on its holiday clothes in order to conceal its wounds.

We spent the long summer entirely at Hancourt and Lentilles. The weather was marvellously fine; every night, under an Italian sky, we went out to admire the famous comet, and I vow I owe it as much gratitude as did the wine-growers for the celebrated vintage it brought them; for it furnished many a subject of idle conversation at that period of my life when it was so often necessary to hide my thoughts beneath insignificant phrases.

Certainly, these were generally serious; but I should be wanting in sincerity if I failed to confess that there were a few frivolous thoughts mingled among them. I often thought of that young empress of whom I had caught so rapid a glimpse, not dreaming at the time that anything would bring me nearer to her. I thought of the emperor, who would speak to me, and to whom I should have to reply, when I was presented to him. The marshal had amused himself by frightening me about the Imperial Court and the great world of Paris.

Autumn came and found us still at Lentilles, where we received the first details of the emperor's journey. Their Majesties had been well received. It was an administrative *tour de force* on the part of the Duc de Reggio. The emperor believed, or pretended to believe, that the country had rallied to him completely; he expressed his great satisfaction to the marshal, who accompanied him to the extreme frontier. The marshal mentioned his marriage projects a second time. "Go," said the emperor, "go and marry Mlle, de Coucy; I give my entire consent."

Without losing a moment, the marshal went to Amsterdam, received the heartfelt *adieux* of that city, crossed Paris, and arrived at Bar, where interests of every kind imperiously demanded his presence. Already war was talked of, and the marshal was informed that he would soon receive the command of an army corps.

The marshal invited himself to breakfast with my mother on Christmas Eve 1811. I rose in a state of great excitement by the pale light of that 24th of December. My mother had only summoned to that intimate breakfast my aunt the canoness, and M. Orisi, a charming old man, her friend and adviser. All was arranged and warmed in my mother's little house by nine o'clock in the morning; my excitement increased from minute to minute, and it had reached its summit when, at ten o'clock, the marshal, accompanied by my brother-in-law, rang gently at the door. I had reckoned on the noise of a carriage to prepare me for the interview; but the travellers had left their equipage and their servants at the post-house, and had come on foot to the Rue de Frignicourt, where we lived.

I awaited the signal in my room. La Guérivière came to fetch me, and his radiant air gave me courage. In a moment I realized that I must try and dominate a childish timidity for which the time was past. The breakfast was gay and charming. The general conversation was resumed in the drawing-room, and the marshal and M. d'Orisi sparkled with a thousand delightful pleasantries. They took a liking to one another, and the dear old man remained till the day of his death the adorer of his new friend. I was very fond of M. d'Orisi; but if he had had no other title to my good graces than his friendly assistance that morning, that would have been sufficient to endear him to me.

Soon, after a journey to Paris to draw up our marriage-contract, which the emperor signed, the marshal announced his arrival for the

12th of January (18 12); he had been appointed commander-in-chief of the 2nd Corps of the Grande Armée, and was shortly to go and see to its organization in Westphalia. The emperor was urging his departure, and he, on his side, urged my mother to such a degree that, in spite of her good head and her activity, she almost gave way beneath the infinite details that bore down upon her. Soon, however, my whole family came to her aid, gathering round us and staying with us until the wedding. My poor Aunts de Lentilles alone were kept at home by their health, unable to face the winter, which was very severe that year. As for me, my children, I knew not whether it was cold or hot.

The marshal informed us that he would be accompanied by almost his entire staff, and that he wished to invite a large number of his relations and of his friends at Bar-le-Duc; and, as on our side too the guests were numerous, we had many lodgings to prepare, and a table of some fifty covers to provide for.

At last the 18th arrived. I was dressed and down in the drawing-room, where the family was assembled, when at eleven o'clock a confused noise made us understand that the marshal had arrived at his hotel. Soon the tumult increased and drew nearer, and we gathered that he was approaching the house. He was preceded by so great a crowd that his *aides-de-camp* had the greatest difficulty in clearing a way for him. A guard of honour, composed of the pick of Vitry society, and commanded by that dear, good General de Possesse, whom you knew, afforded a brilliant mounted escort to the Marshal, who was on foot, in uniform, as were his son, his son-in-law, and all his staff.

On reaching our door, at which stood waiting the men of my family, the marshal stepped from among the gold-laced throng that accompanied him and entered the drawing-room alone. After bowing with the grace and dignity of which your father seemed to have the monopoly, he took me by the hand, beckoned to his friends, and presented them to me by name, commencing with his children; then throwing up a window, without leaving hold of my hand, he told me with him to greet the commandant and the guard of honour. A cheer rose as from one throat, and the crowd joined in the cry of "Long live Marshal Oudinot, and long live the Emperor! "

On the 19th he came and spent some hours with my Aunt Clotilde and myself; this was the best part of the day, on which I had the bitter regret of only catching an occasional glimpse of my mother. At nightfall it was time to think of my *toilette*. The reception was to begin at seven o'clock, the supper was at nine, the civil marriage at eleven, and the religious ceremony at midnight.

Messages succeeded one another to hurry my appearance in the drawing-room, where the marshal and all the guests were assembled. Mme. Morel, my maid, fixed her hundredth pin. At last I followed my mother and found myself in the presence of my betrothed, his children, his officers, and the families and friends of each. As I said, there were several from Bar, including Messieurs Poriquet, Pierre, Buffault, Gillon, the *prefect*, and others, all strangers to my relations and to my Vitry friends; it was natural that a little stiffness should reign at first. The marshal was impatiently awaiting my entrance, which put an end to this state of constraint; not that I was of much use, for I was simply stupid; but I was the cause of a general movement which broke the ice.

After the introductions, some rubbers were arranged; but I well remember that no one attended to his game. My sister teased the marshal by reproaching him with not having made himself smart enough for the occasion. He wore a simple undress uniform. They quarrelled for a moment in fun. Supper was announced at nine o'clock; but just before, we were suddenly dazzled by the reappearance of the bridegroom, who had escaped for a moment and now returned in his full uniform as a Marshal of the Empire. It was the first time I saw him in all his splendour; I was enraptured, and my admiration was in different degrees shared by all the witnesses.

At last the hour came; all was ready at the mayor's; we rose from the supper-table to step into the carriages.

A crowd of people of our acquaintance filled the approaches and rooms of the *mairie*. They crushed with an eager curiosity to catch sight of the marshal, who became the cynosure of all eyes. How proud I felt of him! All the details are still present in my mind; and I distinctly remember hearing at the foot of the stairs the words "The Duchesse de Reggio's carriage!" uttered by the marshal's *chasseur*, who was thus the first to pronounce my new name.

When we arrived at the handsome parish church of Vitry, the scene assumed another aspect; and during the sacred ceremony I saw everything confusedly. The church was brilliantly lighted and, in spite of the lateness of the hour and the terrible weather, crammed with people. I felt, rather than saw, my family grouped behind me, while that of the marshal and all the uniforms were drawn up behind him.

It had been arranged that our country friends, who had not taken part in the gathering of the preceding day, should be invited to the farewell breakfast. Accordingly, on the morning of the 20th, I found assembled in the drawing-room, with my family, Messieurs and Mesdames de Bouvet, Duhamel, de Liniers, &c. Almost all the other wedding guests had left. Some had gone back that morning to Bar; and those from Paris, who were almost all about to join the coming campaign, had hastened back to their families and their affairs in the metropolis.

The end of breakfast was the signal for departure. I anxiously watched the tearful face of my dear mother, vainly repeating to myself that I was only leaving her for a few days.

Soon, the sound of carriages was heard and farewells exchanged. I was pleased to see my sister taking her place in our carriage, which set out drawn by six horses at full speed. The marshal chatted gaily with Christine, leaving me leisure to reflect on those I had just left on my mother's doorstep, throwing me their last *adieux* and blessings.

The gates of the mansion at Bar stood open: General de Lorencez, his wife, Victor, and M. Gouy, the marshal's bosom friend, who had all left Vitry in the early morning, were awaiting us. I also saw, for the first time, Colonel Chevallot, an old and faithful friend whom you well remember.

I had just entered my room when I was roused from my meditation by the sound of a door opening behind me. It was not that which communicated with the marshal. I was quickly reassured by hearing a light footstep and a woman's voice. In the darkness I recognised Mme. de Lorencez. "I have come to ask you," she said, "whether you do not think you should pay my grandfather a visit at home before meeting him at dinner." The kindness of this reminder moved me to tears; and hastening to follow my stepdaughter across the snow-covered avenues of the garden, I let her guide me to the house of my husband's father, in the street now known as the Rue Oudinot. He was a handsome old man of eighty-three; he took me in his arms, and I was happy once more to pronounce the name of father, a word which I had not uttered for five years.

Early the next day, Victor entered my room; but it was another Victor. He did not seek to conceal his emotion. He came to ask me for my friendship; and I had already inwardly promised it him before he asked for it. You know, my children, how constant it has been on both sides. The marshal was charmed with my account of my interview with his son, and touched with the impulse which had led the young man to me.

The day did not pass without some emotions recalling those of the day before. For instance, I was much tried at the sight of Mme. Poriquet, the sister of the late *maréchale*, who entered trembling and all in tears upon her husband's arm. I understood all that this formal visit must have cost her; but I have cause to believe that she guessed the sympathy which her situation inspired in me, for from that day to the day of her death she was my friend.

The marshal's correspondence became more and more active, and the rumours of an approaching war with Russia increased from day to day. My husband said nothing as yet, and I was careful of questioning him as to the day of our separation, the vague thought of which so often, phantom-like, hovered between my happiness and myself.

M. Le Tellier, the first *aide-de-camp*, had gone, but he was replaced by Messieurs de Thermes and Jacqueminot. The latter, who was a native of Bar, kept the whole town moving. So soon as our great dinners were over and all the guests had left, messieurs the *aides-de-camp*, abandoning their full-dress uniforms, swords and head-dresses, organized daily *soirées dansantes*, in concert with the mothers of the young girls of the town.

I must confess, since I am telling all that concerns me, that the first details that reached me of these improvised balls, in which formerly I would so gladly have taken part, made me commit the sin of envy; but I took care not to let this be seen, realizing that I had taken up too serious a position to maintain a girlish attitude. Moreover, a salutary instinct habitually warned me against what was likely to displease the marshal, and I often guessed his thoughts without consulting him.

One evening, however, somebody had thought of playing dance-music in the dining-room after dinner. There had been a number of young married women and girls at this meal; one of the prettiest of the latter was Mlle. Henrionnet, who has since become Mme. Landry-Gillon. This impromptu dance commenced without the marshal's seeming to disapprove of it, and without further reflection I mingled in it. I saw my husband disappear from the room, and soon followed him to his study. The result of our interview was that I gave up dancing for good, if not without regret, at least without a struggle. Besides, events would soon have put an end to this form of amusement, even if my mind had not been made up beforehand.

The marshal had resolved to take me with him, and to keep me by his side so long as the military operations did not assume too hostile a character. You can imagine my delight at learning this plan! Devoted as I was to my husband, I saw at first nothing but the happiness of delaying our separation; but it was not long before I became a little alarmed at the thought of the new era about to open before me. I foresaw that I should not enjoy the marshal's constant presence, as at Bar; and I dreaded lest I should be much left to myself.

The decision taken by General de Lorencez brought me some consolation. He had been appointed chief of staff to the army corps commanded by the marshal, and he too proposed to take his wife with him. Mme. de Lorencez, who was only sixteen years of age, was morally thirty. Habitually silent and reflective, she could never be taken for indifferent, so prompt was the expression in her deep blue eyes. When she spoke, the sweetness of her voice and the charm of her pronunciation atoned for any too positive laconicism of her language. At rare intervals she was capable of the most communicative gaiety. She was religious and charitable, and fulfilled all her duties as a natural thing. Every affection was deep and serious in that loving heart, which embraced all things. And finally her figure, her gait, her whole appearance were alike distinguished.

The want of time and the severity of the season had prevented my making acquaintance with the younger children of my husband. The little girls were accordingly not sent for; both were at school, one in Paris, the other at Nancy. I regretted this postponement, when one day I found Auguste in his father's study. More easy to bring over than his sisters, the marshal had made him come to embrace us before our departure. I see him still, standing by the mantel in his college dress; and even if I had forgotten him, my own son Henry would restore to me his perfect image.

M. Gouy held in his hands, with rare devotion, all the strings of the marshal's numerous affairs. He conducted them better, with more zeal and application, than his own, working from morning to night to put everything on a good footing before that departure which might leave everything to be hoped or feared. At this time there were as many as seven agents of the marshal's diverse interests. All of these, according to his wishes, came together with M. Gouy, who each year summed up the general situation. His penetrating eye discovered any irregularity; he would point it out in his positive and often harsh phrases, without fearing the trouble of this work for himself, nor that which he caused the marshal, whom he opposed without hesitation or scruple whenever he considered necessary.

During this time no one thought (nor did I dream of it myself) of initiating me into the management of this fortune, of which I had but a very confused idea. I had scarcely even ventured to take up my role of mistress of the house; for to give an order of any sort seemed to me a terrible business. All that I saw I thought so beautiful that I took no thought of the reverse of the medal. I therefore let myself live, during these early days, without asking if there were any other duties for me to perform than that of loving my husband and both our families.

Chapter 4

Preparations of War Against Russia

We were a large travelling party, and in order to find a sufficient number of post-horses at every station, it was necessary to spread ourselves on the road. Two *aides-de-camp* were to open the route; then came General and the Comtesse de Lorencez; and the marshal and I next, accompanied by his secretary and all his household, in two carriages with six horses apiece.

At last the day of departure came; and here, my children, began the active and stormy life which has brought me, from excitement to excitement, up to the present date. I have since seen many happy days; immense satisfactions, numerous gratifications awaited me; but these were destined to be mingled with so many trials, and crossed with such terrible catastrophes, that I should infallibly have lost my head had the veil of the future been for a single moment raised before my eyes.

On the 14th of February, two coaches and six awaited us in the court-yard at Bar. They set out before us, filled with the people I have mentioned above, who preceded us as far as the village of Naives. We arrived shortly, in a town carriage, in which my mother, my sister and my brother-in-law had mounted beside my husband and myself. After exchanging our sad farewell *adieux*, I stepped alone with the marshal into the first post-carriage.

Till that day I had always moved in a narrow and monotonous circle. All was new to me; and though the road from Bar to Verdun has nothing very remarkable to offer the traveller, and on this occasion was all covered with snow, I made remarks on everything I saw.

It was night when we pulled up at the Hôtel des Trois Maures. The charm of an inn has long since disappeared from my eyes; but under the circumstances I am describing to you, everything seemed delicious to me. Our gaiety added to the value of all things. The marshal, delighted at returning to a life of activity, seemed radiant, and everyone underwent the same influence.

It was Shrove Tuesday. Our windows were on the street, and we lost none of the carnival uproar that went on beneath. We were wide awake when they came to tell us, before daybreak, that the horses were put to. A chill sleet was falling, and it was not until the sun put to flight the mist that I was enabled to resume my observations of the day before. These amused the marshal, who said to me more than once, "Isn't the world large?"

The same day we passed through Dun, Stenay and Sedan. We were to sleep at Mézieres, the first fortified town I had seen. The ramparts, the draw-bridges, the gloomy archways, beneath which our heavy carriage rumbled, filled me with a fright which tickled the marshal. We alighted at a well-warmed and well-lighted apartment, where the marshal forthwith received numerous visits. I was astonished at the resignation with which he submitted to this performance at the close of a tiring day; but I soon learnt to grow used to it. He knew and received people wherever he went. Notably soldiers of all grades arrived from every side; and their eagerness was explained by the amiable manner in which they were welcomed.

The subsequent days we followed the banks of the Meuse by way of Namur, Liège and Maastricht; and on the fourth we reached the Rhine, which we crossed by a bridge of boats at Wesel. On the sixth day we were to reach Munster, where the marshal was to take the command of the first forces of the 2nd Corps of the Grande Armée. A military reception had been prepared for the general-in-chief; and he was greatly annoyed to find the roads so bad that we were still two leagues from the city when night came to overtake us.

Despite the darkness, I perceived a group of men on horseback, who came crowding round the carriage. Manly, jovial, resounding voices all simultaneously addressed the marshal, who recognized by his voice each of the generals who were to find themselves under his orders. All spoke at once, each gave his name to make sure of being recognized, and in each name the marshal seemed to find that of a friend. Alas! what sad reflections that recollection evokes. Of those ten or twelve generals, all then in the prime of manhood, not one remains alive today, (as at time of first publication).

We reached the gates of Munster, escorted by this distinguished company. The garrison turned out under arms and formed in line to the house of Baron von Drott, where we were to stay. There was no reception that night; but the next morning the entire corps of officers, amounting in all to twelve hundred persons, arrived in full uniform, with the generals at its head, to pay its official visit, and my distress was great when I heard from the marshal that after himself I was to receive these gentlemen, who had asked to be presented to me. I had therefore to summon up great resolution. It nearly failed me, however, at the first step I took in the vast salon, round which was ranged a three-fold row of officers, waiting silently for me to appear among them. Suspecting my shyness, the generals stepped forward at once. They very obligingly surrounded me; I felt my spirits return, and my timidity was thus concealed from the greater number.

Yet another social duty was laid upon me. The French were at that time the masters everywhere, and obtained on every hand an amount of homage which never failed them. It was perhaps to our power at that time that I owed the extreme politeness of the ladies of Munster. Perhaps also, and I prefer to think so, the marshal's great name and pure renown contributed to this cordiality; but the fact is that, on the second night after my arrival, I had to receive, at their own request, an endless number of countesses, baronesses and abbesses. This last title, which at first astonished me, is borne in that country like the two first, and carries with it neither ecclesiastical character nor obligations. The Munster abbesses were, like the other ladies of the nobility, their companions, covered with rouge, with flowers, feathers and jewels. They were all charming to me, and I returned their collective visit at what they called their club, where they met in great numbers one evening to receive me.

Several emigrants of 1791 were also present at our receptions. They had met with so hearty a welcome during their exile from the numerous nobility of the district that many of them had settled down there. Among these were the Comte de Flamarens and the old Comte de Sesmaisons. At Munster, too, I first met the *abbé*, who was then known as the Baron, Louis. He was charged by the emperor with the financial organization of the country; for Munster was the capital of a French *prefecture*, with the Comte de Saillant for its prefect.

We next went to the pretty town of Hanover, where we were to stay. I spent part of our sojourn in visiting the city; and with General and Mme. de Lorencez I went over the famous hot-houses of Hernhausen, a pleasance occupied by Jerome Bonaparte, the King of Westphalia.

On the second day after our arrival, we entertained at dinner a number of French generals, who were gathered in the town, where the cavalry was being rehorsed. To amuse these gentlemen after dinner we played at *reversis*, but although my stepdaughter Lorencez and I were not naturally inclined to disparage or mock at our friends, we had great difficulty in retaining a simultaneous burst of laughter when it came to the turn of General Duverger, one of the four players, to deal. Tall and lean, his hair powdered and dressed into two pigeon-wings, which had quite gone out of fashion, he had the appearance of a mummy in uniform. He only just touched the cards with the tips of his fingers, without moving his elbows, and yet they came to us straight as rain. I never saw anything like it.

I hope that this worthy and antiquated son of Mars paid too little attention to matters of this earth to notice the movements of our youth. Our two husbands, who had seen everything, reproached us at night for our tempestuous gaiety, although they made allowances for the fact that Mme. de Lorencez and I were only thirty-six years old between us.

From Hanover we went to Brunswick, and thence to Magdeburg, where we alighted in a large house on the parade-ground. Marshal Davout had just left it to go forward with his army corps, and in connection with this I will tell you of a singular mistake on the part of his wife, whom he had sent for to see him before he went further. It was before she arrived that He received the order to push forward immediately. The Princesse d'Eckmühl had not had time to hear of this change of plan. She arrived from Paris during the night following our installation at Magdeburg, and, on mentioning her name, had the city gates opened for her, although it was after hours. She simply told the postilions to drive her to the marshal's, and, when they pulled up at our door, she naturally wished to be admitted. This was refused her; she sent for the *aide-de-camp* on duty, and although she did not recognize him as belonging to Marshal Davout, she insisted.

It was then that M. Le Tellier said to her that this noise would awaken *Mme, la Maréchale!* At these words the Princesse d'Eckmühl demanded and obtained explanations, and M. Le Tellier naturally placed himself at her disposal to find her a lodging for the remainder of this night, so stormy for her. She breakfasted with us the next day, and we laughed together at the misunderstanding.

She was at that time exceedingly handsome, very much the princess, and very magnificent in her manners. I have always been on good terms with her; but although our husbands used the second person singular in addressing one another, we never became intimate.

To return to our departure and to our journey, which was resumed by military stages. It was a sign of the war, to which we were drawing near. My husband's carriage, in which I occupied a corner, travelled in the midst of his army corps. These were the orders we had received. Nevertheless, when within two days of Berlin, he thought he would be able to enter it alone; but the Prince de Neuchâtel, major-general of the army and interpreter of the emperor's wishes, hearing of this, reproached my husband, and ordered him to return to the 2nd Corps and make a triumphal entry at its head into the Prussian capital.

France and Prussia, which was nominally our ally, were in a very delicate position. Nobody doubted but that the friendship was forced rather than voluntary on the part of Prussia, and the result proved this to be the case. King Frederic William was to supply a contingent in the event of war with Russia, and naturally to permit the passage of our army. But while awaiting its arrival he had hastened to quit his capital and retire with his family to Potsdam. My husband was fully acquainted with this position of affairs, and his intention in entering Berlin alone had been to spare the King of Prussia the display of a triumphal entry into his capital. The marshal thought it sufficient to accomplish a fact without wounding by the forms with which it was done; but this was in no way the policy of the emperor.

We alighted at the Saken Palace, made ready and furnished for the marshal by order of the King of Prussia, who moreover had sent in a complete domestic establishment: valets, butlers, cooks, footmen, and two town carriages with their horses, the whole to be at the general-in-chief's disposal during the whole length of his stay.

Although surprised and vexed at this munificence, the marshal felt that he was not at liberty to refuse it; and I may add that this constraint bore upon him during all the time he remained in the town, where, as elsewhere, he succeeded in joining the military and diplomatic interests entrusted to him with the consideration due to the power of a sovereign offended in his own country.

France was represented at Berlin by the Comte de Saint-Marsan, a Sardinian by birth and an excellent man, which did not prevent him from being a brilliant and subtle diplomatist. He and your father understood each other capitally from the first A little later there was added to them the Comte Louis de Narbonne, at that time *aide-de-camp* to the emperor and standing very high in his favour.

All the memoirs of the time speak of this remarkable personage. I will only tell you that at a very early age he was Minister of War, for a moment, under Louis XVI., and that he only saved his head by emigrating. Later, when the time came, the emperor gave him an excellent reception, and began by paying some debts of which he had heard. A little later still, the emperor discovered some others, and said to M. de Narbonne, "But, my dear count, have you still more debts?"

"Why, Sire, it is all I ever had." And the emperor paid again, and the dear old man consecrated to him until his dying day, which, alas, was not slow in coming, his devotion, his loyalty and his high intelligence.

It was he who was charged with negotiating the marriage between the emperor and the Archduchess Maria Louisa of Austria. To a profound knowledge of men and things, and a loyal and well-considered scheme of policy, he added a charming wit. He was a man of fine manners, and he restored the tradition of these to the new Court of the Tuileries. I shall never forget, not only the exquisite grace which he displayed in his relations with us, but also the kindness with which he sent me news of the marshal from headquarters, at a time when I was trembling for his safety.

But to resume my story. The marshal was accordingly obliged to ride at the head of his forty thousand men, and I saw them march past from our ambassador's windows. It was a splendid sight! Who could have foretold then that those numerous battalions, that brilliant cavalry, that fine and imposing artillery would for the greater part remain sunk in the snows of Russia, nine short months later?

As I was in Berlin, as it were, as contraband, I remained indoors as much as possible, delighted when my husband's ever multiplying obligations permitted him to join me. In the midst of this immense palace, I by preference used a little silent, secluded drawing-room, which was decorated in perfect taste. It contained a pretty tea-table which I was told had been placed there for me and which had belonged to the beautiful Queen of Prussia.

My health was somewhat indifferent, and compelled me to dine by myself, in order to avoid the fatigue of a table always occupied by my husband's military household and a crowd of visitors. Nevertheless the marshal sometimes insisted on my appearing to entertain some notability brought there by circumstances. In this way I made the acquaintance of Marshal Victor, Duc de Bellune, Marshal Ney, Duc d'Elchingen, and Generals Sebastiani, de La Riboisière and many others, some of whom passed through Berlin never to return.

It was said that the Emperor was preparing to leave Paris to place himself at the head of the forces drawn up in echelon from the Rhine to the Vistula, and divided into twelve army corps, amounting in all to four or five hundred thousand men.

Marshal Davout commanded the 1st Corps; he had under him General Pajol, who commanded the cavalry. The latter had with him his wife, whom I had not seen since she became my stepdaughter. When the 1st Corps received its marching orders, General Pajol resolved to send his wife to join her father in Berlin, so that her journey back to France might coincide with mine. I was much moved when I saw her. Although my friendship with your elder sister was longer in forming than that with her junior, it became none the less sincere, as you were enabled to judge during the short time you were permitted to know Mme. Pajol. Yes, the years developed in her those qualities of heart and charms of mind of which she had brought such fertile roots, and I mourned her the more since she had never given me greater proofs of affection than at the moment when she was taken from us in so crushing a manner.

But to return to the days of our first relations, I must say that we were only in perfect accord in our regrets at the approaching separation from our husbands and our terrible fears of what was to follow. She described to us, with sorrowful energy, her *adieux* at Dantzig, where she had left General Pajol; and she told us that, when her carriage broke down six leagues from there, she had thought herself happy in being able to exaggerate the difficulties of her position in the midst of a disordered country in order to send for her husband to come to her assistance and thus embrace him yet once more in spite of what they had regarded as their final leave-taking. Ah! at that time the *adieux* of soldiers and their families were cruel indeed.

At last the fatal day also approached for Mme. de Lorencez and myself. The order to depart arrived, and while the marshal prepared to set out for Marienwerder, he gave orders and made arrangements to send his two daughters and me back to Bar-le-Duc.

On the 2nd of May 1812, five post-carriages obstructed the courtyard of the Saken Palace. The marshal and General Pajol despatched the three first, which contained us and our belongings, and then stepped with their officers into the two others, which took the opposite direction, proceeding towards the seat of war while we went towards France.

My two stepdaughters bore with them expectations of motherhood which had been denied to me, and my grief at the moment was so intense that it prevented me from thinking of the consolation that awaited me of meeting my family again. Mme. Pajol, who was alone in her carriage, went ahead to order our night's lodging. I followed in mine, accompanied by Mme. de Lorencez, who had begged to be with me. In our third carriage were M. Boudart, the general's secretary, and our women. I saw nothing with my eyes; I only felt that each stride of the horses carried us further away from those we loved, and my grief was such as almost to amount to despair. How I suffered that day! We arrived, shattered body and soul, at our first halting-place, Truïnbrisen, a horrid little town between Berlin and Wittemberg.

It was, I believe, at our third stop that an extraordinary incident occurred. Mme. Pajol, who had already been over the road, traced our itinerary with great intelligence, and tried always to keep in front of us, so as to prepare what was necessary. But this time our three carriages arrived almost simultaneously at the appointed place. It was a lonely post-house, standing at the foot of a mountain. It was still broad daylight, and we perceived a number of carriages with armorial bearings, and a great movement of horses and livery servants in the courtyard. We made for our rooms across this hubbub; but soon we were at our windows to witness the departure of Prince Eugène de Beauharnais, for it was he, on his road to rejoin the Grande Armée. He caught sight of us, enquired who we were, and came up the staircase straightway.

No sooner did we see him take this unexpected direction than a panic seized all three of us. Without knowing what she was doing, Mme. Pajol snatched her sister's cashmere shawl; the latter struggled to retain it; and I vainly sought an outlet for escape. All this was the business of two seconds, and the prince entered before we had resumed our countenances. However, Mme. Pajol managed to reply suitably to Josephine's amiable son, who had all the charm and grace of his mother. He came, he said, "to take our messages for our husbands." But I was and remained stupid. Later I wept for shame and regret. I wrote my confession to the marshal that very night before going to bed, and fell asleep in all humility. I learned afterwards that Prince Eugène, when he met the marshal, showed extreme consideration in the manner in which he related this anecdote.

As we approached Mayence, we heard that the emperor was on the road to join the army, and that we ran a chance of being short of horses. By travelling night and day, we succeeded in reaching Metz before him, and shortly afterwards we reached the end of our journey, Bar-le-Duc.

I visited every corner of my house in tears, and the marshal's room in particular. There everything seemed to speak of him. I even seemed to recognize the smell of his pipe, and hugged the illusion. There are moments in life when one loves to accentuate one's sorrow!

At last the marshal's first letter arrived. The sight alone of his handwriting on the address caused me so great an emotion that it was long before I could grasp the meaning of his expressions of affection. There is something more sacred in the written than in the spoken word. It is as though nothing could destroy or alter what is thus sworn to us. Mme. de Lorencez also had a charming letter from her husband, who was not to leave mine. It was not the same in Mme. Pajol's case; the 1st Corps, to which the general belonged, seemed destined to strike the first blow, whereas the marshal, who had arrived at Marienwerder, had not as yet received his marching orders, and for the moment I breathed again.

Soon M. Gouy arrived. He came to install me in the position which he wished to see me take up at the head of that household in which, so far as authority was concerned, I had till then remained a mere nullity. And at last came my mother, accompanied by M. and Mme. de la Guérivière; and in the happiness of this meeting and the busy life I led I found the only salutary remedy for my increasing distress. During the war, naturally all amusements were suspended. My uncle brought with him Enguerrand, that charming boy, who came enraptured with joy at the promise that on his leaving Saint-Cyr, where he was going, my husband would take him as his *aide-de-camp*. Alas!

The whole army had crossed the Vistula; and as it advanced upon the Niemen, letters came with less frequency.

It was about this time that I was told one morning that the mistress of the boarding-school at Nancy to which my husband had sent my little stepdaughter Stéphanie, had arrived at Bar with the child, whom I took to live with me at home. Her little heart opened out to me; and from the very first day commenced that intimacy between us which nothing has ever broken.

At last war was openly declared, and our army marched beyond the Niemen without as yet finding the opportunity for the great battle which everyone was expecting. Slight and partial engagements alone fed the ardent interest with which the letters and newspapers were received. In those days the post from abroad came only four times a week. Those were moments of fever when it arrived, and the intervals were days in which we painfully vegetated and counted the hours.

I was expecting a bust of my husband, which an artist of some talent had executed in Berlin during our stay there. One day a large case arrived from Germany. I dragged my mother away to come and see it opened. Palpitating with eagerness I saw the lid removed, and then the first, second and third covers of paper in which it was wrapped. What was my horror at seeing one of the plaster shoulders smashed and ready to fall from the body. A fatal thought seized hold of my imagination; and it was realized but too well, for a few days later the marshal had his shoulder shattered by a ball of grape-shot!

******

After a halt at Marienwerder, on the Vistula, Oudinot crossed the Niemen, with the rest of the army, above Kowno (24 June). He was to form the left with the 2nd Corps, received orders to cross the Vilia, and directed himself towards the north upon Vilkomir. His first engagement at Deweltowo, on the morning of the 28th, revealed to him from the commencement the nature of this deceptive war; it was hardly possible to touch Wittgenstein's rear-guard, although this sustained a severe check; and the enemy dispersed, protecting himself against us by means of his endless, desolate and forbidding plains.

******

The emperor with the Grande Armée followed the line of Moscow, endeavouring to provoke one of those battles of giants which he had always been able to turn to his advantage; while on the left he had detached the corps of Oudinot and Macdonald[1] in the direction of St Petersburg. The army opposed to my husband was commanded by Wittgenstein, the Russian general-in-chief. He had at last resolved to deliver the battle which had hitherto been refused to the Grande Armée; and several combats had taken place. After one of the first of these, the marshal wrote to me, with no other details, "Be easy, my dear; the bullets refused to touch me, because my bones are too hard." A joke which failed to enliven me, I assure you. But his letters came more and more irregularly. Sometimes, after long days of anguish, they would be delivered to me in a heap. Then I lost my head, broke all the seals at once, and gazed at the pages spread out before me with

1. *Recollections of Marshal Macdonald, Duke of Tarentum* by Jacques also published by Leonaur.

frightened eyes which distinguished nothing.

I was in this mood when one day I received a letter written on sugar-loaf paper. It bore the stamp of Vitebsk, and the writing was unknown to me:

Vitebsk, 3 July.

> You gave me leave, *Madame la duchesse*, to write you one note for each victory. I beg a thousand pardons for delaying so long; but here is one, with every condition fulfilled; and as you may well believe, it was our Bayard who won it. Alas, I was not there; but I have at least the happiness to announce to you that, at the cost of a scratch on his hand, he has just taken twenty pieces of cannon and three thousand men, and the barbarian has killed four thousand.
>
> With this, *Madame la duchesse*, accept the respectful homage of your old servant,
>
> (Signed) L Narbonne.

I was deeply touched with the fulfilment of this promise, which I had taken for one of those obliging speeches of the man of the world. The details were soon confirmed by the marshal himself, who only suppressed the scratch, of which he never spoke to me. His letters were always full of affection for me; but they were written at a gallop on every odd and end of paper he could find. They smelt of powder and the bivouac. Sometimes also I received news of the Grande Armée from Moscow through Victor, my stepson, an officer in the *chasseurs* of the Imperial Guard and permanently attached to headquarters."

★★★★★★

Oudinot was alone at the head of an important command, far removed from headquarters, and, with the exception of instructions which became daily more rare, was left to his own initiative. This honour came to him in the most thankless, unknown and desolate country in the world, and at a time when there blew as it were a bitter blast of bad luck, the forerunner of vaguely foreseen disasters. Many another, senior to him and rocked till then by success, was suddenly to awaken in surprise and find himself an unlucky officer in these last great sorrowful years.

He nevertheless bore a good countenance in spite of the overpowering fatigue. The heat was like lead on that unsheltered soil. He himself said that he had never suffered so terribly, even in Italy; not suspecting that, through the bitter irony of that climate, we should be ravaged in three months' time by the two contrary excesses of temperature. His officers, who worshipped him, and who suffered at seeing him thus oppressed, went out at night into the neighbouring woods and gathered branches which they planted over his head, so that this improvised arbour might bring him some relief at waking.

Napoleon, after vainly endeavouring to hem in Prince Bagration in the south, returned north to attempt a similar manoeuvre against Barclay de Tolly, whom he wished to hold in check behind the Dwina. He himself established his headquarters at Glouboukoe, between Drissa and Polotsk. Oudinot, who was already on the Dwina, marched up the river by its left bank and fiercely cannoned the enemy at Dwinaburg. Only Barclay also had fallen back, according to the prudent tactics of the Russians; and Napoleon, deceived, but fascinated by the mirage of Moscow, plunged eastwards into the country of the devastating *steppes*. He ordered Oudinot to resume his movement upon St Petersburg and to continue to press against Wittgenstein.

The Duc de Reggio crossed the Dwina at Polotsk, and the Drissa at the ford of Sivotschina. On the 29th of July, Legrand's division, which formed the advance-guard, was sharply attacked by the enemy. The marshal flew to its assistance, maintained the combat at every point, drove back the Russians with the bayonet, and would certainly have crushed them, if they had not succeeded in taking refuge in a small wood, where they were able to mask themselves under cover of their artillery. Their advantageous position prevented us from continuing the fight to good purpose. Oudinot saw that it was no use insisting for the moment; but he did not despair of enticing the enemy into making some dangerous mistake. Feigning a retrograde movement, he crossed back to the left bank of the Drissa, and there established himself in a strong position.

The Russians, growing bolder, committed the imprudence of crossing the river on the night of the 31st of July. So soon as he perceived this, the Duc de Reggio completed his measures: the artillery crowned the heights; a regiment of infantry ensconced itself in a coppice on the left of the road; the light horse occupied the right, and the *Cuirassiers* remained in reserve. He gave orders to let the enemy advance within reach of the cannon, and then, when the moment had come, to charge.

The following is an extract from the report he addressed that night to Berthier:

Besala, 1 August 1812, 10 p.m.

The Russians at first offered a sharp but useless resistance. They were overturned in a moment and thrown into the Drissa, leaving in our hands fourteen guns, thirteen wagons, and over two thousand prisoners. We drove them fighting before us for three-quarters of a league to the river; the ground is covered with their dead. I have seen few battlefields offer so great a display of carnage.

Unfortunately Oudinot was not in a position to profit by his success. The 2nd Corps had suffered greatly since joining the campaign; fatigue, privations, combats, dysentery and desertions had in a very little time reduced it to half its strength, and it numbered little more than twenty thousand men. Even when reinforced on the 6th of August by the thirteen thousand Bavarians, led by General Gouvion-Saint-Cyr, it was difficult for it to take the offensive as the Emperor wished. Nevertheless, a few days of repose enabled it to resume its movement northwards.

The marshal crossed the Drissa once more and advanced upon the Swaina, which separated him from the Russians. He tried in vain to draw them into fighting. Then, not feeling very sure of his position, and fearing lest his right, which he was unable to guard, should be turned, he resolved to retrograde and to place himself close to Polotsk, between the Dwina and its affluent the Polota. Wittgenstein, who was watching all our movements, retiring when we advanced and advancing when we retired, thought the moment favourable to attack. On the 16th, he was kept at a respectful distance.

The next day, the 17th, the combat was renewed at eight o'clock in the morning. Oudinot resisted energetically, while accentuating his retreating movement upon the left bank of the Dwina. Our troops were exhausted by their marches and counter-marches and scorched by the heat, and at two o'clock a battalion of *voltigeurs* gave way. The marshal, rushing to make it return to its position, was struck seriously in the shoulder by a ball of grape-shot and obliged to hand over the command to Gouvion-Saint-Cyr.

He was carried to a Jesuit convent, where the Fathers gave him the first necessary cares, and from there, as he was incapable for the time of returning to the head of his troops, he was moved to Wilna, where he arrived on the 20th of August. There he was soon joined by his young wife, who did not hesitate to face the journey.

******

The Comtesse Pajol had left for Paris, accompanied by Mme. Poriquet, who, with a solicitude worthy of a mother, wished to be present at the moment of her confinement. In order to spare her as much fatigue as possible, I had lent her my firmly-built and easy-going travelling carriage, which my husband had given me and which I had used for my journey from Berlin. I had kept hers, which was less comfortable and half worn-out with long service. You shall see why I mention this trifling circumstance.

It had long been agreed between my husband and myself that I should proceed before the end of the summer, without him, alas, to pay my wedding visits to Lentilles and Hancourt, stopping for a few days at Vitry to renew acquaintance with my friends there; and I relied upon this latter diversion to assist me in passing a few days of this terrible period. For my alarms seemed more and more well-founded, and there was general anxiety about the march of the emperor, who was penetrating beyond all expectation into those distant regions. People were beginning to ask how and when we should get out of it; and this first doubt of the infallibility of our star astonished every one painfully.

However, while awaiting the post, we were to make an excursion to all our favourite spots in the neighbourhood. I had been ready some time, and was waiting for the others in the drawing-room, when my mother entered.

"How fine you are!" I said, noticing the beautiful costume she had put on that morning. It was a cambric *peignoir*, lavishly garnished with lace.

"I may have looked fine this morning," she replied, "but——"

It needed no more to apprise me of a misfortune; and I at once believed the worst. And when, after striking the first blow, they endeavoured to add some details, I uttered such loud screams that it was some time before my family, grouped around me, could make themselves understood. At last my uncle shouted into my ear:

"But he's only wounded!"

I heard him suddenly, and opened my eyes, which till then I had kept closed, as though to keep out the dreadful news.

My uncle showed me the *Moniteur*, and through my sobs I read a paragraph which I have not before me, but of which the following was the purport:

"On the 17th of August, at the moment when the Duc de Reggio was ready to reap the fruits of victory, he was struck down by a ball of grape-shot in the shoulder. The wound, though serious, is not hopeless. The marshal has been carried to the rear of the army, and he will be taken to Wilna."

"I must go to Wilna at once," I cried. "Mother, uncle, you must let me go."

"You shall go," they replied.

"Yes," added my Aunt Clotilde, "and my husband shall accompany you—"

Great grief is always selfish; I at once accepted this great sacrifice without calculating its extent for my uncle and aunt.

"Let us go, let us go! "I cried. "My God, shall I find him alive?"

During the crisis produced upon me by this terrible doubt, some of them waited on me, while others occupied themselves actively with the arrangements for my departure. An hour later, we were on the road to Vitry, and in spite of the darkness and the roads, which were soaked by a storm, in spite of the flood of the Marne, which we had to ford, we made good progress, and in the middle of the night we reached Vitry, where we were expected.

"Did you meet the second post which we sent you yesterday evening?" asked Rosalie, running up to the carriage. We then learnt to our despair that the trouble and eagerness we had displayed would turn against us.

A fever of impatience overcame me when I learnt that that messenger was the bearer of a letter from the army. It was sent to me from Bar by Mme. de Lorencez, who did not lose a moment, and sent her own coachman with it. We all counted the moments until he arrived. At last a paper was placed in my hands upon which I recognized, though I could not read them, a few lines in the marshal's handwriting. "He is not dead, he has not lost his arms!" I cried. This was all I was able at first to grasp.

The precious document was passed from hand to hand, and when I had recovered sufficient consciousness, I read as follows:

> My Eugénie, if you learn of my wound through any other channel, do not be alarmed at it, for it will not, I hope, be dangerous. However, it will compel me to withdraw to the rear and to leave the army. I shall not be able to write to you, because of the lack of communications (20 August).

Although weak, the writing had not lost all its character, and I breathed again.

To this letter General de Lorencez had added a very precious note, containing these words:

> *M. le maréchal* has charged me to recommend you not to undertake so long a journey to join him; but believe me, follow the impulse of your heart.

If I had not already made up my mind, the general's letter would have settled the matter. I now thought only of reaching Bar. I arrived there in the morning accompanied by my mother and my uncle; but a cruel hindrance awaited me there. My travelling-carriage was in Paris, and I was assured that the one which Mme. Pajol had left me in temporary exchange could never resist a hurried journey of six or seven hundred leagues. We should have run the risk of breaking down a score of times. I had no chance but hastily to despatch an intelligent servant with injunctions to bring me back my *berlin*, of which I foresaw the usefulness to my dear wounded.

The posting arrangements were at that time perfectly organized, especially if one paid the postillions well. And yet three days passed between his setting out and his return. Three leaden days, which were spent by all around me in making preparations for the journey in which I was utterly incapable of assisting. I only remember having twenty bottles of claret put into the boot of the carriage, before which I would readily have prostrated myself when I saw it arriving on the morning of the 12th of September.

The day was spent in loading it, and our departure was fixed for six o'clock in the evening. At last the postillions' whips gave the signal. Every one rose in tumult and followed me. The horses galloped off so fast that it was not until we reached the village of Naives that I recovered my spirits. There, at his old mother's door, Jacqueminot the senator stood waiting for me, and handed me—he crying too—his messages for his son. In those days no one was certain that a message addressed to a combatant would reach its destination.

The weather was magnificent; we travelled at high speed, and I felt the better for it; for a forced movement is perhaps the most powerful alleviation of the great sorrows of the soul. Besides, did not each turn of the wheels bring me nearer the one spot in the universe towards which all my thoughts were directed?

At five o'clock in the morning we reached Metz, and knocked at M. Gouy's door. His wife and he were soon up; and our faithful friend said to me, "I felt certain, even if you had not let me know, that you would start for Wilna. I have got ready for you, in case you need them, six thousand *francs* in gold. Will you have them? Here they are."

I had the necessary funds, however, and could only thank the dear good man.

On the morning of the 14th we arrived at Mayence, resting for a moment only at the Hôtel des Trois Couronnes, so well known to all the army. But our fatigue was so great by the evening that we took a few hours sleep at Hanau. This was our only repose between Bar and Berlin.

So soon as we arrived at the capital, I sent in all directions for news. What was my surprise to see the Comte de Saint-Marsan, our ambassador, come hurrying up to me with a letter for me from my husband in his hand. Before asking how he had come by it, I loaded the excellent man with blessings! My husband told me in a few lines, and in a firmer handwriting, that he was bearing his journey well and travelling slowly to Wilna.

To explain the delivery of this letter I must tell you that I had written from Bar to the Duc de Feltre, the Minister of War, telling him of my departure, and asking him for some kind of chart of the road which might facilitate my journey in case of difficulties. The Minister of War had made known my departure along the road that I was to travel, through the auditor to the Council of State who regularly carried the official news from Paris to the Emperor. I believe one of these gentlemen used generally to leave every week. They often crossed on the road, and invariably stopped at the French Embassy in Berlin. M. de Saint-Marsan, when going through the bag of the returning auditor, took out to give to me the letter of which I have spoken. "I have made known your departure," said the count, "and as, in spite of your diligence, my young men travel still faster than you do, your arrival will be announced beforehand to the Duc de Bassano, and consequently also to your husband."

This news was so good that I decided to yield to my uncle's persuasion and to stay one day in Berlin. The opportunity was taken to mend my carriage, which had been greatly tried by the three hundred leagues we had travelled, and also to fill it with provisions, which I gratefully accepted at the hands of the kind friends I had found there, although I was then far from suspecting the penury that was soon to threaten us.

The second notable person who came to see me at my hotel was

Marshal Augereau. It was the first time I saw the husband of my fair compatriot. He was tall and broad, spoke loudly, and reminded me a little of the drum-major whom I had always regarded in my childhood as the chief of a regiment. I spoke to him of his delicious wife, of whom he showed me a charming miniature. He was thinking of sending for her to come to him, and in rather strange terms, which, however, were quite natural with him, he said, "I have told her to get her doeskin breeches ready for the journey."

But altogether the Duc de Castiglione was not only very obliging but full of solicitude for my welfare; and taking my uncle aside, he urged him most expressly not to allow me to travel at night beyond Custrin, the first place at which I was to sleep. "Yield to no entreaties, for the road that follows is the most difficult part of the *maréchale's* long and painful journey. Once beyond the Oder, you may find it covered with the highwaymen, deserters and robbers who usually follow in the wake of an army." My uncle took his advice and followed it.

On the third day, I took leave not only of our ambassador and of the marshal, but of a number of other superior officers, who had all, from devotion for my husband, shown me every kindness.

Berlin passed, one finds the deep sand which makes travelling so difficult. Nothing seems to me more melancholy than the country between the Prussian capital and the city of Custrin, a fortified town on the Oder. General Fournier d'Albe was in command of our garrison, and warned by my courier of our arrival, he sent a messenger to beg me to come to his house, where the most amiable reception awaited me. "In this sad exile," he said, when he had installed me in his best rooms, "my only consolation is at least to be of some use to those joining the army."

From Custrin we travelled to Marienwerder. The sand grew deeper. The relays were irregular, and at long distances; at each we increased the number of horses, but the poor worn-out teams went no faster, and night fell as we descended through a gloomy forest towards the bank of the Vistula. As the slope was a steep one, we alighted from the carriage, and it was not till that night, when we had reached our lodging, that my uncle told me he had distinctly seen a large wolf a few paces from us, in that forest which seemed so wild that it might have been the undisputed domain of those redoubtable inhabitants.

We crossed the river on a bridge of boats. Had I then been travelling for my pleasure, I should have keenly regretted seeing nothing of that country, which had already been covered by our armies in a former war. But, as you know, I was absorbed in the present. I observed, on reaching the inn, where my courier had preceded me, that everything was brightly lit up, and that there was a general air of movement; and I soon learnt that this was in our honour, or rather in memory of the marshal, who had recently, at the head of his army, left so good a reputation for equity in strength that they did not think they could ever do enough for one bearing his name. However, they charged us pretty dear for the splendid repast and the room of fifty covers in which my uncle and I supped *tête-à-tête* amid a multitude of candles. This was our last acquaintance with luxury and civilization.

I will cut short the details of our painful journey across that endless sand, interspersed with a few pine-forests and a number of ponds, and bring you within sight of the Baltic. For six leagues we followed one of its arms called the Freschaff. Wretched fisher-huts form the only dwellings of these melancholy shores, giving all the greater brilliancy to the town of Königsberg when it comes into view with its port and its many steeples.

At any other time, the sea, which I now saw for the first time, would have aroused my keenest interest. But I saw everything through the medium of a single idea, and my first thought was to ask the French general commanding the district for news that might interest me.

General Loison commanded at Königsberg, and he was at my hotel within half-an-hour after receiving my message. He began by reassuring me as to the marshal's health, without, however, giving me the details I wanted.

"But where do you expect to find the marshal?" he asked.

"Why, at Wilna," I replied, in alarm . . .

"He is no longer there, *Madame*."

A thousand confused and terrible ideas traversed my mind before I had found time to question him afresh. I felt as though I were going mad, but my uncle, more calm, elicited the facts. It was a vague rumour which had reached General Loison, who was not even able to say in what direction the marshal was travelling.

"Perhaps he is returning," I cried; "and how do you know I shall not meet him on the road?"

"No, *Madame*," replied the general; "if your husband has moved, it would not be in this direction."

"Well, I shall follow him, wherever he is!" I cried, in my despair. "No, I have not travelled five or six hundred leagues, and undergone all these days of torture and uncertainty, only to retrace my steps; and if it is only for an hour, I mean to see the marshal."

I had had courage so long as I was travelling towards a fixed point, to which each step brought me nearer. But now! And moreover I also heard that the emperor had forbidden all wives of officers, of whatever rank, to go beyond the Vistula; whereas I was approaching the Niemen. In proof of his statement, the general told me he had been requested by the governor of Wilna to find a lodging at Königsberg for his wife, whom he had been obliged to send back from Wilna, where she had followed him in all confidence.

"We must put our trust in God," I said to my uncle, as we climbed into our carriage at daybreak, in pouring rain. This downpour, which made our moods still gloomier, continued for three consecutive days, and greatly increased the difficulties of the journey. We no longer drove through the thick sand which we had found from Berlin to Konigsberg, but over thick mud, in which we sank up to the hams of the wretched little horses of the country. This part of Prussia is said to be fertile and prosperous, but I was not there to study the country. The execrable roads, the delays necessitated by our having to find horses where there were so few, had upset all the arrangements for our stoppages; and I do not know exactly how much time was spent over this second part of our journey, which was drenched in the most abundant rain I had ever seen in my life. It redoubled in force when, long after nightfall, we arrived at Insterburg.

The first lodging at which the carriage pulled up was occupied entirely, we were told, by a detachment rejoining the army. It was the same thing at the second, and so on; and I since learnt that no less than ten thousand men were stationed that night in the little town.

My poor servants, who had received the torrents falling from the skies throughout the day, excited my warmest pity; and I must confess that we were all worn out, body and soul. It would have been very cruel to spend that night without shelter. At last we took a great resolve, and Carl, a young Prussian footman, was sent to knock at the door of the commandant of the town.

My uncle slept outside my door, for want of a bed; but at least he was sheltered from the deluge, which descended more fiercely than ever. We set out before daybreak. It was pitiful to behold the difficulties of our progress through roads soaked through with the rain. However, we arrived without any accident at Gumbinnen, where we found a lodging. The next day we noticed that the route we were following bore more and more traces of the disasters which war brings with it.

Not only did the horses become more scarce, but their owners waxed very distrustful (we had long passed the limit of the postal administration, which had become wholly disorganized).

Every villager wanted to follow his animal, to be quite sure that he should get it back; and one day I had four postillions to eight horses. And such horses! And such postillions! The first were harnessed with odds and ends of ropes and cords; the second, dressed in sheepskins, resembled savages.

Food became scarcer as we advanced, and one morning we were very happy to find at the bottom of a locker a remnant of sausage which had formed part of the presents of our friends at Berlin. We were really famished when we arrived at Marienpol. The distressful air of the country boded no good. We were therefore agreeably surprised when we saw appear at the door of a tumbledown inn a prepossessing Frenchwoman, who offered us two chickens, which we seized upon without waiting to have them cooked, reserving them for our supper at Kowno, where we hoped to arrive that evening.

Kowno, on the banks of the Niemen, the last river I should have to cross, seemed to me the outpost of my destination.

We pursued our slow and unequal progress along roads that were no longer traced. Night surprised us at the most wretched lodging we had yet met with; we were compelled to stop.

As I contemplated the repulsive bed they offered me, I asked if it was the best they had.

"Yes," they replied, "because the best room is occupied by the princess."

"Who is that princess they speak of?" I asked my uncle, who enquired and found it was the Princess of Hohenlohe, wife of the Dutch general, van Hogendorp, then governor of Wilna. Yes, it was the poor woman who had been sent away from that town by order of the Emperor! I so greatly pitied her fate that I did not even secretly think of envying her better accommodation; but I was resolved not to leave without seeing her. I made them bring one of the two little mattresses which my carriage contained, and spread it on a sort of bench in a room on the ground-floor which opened upon the street.

My uncle slept in the carriage, after having it brought up against the window, and overcome with fatigue, I soon fell asleep. But I awoke with a start at the sudden entrance of a man into my room, smacking his whip and swearing. At my first scream, Mme. Morel, who was sleeping on a pallet near mine, fell upon him like an hyena. He was so taken aback that he fled for his life. That was all; but I was unable to get asleep again. We learnt the next day that it was only an army courier demanding horses.

This alarm, combined with my desire to see Mrs. van Hogendorp, kept me awake till daybreak; and as soon as my ear caught the first movements announcing her departure, I went upstairs to the "best room" which she occupied. What a hole! . . . I there found a delicate and distinguished woman dressing a poor little girl of six, who seemed to have nothing left in her but her breath. A number of lady's maids were making up parcels, and no one seemed astonished at the eagerness with which they were preparing to leave that hovel. On hearing my name, Mrs. van Hogendorp, when she had recovered from her astonishment, hastened to give me news of my husband in these words:—

"I left him about six days ago. His wound is doing well; but he has not yet thought of leaving Wilna to return to the army, for in spite of the improvement of which I speak, he would not for the present be able to ride his horse."

I left Mrs. van Hogendorp, after wishing her, from the bottom of my heart, health, happiness and a speedy meeting with her husband. Alas! none of my wishes were fulfilled, for the child died six months later, and the mother followed her after a short interval. At Kowno, I found an *aide-de-camp* of my husband's, who, by the latter's orders, had been awaiting me for the last twenty-four hours. It was M. Jacqueminot. With his usual activity, he had got together an excellent team of horses from the artillery stationed in reserve at Kowno. This would enable us, without having recourse to other means, to cover the twenty-five leagues which still separated us from Wilna, thanks to the relays prepared before-hand.

M. Jacqueminot joined us in our carriage, and at last I was able to hear the details I had so longed for. He confirmed those which I had already received at Berlin through M. de Saint-Marsan. It was the latter who had announced my arrival, and "for the last five days," said the young man, "the marshal is exciting himself while waiting for you; let us hurry."

"But," said I, in great distress, "will he send me away?"

"He has not the slightest wish to do so," he replied, laughing; "but the Emperor—"

"Oh, I know," I said; "but let us get on . . . the first thing is to arrive."

At that moment it became necessary to alight in order to push back the carriage, which had left the road. It was so dark, one could distinguish nothing. M. Jacqueminot took one of the lanterns, went ahead of the horses, and succeeded in bringing us back, not to the road, for there was none, but to the line of disasters which served to guide us. We followed him on foot, with sand up to our ankles, when M. Jacqueminot returned to tell us the result of his investigations, and urged us to hurry back and resume our seats in the carriage. But when, by the light of his lantern, he saw me painfully drawing my feet from the sand, he burst into one of those fits of laughter which he often indulged in, and which contained more sarcasm than gaiety.

"What a strange circumstance," he said, "is your presence in the midst of this desert, *Madame la duchesse!* Oh, that all-devouring ambition which leads us to the end of the world, which disorganizes every existence and paralyzes every industry! And to what will it bring us? We are all done for."

This diatribe, the first I had heard uttered against the emperor since my marriage, this violent discontent on the part of a man who was as brave as he was enthusiastic, petrified me with surprise. I listened in silence.

"Yes," he continued, "misfortunes without end have already reached and are increasingly threatening our army (the emperor was then marching upon Moscow), and I do not know which of us will ever see France again."

At last we perceived the lights of a house, before which the horses pulled up. I was taken through several rooms which seemed to have been devastated before being finished. It was a real shed, with neither floor nor ceiling; but the most pleasing reception awaited me there. Mme. Oguinska, a charming woman of about thirty, met me with amiable alacrity. She spoke French, like all her compatriots, with remarkable ease. She made her excuses for all that I might find wanting in her house, owing to its position. It had served as the headquarters of the various armies which had followed one another along this route, and I understood that this was not calculated to revictual the place. But this sad incident of the war was not, on the princess's part, the object of any direct or covert complaint.

At that time, the Lithuanians, including the women, were all under the charm of the keenest hopes. At the commencement of the campaign, they had rushed in rapture towards the emperor, seeing in him, as they thought, the restorer of their liberty. Poland had offered him on every side men, arms and homage. And as yet nothing had formally belied the hope which they had conceived.

I slept little, and as I had taken my leave of the mistress of the house the evening before, I set out without delay at daybreak. But the roads, ploughed by the artillery, were worse than those we had followed so far. We made hardly any progress. I should have liked to help the horses to drag the carriage. I tried to restrain my impatience, but it stifled me.

Towards mid-day, M. Jacqueminot found a country cart in a sort of farm which had been left standing, and decided to go on in front. "You have no longer anything to fear," he said. "I will try and quiet the marshal's impatience by announcing your arrival. I only recommend you," he added, addressing my uncle, "to take precautions against the rapid descent which you will meet with two or three leagues from here."

After his departure, we preserved a profound silence. A keen joy sometimes closely resembles pain, and nothing can issue from a heart when its impressions are too vivid. As it reached its summit, our emotion was not of a nature to find expression; but we were suddenly relieved from the indefinable position by the sight of a long and rapid slope, at the top of which the carriage had stopped, and throwing my eyes over the plain which it commanded, I uttered a piercing cry. Wilna lay before me.

Leaping with joy, I descended this mountain on foot, this white and icy mountain, which, two months later, was to come, like a great ghost, between France and our army, of which almost all that remained lay down in death at its foot. But now nothing could diminish my transports. And yet, during the two leagues that remained for us to travel, we found many a portent of the hideous disaster which was drawing nigh. Among the wreck of artillery trains bordering the roadway were a number of dead horses, some already reduced to skeletons, others to a state of corruption which sent a fetid odour through the air. But I had arrived! and for the moment I was proof against any other sensation.

Suddenly I heard a horse's hoofs.

"Ah! M. de Thermes!" I exclaimed.

He had been despatched by my husband to make me come faster.

"Hasten, *Madame la duchesse*, hasten," he said, at the carriage-door. "Since Jacqueminot's return, the marshal is counting the minutes. And then, you should hurry to get out of this atmosphere; "and the young man galloped off gaily, adding, "I am going to announce your arrival."

He disappeared from sight as the carriage rolled on to the paving-stones of Wilna.

I recognized servants in the marshal's livery. The carriage rolled into the courtyard, and I saw him . . . him, with his most gracious expression. He stretched out his only free arm to embrace me; the other was in a sling. His face was pale, but what matter? He was there. I kissed him; he spoke to me with infinite tenderness. What a moment of happiness!

He next turned promptly towards my uncle and thanked him, with his captivating courtesy, in words which will never leave my memory. All the staff and a crowd of people whom I did not even see were witnesses of this meeting, which sounds so cold when told with the pen, though its memory was burnt into my heart. We all climbed the staircase, and leaving behind us the multitude who followed us, we three entered his room, and there followed the reciprocal questionings, the cross-fire of enquiries and replies which are the delights of reunion. A few favoured friends were then gradually admitted, but I did not complain. When one is happy, one loves and receives everybody. Besides, all those who accompanied the marshal excited my interest, down to his servants, headed by the brave and worthy Pils.

We dined in private, but the conversation of us three was sometimes interrupted by the bursts of noisy festivity of the staff, who were dining in full mess in the next room. The marshal evidently enjoyed this gaiety, while paying my uncle the most delicate attention. My heart swam in happiness; everything smiled to me. The marshal's voice alone did me so much good that I tried to make him talk without stopping. The sight of his two arms fixed safely to his shoulders after that wound was a special delight.

Quite unable to eat, I asked for something to drink. They gave me some red wine and water, which made me pull a horrid grimace.

"Ah, ah!" said the marshal, "you don't like wine made without grapes."

This reminded me of my twenty bottles of Bordeaux. They were unpacked and brought up, and I presented them in triumph to my cripple. He had one placed on our table, but sent the nineteen others to his staff, whose joy and animation were redoubled. I was certainly charmed to be of use to them; but I must nevertheless confess that I regretted the rapid disappearance of this little comfort, which I had brought for the marshal, and I did not quite know what to reply to the thanks the gentlemen came and offered me.

We were still at dinner when a dazzling elegant entered the room. It was the Comte Adolphe de Maussion. As an auditor to the Council of State, he was attached to the office of the Duc de Bassano, and in the minister's name, came to ask for news of my arrival.

"You see her before you," said my husband gaily. The young man bowed low, saying he would go and carry the news to his chief who was just sending a courier to the emperor. I feared that these words meant that I should be sent away. All my fears returned for the moment; but I was in too great need of happiness to permit the thought, and I drove it away, saying to myself that the distances were enormous, and that many bright days would pass before the dread command could reach us.

I was agreeably surprised to find nothing in the marshal's mood or conversation to confirm the sad account and melancholy prognostications of M. Jacqueminot. My husband, who had assisted at nothing but triumphs since his entrance into a soldier's career, was the last to certify our disasters; and even when he touched upon them slightly, he yet sought to conceal them. When at last he was compelled to believe them, he continued to do so from rage and distress.

Moreover, he allowed no one to repeat anything to him on hearsay, when it was unfavourable to our arms. He received no news except that given by the Duc de Bassano or furnished by his chief of staff (General de Lorencez) on the movements of the 2nd Army Corps. On this side nothing alarming had happened during the first half of October. After Marshal Oudinot had been wounded, his corps had been placed under the command of Marshal Gouvion-Saint-Cyr, who had remained on the Dwina, where he maintained himself advantageously against Wittgenstein's army. Consequently everything was satisfactory there.

The day after my arrival, I received many visits: first that of the Duc de Bassano; then came M. Bignon, a very clever man, who was also fulfilling a diplomatic mission, with the title of Imperial Commissary. Next, all the wounded who had left the army temporarily in order to be cured at Wilna.

I also made the acquaintance of some charming women of the country, not only Lithuanians proper, but coming from every part of Poland to be at the centre of politics and of the news of the moment. They first called upon me, and I gladly returned their visits.

We also accepted, my husband, my uncle and myself, the invitations of our two diplomatists. They alone kept house; the natives had enough to do in keeping up their cause, to which they eagerly sacrificed more than their incomes. For instance, all these charming ladies gathered at Wilna lived in privation in order to assist their husbands to keep up the regiments raised at their cost and commanded by them, their sons or their brothers. Yes, cashmere shawls, plate, pearls, diamonds, all went successively to be swallowed up in the vortex of a war from which those noble hearts and vivid imaginations refused to draw anything but hope.

The first function at which I assisted was a great dinner, followed by a crowded reception, at the Duc de Bassano's. The Minister enjoyed all the Emperor's confidence. He held and pulled, by his master's direction, all the wires of European diplomacy. Like the Comte Louis de Narbonne, he had preserved the old-fashioned way of doing the hair. He carried his powdered head well and loftily. He was tall in stature; his demeanour was grave; his movements slow; his words rare and measured. Altogether he was an imposing figure.

The month of October had been magnificent, but it was drawing to an end, and not everyone was illusioned by its deceptive mildness. The interviews between the Duc de Bassano and my husband were redoubled.

Often, during these fine October mornings, my husband and I would set out alone to explore the neighbourhood. Certainly the charm of these drives did not lie in the localities themselves. Wilna is situated in a dry, sandy country, and surrounded by hills deprived of all vegetation. The Wilia winds through the country in vain; it does not seem to fertilize it. A few brick towers were to be seen upon the heights. They were half demolished: destroyed, not ruined.

The streets of Wilna were dark and dirty, and the Jewish population, which was in the majority, did not brighten the picture. There are, however, a number of domes and steeples, which rise up brilliantly from the thirty-six convents that the city contains.

To this repulsive Jewish population were added our sick and convalescent soldiers. These dragged themselves through the streets or lay stretched in the sun. Nothing is sadder to my mind than a sick soldier, because, to the physical suffering expressed on his face, must be added the home-sickness which is so cruel for the rich and so intolerable to the poor.

One morning, my husband and I had reached on foot a clump of fir-trees which had attracted us, because any vegetation was so rare. We were chatting merrily when we suddenly stumbled against a heap of earth. It was a tomb! Then another, a hundred others. . . . We had lit upon the graveyard of a military hospital. We turned short, and not far away we found a canteen, in front of which our soldiers, ready to rejoin the army, were dancing with the canteen-women.

Meanwhile, as the days passed by, a vague anxiety began to manifest itself. The entertainments continued. The diplomatic faces remained impassive; but I perceived that the private conferences between the minister and my husband became much more frequent. Treated almost as a child, I was told of nothing; but one morning, I believe it was on the 29th or 30th of October, I noticed such a going to and fro; the marshal, in a low voice, gave so many different orders to his officers; his people, too, moved about to such an extent that I had a presentiment of departure, and all my doubts were dissipated when I saw him arranging his war-charts and telling Pils to put them in his boxes.

The departure was irrevocably fixed for the morrow, and the hateful preparations for a long journey upset the house from top to bottom. I felt inclined to scold all the people who were busying themselves in these preparations; I was shocked at the careless air of some and the contented air of others. The *aides-de-camp* in particular rejoiced at resuming the campaign, and I detested them for it.

What a dinner! what an evening! what a night! At daybreak the carriage rolled heavily beneath the archway. The marshal embraced me silently, sadly, and after recommending me afresh to the care of my uncle, drove off, leaving me a victim to genuine despair. I was ill for several days.

It was the news of a wound received by Marshal Gouvion-Saint-Cyr that induced the Duc de Reggio to resume his command of the 2nd Corps without waiting for orders or instructions from the Emperor, whose movements and plans were at the time unknown. The 2nd Corps had evacuated Polotsk, and your father was to rejoin his troops during their retrograde march upon the Beresina.

The fine weather was past, and November opened in mist. My uncle tried to distract my thoughts by every possible means. He read to me. He made me take a piano-mistress. I agreed to everything, but without zeal or attention. Then my uncle suggested that I should take drives. The marshal had left me eight of his horses, which, well fed and cared for, were later to render us immense service. But for the time they were a luxury.

Already the first snow lay on the ground, when one morning, huddled in our calash, and going at a great rate, we were shaken from our lethargy by a sudden swerving on the part of our horses, who had seen a corpse, which they refused to pass. This was the beginning.

The incident did not increase my taste for driving; however, I could not refuse when the Duc de Bassano invited me to the review of the Neapolitan Guards, who were passing through Wilna to join Murat. These light and brilliant troops manoeuvred before us for an hour or two. It was their farewell to the world; for, a few days later, the cold having increased, men and horses gradually melted away like snow beneath the sun. Not one reached his destination. Troops were constantly being sent to the army, but none ever returned.

A silence as of death reigned at the Duc de Bassano's and at my own house. He often came and communicated his forebodings to me. Each succeeding day, each added degree of frost increased the melancholy of the position. In the third week of November, the thermometer was at 12 degrees, and it could not but go lower still.

Our letters from France had brought us nothing but news of peace and health; but one morning I was seized with horror on reading in a letter from my sister of the inroads of a mad wolf who had bitten nineteen people in the town of Bar, of whom seventeen had succumbed to hydrophobia.

I was interrupted by a visit from the minister. "There are also," he said, "wolves in Paris." He had just heard of Mallet's conspiracy. "Look at my position," he said. "Paris is in uproar, and what news can I send to calm it? Instead of the victories to which they are accustomed, the reports of which would make an instant diversion, am I to tell them that at this moment we are ignorant of the fate of the emperor and the Grande Armée? Will it be sufficient to repeat the last reports which I have read from Moscow, and which I have already sent home? And yet I must write to Paris, which is so exacting and so impressionable; and, on the other hand, I must keep a good countenance here before this diplomatic body, whose eyes are always open, watching my movements. I must continue to keep the Polish ladies dancing: they persevere in their hopes and will perhaps be undeceived all too soon. That is my position, which becomes more difficult day by day."

Very gloomy days succeeded to this revelation of the Duc de Bassano's. Nothing was able to draw me from my sombre meditations. I had been warned by the minister that all the ladies who had taken refuge at Wilna would attentively follow my impressions and my movements, and I must therefore force myself to make no change in my mode of life. Since the marshal's departure I had ceased to appear in public, but I paid and received morning visits, and in addition to the Lithuanian nobles, I saw much of the superior officers on duty in the town, and also of the convalescents who were completing their cure.

Count and Countess Abramowietz were among our most frequent visitors. There was a curious detail, rare everywhere except in Poland, connected with the countess: this was her fourth husband. All four were living. I will not undertake to excuse the religious position, so revolting in itself and so strange in a Catholic; but the Duc de Bassano explained the civil position to me by the elasticity of the law, which in every Polish marriage-contract leaves an opportunity for a declaration of nullity or a separation. Among these four husbands was, I heard, one Frenchman, the Comte de Montholon; and I believe, although I am not sure, that it was he who followed the emperor to St Helena.

Mme. Abramowietz, apart from the oddness of her position, was a most kind and charitable woman, and the charm of her mind and manners would infallibly have attracted me, if those three first husbands had not so often sprung up between us. But he who at that time reigned over her actions and her heart certainly deserved all the affection she bore him, as you can judge by the following anecdote.

As you know, communications were interrupted with the army generally, and particularly along the line to Moscow. The Duc de Bassano, anxious to inform the emperor of the Mallet affair, and fearing to deliver the details to the chance of seizure which all his despatches ran, was eagerly seeking a means for the safe conveyance of his important news. Count Abramowietz delivered him from his perplexity by offering to undertake the risk and perils of the journey in question.

"But how will you set about it," asked the duke, "so as to avoid the risk of capture?"

"That concerns myself," he replied; "but I can assure you of this, that if your despatches do not reach the emperor, no one else shall ever know the contents."

Thereupon the Duc de Bassano suggested that I should take advantage of this opportunity to write to the marshal. It seemed evident to us that the latter was returning, in concert with Marshal Victor, to the point of junction with the army of Moscow. I accordingly handed my letters to the brave traveller.

A long time passed after his departure. One Sunday, during mass, I was told that M. Abramowietz had returned. You can imagine the excitement with which I called at his house. Soon M. Abramowietz, who had naturally gone first to the Duc de Bassano's, came and brought me both letters and verbal news. The whole was reassuring, and I saw that we had well judged the position in assuming that the 2nd and 6th Corps had joined the emperor.

Either from prudence or from the inrooted sentiment of the Poles, which closed their eyes to the real state of affairs, M. Abramowietz wrapped himself in great reserve, at least in so far as I was concerned, and gave me no clue to what he had perhaps already communicated to the Duc de Bassano. He had arrived almost at the moment when the corps of Bellune and Reggio were joining the emperor, and he must certainly have obtained a true idea of the position. But the story of his journey was told me. Knowing the country perfectly, he had decided to put the partisans off the scent by crossing the various lakes, which he hoped to find entirely frozen. When he reached the first, he sounded the thickness of the ice with a long iron-shod stick. The trial did not seem satisfactory; but, "What matter?" said he. "I am only risking my life, and if I am drowned, the despatches will disappear with me. Forwards!"

It was in this spirit that he took the first few steps upon the ice, which cracked beneath his feet and left the gulf open behind him. By running lightly and speedily with the aid of his stick, he went forward full of hope and ardour, closing his ears to the fatal sound which threatened his life at each movement he made. But God protected him. The gulf did not open before him; he left it behind and did not look back at it. Had he been swallowed up, his wife, his friends, his country would never have known his fate, and this modest courage, the courage of duty accomplished, would have remained unknown.

Days of absolute silence followed upon the details you have just read. No direct, no official news reached us from the army, which we knew to be marching towards Wilna. The cold increased, and all our hearts were wrung when we thought of that mass of men tramping along between the snow, which covered all things, and the grey sky, which was no longer pierced by a single ray of the sun.

CHAPTER 5

Battle of Borizow

The 2nd Corps, commanded for the second time by Oudinot, who had rejoined it on the 4th of November after the wound received by Gouvion-Saint-Cyr, was growing weaker and weaker, while the enemy on the other hand was receiving reinforcements. He was compelled to retire and endeavour to rejoin Marshal Victor, and he hoped at Borizow, on the upper reaches of the Beresina, to make himself master of the only road which could afford a passage to the Emperor and the wretched remnants brought back by him from Moscow. Which of the two, Oudinot or Wittgenstein, would become master of that little water-course, but lately an insignificant stream, now a fatal gulf? The Duc de Reggio and the Duc de Bellune possessed the only solid and organized bodies of troops remaining in Russia, but their united effective strength scarcely amounted to a total of twenty-five thousand men. They vainly attacked at Smoliantzy, and were unable to break through the enemy. At the same time the Polish General Dombrowsky, who was holding the bridge of Borizow for us—our last hope!—lost it after a sanguinary combat.

The sudden arrival of Oudinot almost restored the position. He swooped upon Borizow, surprised General Pahlen's advance-guard, killed or took prisoner twelve hundred men, and rushed upon the bridge. . . . Too late! The Russians, unable to hold it, had set fire to it as they fled.

Fortunately, General Corbineau, who had been separated from the 2nd Corps since the retreat, and who had fallen back somewhat at haphazard, observed some peasants fording the Beresina opposite Studianka, three leagues above Borizow. So soon as he was informed of this, Oudinot hastened to send Corbineau with this valuable information to the emperor. Napoleon at once adopted the idea of using the ford at Studianka, and in order to deceive the enemy, ordered feigned works of passage to be executed on other points below Borizow.

He arrived at seven o'clock in the morning on the 26th of November at the village of Weselowo, on the left bank of the Beresina, opposite Studianka, which is on the right bank.[1] He said to Oudinot, who had already begun his preparations, concealing them as much as possible:

"Well, you shall be my locksmith and open that passage for me."

At the same time Berthier, seated in the snow, wrote out the orders of the day.

Corbineau crossed with a few cavalrymen, who, taking foot-soldiers behind them, occupied a small wood on the right bank, after dislodging some Cossacks. At the same time General Eblé's pontoniers, plunging into the water up to their shoulders, and surrounded with ice which crystallized around their chests, drove in the piles intended for the foundations of two bridges. The right one was finished at one o'clock in the afternoon on the 26th, the left three hours later. Oudinot's corps crossed forthwith to the right bank, took up its position with two pieces of ordnance, threw itself upon the Russian troops commanded by General Tchaplitz, dispersed them and drove them back beyond Brilowa, and thus assured a free passage.

That night Oudinot slept upon that terrible ground, with no other shelter than some boughs of trees. There was not even any straw, and nothing to drink but melted snow. We resume the Duchesse de Reggio's narrative:

******

Despite my sinister presentiments, I did not dream of leaving Wilna. There was much talk among the refugees of a speedy retreat to Warsaw; but in no case should I have followed that route, since the one which my husband had prescribed for me by way of precaution in case of need ran by Kowno and Königsberg. But the Duc de Bassano, who was responsible for my safety to the marshal, and who felt certain of having time enough before him to retreat, did not think it necessary to send me on ahead, which would have been an evident signal of distress for the whole town.

We thus came to the 2nd of December, the anniversary of the emperor's coronation. Eight years had passed since that event, which they

---

1. Thiers is wrong in describing Studianka as on the left bank (Vol. xii.). A note of Victor Oudinot, an eye-witness, confirms the above detail.

proposed to commemorate once again. The day rose still more misty and frosty than the preceding ones. My uncle and I in gloomy silence were awaiting our sad breakfast, exchanging, not without effort, a few words with the excellent M. Verger, the marshal's war-commissary and private secretary. An enormous weight seemed to crush us all three, when suddenly the door burst open, and there appeared before my eyes a sort of phantom, which resembled M. Le Tellier. I gave a scream and darted towards him; he took my two hands, placed me in an easy chair, sat down by my side, and, keeping my hands in his, said in a hollow voice:

"I bring you news of your husband—"

"Ah, God pity me!" I cried.

"Calm yourself," resumed the *aide-de-camp*, "he is alive, he is coming, but . . . he has received . . . he is wounded again . . . a little."

I had felt the blow at M. Le Tellier's entrance, and I remained dumb, without strength or words to ask for details. In vain M. Le Tellier put four lines written by your father before my eyes: I could distinguish nothing. He then read out to me, and I understood. The words speaking of a return to France revived me, and I returned to life.

"Come," I said to M. Le Tellier, "let us go, let us go and meet him."

"Ah, as to that," he replied, "I have my orders, and you shall not leave this place."

"We shall see about that," I answered. "Do you think I will wait quietly and not at once take him all the help he stands in need of?"

"He foresaw your project, *Madame*, and he has so rigorously prescribed my line of conduct that I will not let you go even if I have to lock you up to prevent you."

My uncle took the young man's part, and I had to bow my head, and resigned myself to letting M. Verger go alone, the kind man offering to carry at once to the wounded hero all that I could think of as useful for him.

When all my arrangements were made, I greedily asked M. Le Tellier for details. He took care to hide from me, as much as possible, the gravity of the wound, and thus left me the strength and presence of mind to listen to the rest.

"Where is the emperor? where is the army?" I asked.

"The emperor!" he replied with a sombre air. "It is his victims that we have to think of. His vast, mad enterprise, his boundless ambition, his unequalled selfishness have cost us 400,000 men, . . . You ask me for news of the army, *Madame*: it no longer exists . . . Look at me: I am one of the strongest, one of the best clad of those who, in small numbers and by a miracle, have escaped that immense disaster!"

Tears of rage and despair sometimes interrupted the young man's vehement words. During two consecutive hours, my uncle and I listened to the terrible story of the retreat from Moscow. He told it us by hearsay up to the moment when, with his own eyes, he saw the 2nd Corps joining the scared remnants of the Grande Armée. This junction, to which should be added that of the 6th Corps (under Marshal Victor), began on the 20th of November and was not completed until the 25th.

It was on the 24th, after his junction, that the Duc de Reggio sent three hundred men to Aukoholda to pretend to build a bridge over the Beresina, while in the succeeding night he began, with all possible secrecy, to construct the real bridge opposite Studianka.

On the 26th, Marshal Oudinot was the first to pass. The emperor followed him on the 27th. Wittgenstein pressed our retreat on the rear, while Tchitchakoff's corps awaited us on the French side. Therefore, but for Marshal Oudinot's clever ruse, but for the false bridge which deceived the admiral and made him concentrate his forces on a distant point from that at which we really proposed to cross the Beresina, our army with its leader, pressed before and behind by the Russians, would have been lost.

It was your father, my children, who saved what returned from there, as has been universally acknowledged.

In spite of the decrease in numbers, this crossing took longer than if it had been the case of a well-organized army; and it was not over when Tchitchakoff, realizing his mistake, hastened up to meet us, while Wittgenstein was upon our backs. It was then that the crossing of this fatal river assumed a character of horror of which no bare narrative can give you an idea, and which I will not here attempt to describe to you.

★★★★★★

On the 28th snow fell so thickly that people could not see each other at a distance of thirty paces. Oudinot tried to hold in check General Tchitchakoff, who marched up from Borizow along the right bank of the Beresina. Our men were skirmishing among the woods interspersed with clearings. A company of Cossacks, springing from the whitened soil, attacked our artillery, and the Duc de Reggio sent an *aide-de-camp* to the rear to bring up a squadron of *cuirassiers*. He was waiting impatiently amid a hail-storm of bullets, gay in spite of the danger, and humming at the projectiles, between his teeth, "You shan't catch me just yet." Everybody was looking out expectantly for the *cuirassiers*, when suddenly the marshal fell from his horse.

★★★★★★

While our men were being crushed upon the bridge, or dying beneath it, drowned, frozen, or cut to pieces by the floating ice, your father marched forwards, fighting. On the 28th, in the wood of Zameski, he received a bullet which passed through his body. His foot caught in the stirrup, he was dragged with his head on the ground by the startled horse, until one of the *aides-de-camp* flew to the animal's bridle and prevented a greater misfortune.

The marshal had been shot from below; the bullet had entered low down in his side, but in consequence of the destiny which has always multiplied dangers of every kind about your father and yet preserved his life, the bullet, notwithstanding the long course it had taken, struck no vital organ.

The wounded man was conveyed, as best he could, through the thick of the battle. He had lost speech but not consciousness. The sad news soon reached the emperor, who was close at hand. He at once ordered his whole surgical and medical staff to be placed at the marshal's disposal, and sent him his son Victor, who was in the *chasseurs* of the Guard.

The marshal refused to be bound down. Pils gave him a napkin to bite into, and the operation commenced. In vain the knife probed to a depth of six or seven inches; it could not reach the bullet, which was never extracted.

The sufferer had not given way either physically or morally. He heard all that was whispered about him, and notably Dr. Desgenette's remark: "If he vomits, he's a dead man." This accident did not take place, and at last they were able to apply the first bandage. But it became necessary almost immediately to move the martyred man, in order to get him away from the field of battle. Amid the terrible cold and dangers of every kind, he had to undertake a journey of nearly a hundred leagues.

I must here explain that M. Le Tellier had spared me as much as possible in what concerned the principal interest I possessed in his story; but he did not detract from the dark side of the rest of his picture.

"And now," he asked, "what is to become of us, supposing the remnant from the Beresina holds out in part against the increasing cold, the unappeasable famine of this desolate route, and finally the Russians, who are pursuing us methodically and in good order? Granting, I say, that a morsel of the Grande Armée reaches us here, what are we to do with it? Under what conditions and how are we to regain our frontier? And yet," repeated the young man furiously, "we have not once been beaten by the enemy. We have only yielded to the force of cold and hunger; but as to the Russians, each time, during the retreat, that we faced about, we beat them.

"When the foundations of that historic bridge, the sole hope of safety offered us, had to be laid in the Beresina, at the voice of their chief those men of duty and resolution marched silently into the water, never interrupting their work save to turn aside the huge pieces of ice which threatened to cut them in two like a sword. They drove in the piles, the ground-work of the construction, and went on striking their blows until the moment came when they felt death seize them. Not one came out alive, but others stepped in to complete the work—the work of a day which should leave an immortal memory!

"Long deprived of its daily nourishment, the army suffer cruelly. Your husband and his staff feel the effects of this privation; but perhaps worse still is the absence of sleeping accommodation in this infernal temperature. With no other covering but our cloaks, we have long been sleeping in the snow. We have returned in rags."

I looked at him with greater attention. His always handsome but tragical face now had something so sombre that I was astounded. When he had appeared to me two hours before, I thought I saw a phantom; and indeed his hollow cheeks, his look of despair, the smoke from the bivouacs incrusted in his skin gave him an air that was quite cadaverous. His clothes were worn, tarnished, almost colourless. His boots were split and fastened with string; in fact the catastrophe which he had so eloquently described seemed personified in himself.

"But, after all, where have you left the marshal?" I asked.

"Making for Wilna," he replied. "With him in the carriage are his son, a doctor, and an *aide-de-camp*; on the box are Pils and a footman. He is surrounded with an escort, which has become necessary because of the Cossacks who infest the whole country we have to cross. You see, *Madame*," he continued, "that it is impossible for me to allow you to run the risk of such a journey."

"But in Heaven's name," I replied, "is the risk not equally great for my husband?"

"No, because he has an escort which you would be without. I repeat, the marshal's life and journey are safe."

In spite of his state of exhaustion, M. Le Tellier would hardly take time to eat, or even to change his clothes, before going to inform the Duc de Bassano of the general condition of the wreck of our army. He had nothing now to conceal, and the young man unrolled before the minister the black and terrible picture which had passed before my eyes. After that he withdrew into absolute silence, by reason of the command the marshal had laid upon him to reveal the story of our misery only to those entitled to hear it. I was reassured as to the life of Victor, who was accompanying his father. I knew also that Generals Pajol and de Lorencez were both alive, and retained their appearance of command.

The minister's silence, and ours, failed for long to stop the dull but significant rumours which began to spread about the town of Wilna. The news of this second wound of the marshal's was alone a serious omen, which at once brought me many marks of sympathy. What the Duc de Bassano had foreseen was now realized; alarm reigned on every hand, and people came to me to know what road I meant to take, before deciding which they would follow themselves. The night which came after that terrible day of the 2nd of December seemed very long to me.

On the morning of the 3rd, my uncle entered my room, followed by Mme. Morel, who obliged me to take a little chocolate, an incident I should certainly not have mentioned if what I left had not gone to relieve a starving man, who threw himself upon the tray carried off by Mme. Morel. I heard a mingled sound of voices and clattering china in the next room, and I had no time to make enquiries when my uncle, who had hurriedly left me, returned with Victor. The latter forestalled all apprehension on my part by calling out at the door that his father was no worse, and that he had come to announce his probable arrival for the next day.

My satisfaction at this news very soon dispelled the momentary terror with which I had been seized at sight of the traveller. Victor was really dying of hunger, and it was he who, seeing the remains of my breakfast leave my room, had fallen upon it like a wolf upon its prey.

"Well!" said I to Victor, "I can gain twenty-four hours by going to meet him; and since you arrived without any obstacles, why should you put any in my way?"

My stepson was no more ready to be convinced than was M. Le Tellier, and you will understand why when you read what follows.

"In the first place," said Victor, "it was providential that Le Tellier and I succeeded in escaping the Cossacks scattered over the road. But listen now to what Le Tellier was not able to tell you, and thank God that we escaped the many dangers to which my father was exposed shortly after despatching his first *aide-de-camp.*"

The extraordinary incident that had occurred was this:

Lying in his carriage, which was occupied besides by his son, an *aide-de-camp* and his surgeon, the marshal travelled under an escort of infantry. At first they proceeded slowly and cautiously; but on the second day, as the road apparently continued clear, the wounded man determined to try and hasten the painful journey, and gave orders to drive ahead of the detachment, and trot to the next resting-place. This was the village of Pletchnitzy.

The marshal was placed in a room warmed by a stove. He thought himself alone, and was waiting on a pallet for Dr. Capiomont to prepare the dressing for his wound, when a cannon-shot shook the wooden shed in which he lay, and caused the victim to be struck by a splinter of the partition. At the same time, four or five Jewish children were tumbled off the top of the stove, where they had heaped themselves up to enjoy the heat unobserved. Thereupon Victor entered with the other gentlemen, and told the marshal that the village was surrounded by five hundred Cossacks, with two pieces of artillery, one of which had already given news of itself.

On our side they were twenty-five to thirty, all told, to defend that fine prize, a Marshal of the Empire! Will you believe that your father, over-excited at the thought of being taken prisoner by the Cossacks, insisted on being set upon his horse. He was not able to keep himself up, and was carried back almost fainting to his wretched bed, while all the others hastened to the defence. They made use of everything that came to hand to form a sort of barricade around the house. During this time the marshal had recovered consciousness, and he found by his side the wife of the military *intendant*, Martouret, who had, at her own risk and peril, followed her husband throughout the campaign. She had borne with surprising courage the unequalled trials of this retreat. Her health had been able to withstand it; and she had made herself useful and serviceable to everyone.

On recognizing her, the marshal made her give him his pistols;

and from his bed, aiming through an opening opposite, he fired at the Cossacks. His shots were lost in the general din. The struggle was a keen one, for each was determined to be killed rather than surrender. But whether this obstinate defence imposed upon the enemy, or whether they were ignorant of the marshal's rank, which would have been so fine a trophy for them, they failed to profit intelligently by the situation, and gave time to a remnant of a French column to arrive. So soon as they perceived it, they thought of no more but to seize any horses that they could find; and the adventure ended in a flight, rather than a retreat, on their part. Naturally, it had heated the wounded marshal's blood, and while thanking God for the sort of miracle by which he had been saved, he passed a very bad night.

Under any other conditions, the continuance of his journey would have been regarded as impossible; but at that time the word had been erased from the dictionary! They took the road therefore the next day, but slowly, and surrounded by an escort, which they no longer felt tempted to go beyond.

This day of the 3rd was spent by my stepson in relating, and by my uncle and myself in listening.

Several of the marshal's officers went ahead to assure me of his speedy arrival. It was high time, for the thermometer had descended to 18° below zero; and I saw, with alarm, night approaching, when the sound of the carriage under the archway was heard. I hastened to the door: it was open, and nothing came out of it. The servants seemed frozen to the box. At last, with great difficulty, the marshal, broken by his sufferings and stiff with cold, was lifted out of the carriage. They offered to carry him up the stairs, but he refused, and bent in two, unrecognizable from head to foot, he arrived prostrate before the fire which awaited him.

I was then able to realize the unspeakable change which a serious wound, accompanied by keen moral suffering, had brought about in so strong and vigorous a constitution. But it was no time for reflection. A warm bed was at once made ready, and I was present at the dressing of that open wound, which refused to give up the projectile, although it got rid gradually of all that had entered with it. Shirt, vest, uniform, *astrakhan*: the bullet had carried all in with it; and it was not until his vigorous organization had expelled all these foreign bodies that the wound could be expected to heal. As yet we were only at the commencement.

When he had rested, the marshal asked for food, and wished to have it served at his bedside, to which he naturally invited his travelling companions. They were fairly numerous and all famished. At the sight of the clean table-linen, of the plate, and the candles, and still more upon scenting the succulent dishes which I had taken pleasure in having prepared for them, there was an hurrah of surprise as well as satisfaction; and to my great delight it was the marshal who led it.

"Is it not a dream," he asked, "to find a well-supplied table again?"

And thereupon followed the distressing details of their privations. They were long over their meal, and I felt inclined both to laugh and cry at all that I saw and heard.

The marshal had a good night; but the next morning his bed was besieged, not only by all those who had remained at Wilna, but by those who began to arrive in disorderly crowds. It was the commencement of the rout; and your father, who was unable to understand any movement not based upon duty and discipline, was keenly irritated on each fresh occasion. Nothing could persuade him of the terrible truth, of which evidences lay on every side, that there was no army left.

Every day brought into Wilna masses of sick and wounded, of soldiers without chiefs, and chiefs without commands. Convoys of dying soldiers, heaped up in the wagons, were unable to find room in the overcrowded hospitals. The governor, losing the little head he had left, put neither men nor things in their right places, and thus increased the chances of the terrible disorder which broke out a few days later, when the shadow of a few apparently still organized bodies presented itself in its turn.

The marshal, knowing thoroughly what provisions of all kinds Wilna contained, insisted that we could and should defend ourselves there long enough to recover and reorganize ourselves a little. On this subject he had lively discussions with all the heads who surrounded his bed: Marshal Gouvion-Saint-Cyr, General Pajol, the Duc de Bassano.

The last, on the third day after my husband's arrival, came earlier than usual, and expressed a wish to speak to him in private. The interview was a short one, but of such a kind that, on separating, the two bade one another a special and eloquent goodbye. I met the minister as he was going out. He took me aside, and, in a low and eager voice, said:

"I have just persuaded the marshal to set out today. Hurry your preparations as much as you can; you have not a moment to lose."

"But how," I asked, "did you succeed in obtaining so prompt a decision from the marshal, who only yesterday argued against all of us that we should defend ourselves here?"

"Ah!" he replied, "my argument was convincing;" and lowering his voice still more, he added, "The emperor passed us last night on his return to France."

I felt as though in a dream; but I understood that this was not the time for comment. I took leave of the minister, and he of me. He was to start the next day, and strongly urged us to precede him. As to your father, I found him in a state of violent excitement. He was furious at recognizing at last the impossibility of the struggle; and once compelled to give way, he wished to leave at the earliest possible moment.

It was on this fatal day and during the subsequent night that the thermometer fell from 18° to 28° below zero!

We left Victor behind, to our great regret; but he wished to wait for the chance of official instructions arriving. General Pajol had gone ahead of us. General de Lorencez, retained by the shadowy remnant of the 2nd Corps, of which he represented the staff, was one of the last to take the road for France.

The marshal was carefully packed into my comfortable carriage, with me by his side and Madame Morel opposite, while my uncle and Messieurs de Bourcet, Jacqueminot and Capiomont installed themselves in the marshal's carriage, which was much less roomy than the other. The three last were attacked in different degrees by dysentery, one of the diseases which were ravaging the army; and a fourth victim of this scourge came and asked their pity, saying that the place on the box which was destined for him would be his death. This was M. Rouget, the marshal's *maître d'hôtel.* The four of them were already crowded; but, as I have said, the word impossible did not then exist. They made room for the unhappy man, who sometimes on his knees in the midst of them, sometimes partly stretched upon their knees, twisted about in pain, and aroused all their commiseration.

The box of this second carriage was occupied by two of our servants; on the box of ours sat Pils and the cook. After we had taken a sad farewell of Victor and of all the half-frozen wounded who crowded into our apartments at the moment of departure, the carriage-doors were closed. It was time, for the cold was already nipping us.

The carriages moved and soon scattered the snow like dust. We had an escort of twenty *cuirassiers*, perfectly mounted, and wrapped in their great white mantles. But except a few white-faced Jews shivering as they hastened to their speculations, with which nothing ever interfered, we encountered not a living being on our way through the streets of that town which I had entered with so glad a heart two months before.

Brave M. Le Tellier, with his phantom face, declaring himself the soundest of his comrades, had wished to perform the service of this terrible day, and he galloped actively beside our carriage. He kept his place while, little by little, I beheld the number of *cuirassiers* of our escort diminish. Did a single one reach our first bivouac? I am unable to say, because the night put an end to all observation. I only remember that the last two soldiers I was able to see had their long moustaches stiffened by the icicles formed from their breath.

Soon all grew confused in the darkness, but not too soon, however, to prevent me, when we reached the foot of the well-known mountain which we had to ascend, from distinguishing the soldiers lying stiff and stark along all the slope which they had vainly endeavoured to climb. They had fallen down, overcome by the cold; and there, when one fell, he did not get up again. . . . A few pools of blood had escaped from their chests and nostrils and stained red the snow.

Nothing has ever been able to efface from my mind the terrible impression I retained of this ascent across this field strewn with the dead. And yet it was but the commencement of the end.

Our rough-shod horses quickly surmounted this steep and forbidding incline, and soon we had left the awful spectacle behind us. The marshal kept a profound silence; he felt instinctively all that I must suffer from what I saw; but he suffered too deeply himself to question me. We went like the wind along this table-land, which we had traversed with so much difficulty a few weeks ago. But the snow had smoothed the roads . . .

Soon I was able to distinguish nothing upon its whiteness save the figure of M. Le Tellier, who continued to gallop by the carriage door. I could not say exactly at what time he stopped the carriage, crying that he was going to prepare a lodging for us in a building of which he had caught sight. He soon returned. "Quick, *Madame la maréchale*," he said, opening the carriage door, "out you come." Seized by a horrible feeling of this deathly temperature, I asked myself how my wounded husband would bear it. Our unfortunate servants, stiffened by the cold on their outside seats, nevertheless retained the energy to do their duty. The marshal was carried upon one of his mattresses, and we moved towards a kind of shapeless shed, which at a distance seemed to me to be surrounded by a number of great black circles drawn upon that eternal snow. They consisted of men, who were all still moving then; but the next day . . .

The half-burnt post-house which M. Le Tellier made us enter had been crowded during the daytime not only by those who were returning from the army and who had been able to resist the cold so far, but by those who were travelling in the opposite direction, and who had come from Königsberg in order to rejoin what they still called the army. It was the staff and the last portion of Loison's division, which the emperor had sent for. The general and his officers had sought shelter in this house, the only one left standing on that devastated road, and part of it had been demolished to provide firewood for the bivouac which we saw before us.

So great was the crowd that M. Le Tellier had the greatest difficulty in penetrating. He struck some and stepped upon others, shouting to everyone that Marshal Oudinot, who was dying, was also entitled to a place. No one listened; no one made way or moved. He stormed in vain; but before long he perceived that several among them were dying, and some already dead. He tried to drag outside a number of the latter, so as to make room for us; but those who remained took advantage of his exertions and, with the brutal selfishness which was the only sentiment left to most of them, stretched themselves more at their ease.

However, after crossing the first room in which reigned this frightful confusion, we penetrated to the second, which was filled with General Loison's officers. These were so closely packed that they could neither lie down nor sit, and they stood up so as to occupy less room, including the general, who, in the name of my husband, obtained just sufficient room to lay before the fire the little mattress upon which he reclined. I sat down at the foot of the mattress. The other occupants of our two carriages found shelter somehow, as did also poor Mme. Abramowietz, who, driving alone in her *calash*, had followed our fortunes.

Dr Capiomont tried to dress the sick man's wound; but everything froze beneath his hands, and he had to give up the attempt. We tried to use the provisions brought on one side from Wilna and on the other from Königsberg; but everything—bread, wine, ham, poultry—was frozen, and could not be thawed even when put before the stove. A slight dampness was all that appeared on the outside of the eatables; the inside remained as hard as stone.

None of us who were packed into this room were able to sleep, since it was a condition of admittance that one should remain standing. For a moment I saw General Loison, who was standing over us, close his eyes and sway to and fro above our heads. His fall would have crushed us, and I thought it best to warn him.

We suffered so much where we were that it was easy to imagine how things were going outside: we felt Death all around us. . . . The fire in the stove grew low for want of fuel; but where and how to find any? It was almost risking one's life. That good Dr. Capiomont ventured out, however, and I can still see him returning in triumph with a part of a cannon-wheel, which blazed up and gave us the necessary energy at the moment of departure.

Again it was M. Le Tellier who came to give us the signal. Day had not yet broken; but it was high time to restore to movement our people and our horses, which had escaped by a miracle from the disasters of the night. Besides, the snow showed up only too well all that surrounded us. The marshal was carried quickly to his carriage; but however briskly the rest of us followed him, we had plenty of time in which to take in the sight that met our eyes. The bivouacs of the night before stood out black against the snow; but all was extinct and motionless. How many of the men were dead? How many dying? I know not; but it is notorious that this night of the 7th of December 1812 was one of the most deadly, and that its ravages on the remains of our army were terrible.

Shut up in our carriage, between the grey sky and the white ground, we felt as though we were wrapped in our shrouds. The pale sun, which had shown itself at moments the day before, now refused to appear; and although in such cold as this it has no power to prevent freezing and death, it at least prevents despair.

You know how desolate I had thought this road when we travelled by it before. Now we saw not a single inhabitant near the ruins of which I have spoken to you. Only, at rare intervals, there rose a few blackened chimneys, which I sometimes took for Cossacks on the lookout. The scattered fir-trees caused me the same fright. I then pictured my husband as a prisoner of war, and was sure that he would never recover from it. My apprehensions were increased by the presence of my uncle, whose serenity never diminished in the midst of this calamity which I had involuntarily brought down upon him.

I often thought of his wife and children seated around that fireside from which I had perhaps torn him forever. . . . Then I would lose my head when I thought of my responsibility; for, as you can understand, we were all there from duty: my husband and those of his profession followed their destiny; I was accomplishing mine; but in my uncle's case, he had forced his, through sheer devotion for myself.

We were not able to communicate often between the two carriages, for our people, dulled with the cold, could not easily serve as messengers. They only protected themselves against the frost by sitting huddled on their box, and covering as far as possible their feet, hands and noses. Our escort had disappeared. M. Le Tellier alone rode by our side, as on the day before.

I do not know how we managed to live during this day of travel; the cold absorbed all our faculties. At nightfall, M. Le Tellier made us turn sharp off to the left; for he had a marvellous power of finding his way, in spite of the uniformity which the snow seemed to produce. We drove into a village called, I believe, Tchismori. The houses were standing; it did not offer that appearance of devastation which we had so long had before our eyes. The carriage pulled up before the house of the priest, who quickly put at our disposal two little rooms, of which one was heated by a stove.

Soon we were gathered round a copious dish of potatoes, which to tell the truth, constituted the first nourishment we had taken since leaving Wilna. The warmth had restored to our stomachs a part of their faculties, and those of us who had been attacked with dysentery experienced a racking pain resembling sudden hunger. All of us, excepting my uncle, showed signs of real suffering and great irritation. But he, the excellent man, had preserved his sweet and equal temper, and I gladly perceived that till then his health had withstood every trial.

At daybreak we were all on foot to enter the carriages which were ready and waiting for us. In spite of the comparatively good night which the marshal spent, the doctor was not content with the state of his wound. It had inflamed and caused him so much pain that he did not know what position to take in the carriage. And yet it was necessary that we should push ahead . . .

M. Delamarre, the marshal's *aide-de-camp*, had joined us at Tchismori during the night. Although he had left Wilna only a few hours after us, he had new and melancholy details to give us. He had witnessed the increase of the tumultuous disorder which we knew to have begun in the town. The mountain was becoming more and more encumbered; and they were preparing to burn the wretched remnants of our lodging of the night before.

General de Lorencez had not yet returned to Wilna; Victor was still waiting there with a few wretched remnants of his regiment; General Pajol alone, compelled by his wound to return, followed us closely. He soon joined us in a Jew's cabin where we had been obliged to set down the marshal, so as to try and dress his wound, which was becoming more and more inflamed. He should have had poultices, but they froze in the doctor's hands. The latter, however, succeeded in giving some relief to his patient.

At nightfall we reached Kowno, and alighted at the house of the military *intendant*, M. de Baudecour. He had stayed with us at Bar, as well as his wife, who accompanied him as far as Mayence, when he set out to join the Grande Armée eleven months earlier. He busied himself in seeing to the comforts of the marshal and myself with extreme kindness, but it was not until I had seen my husband receiving all his first cares that I perceived the violent grief that seemed to oppress our host. My evident anxiety made him speak, and he anticipated my question by saying, amid a torrent of sobs:

"I have lost my only son during this retreat, and I have only learnt it two hours ago."

A mournful silence succeeded this revelation. What could we say to the heart-broken father? My eyes did not leave him. He soon actively resumed the duties demanded of him by hospitality, but his domestic arrangements did not second his kind intentions. The space at his disposal consisted of but one decent room, that in which we had been received. It was at the same time sitting-room, office, and entrance-hall; for it was preceded by no sort of passage, and you can understand that it was impossible to ask people to wait outside in the cold. You can imagine the pressure put upon the poor military *intendant*, who had to attend to so many diverse and urgent matters, and, who, moreover, wished to have dinner served for us. The stove gave out a great heat, and the crowd was stifling.

On leaving Kowno, we crossed the Niemen, which was covered with thick ice, and reached the well-known slope, which was like that of Wilna on a smaller scale. Our poor horses were just able to drag us out of this difficult place, where a few days later the swords were broken of the valiant captains who had succeeded in carrying them so far. It was at Kowno, in fact, that Ney gave up the retreat, if that was still the name for the shadow of a command which he strove to wield till the end over the few scattered remnants he had kept together on the march. They broke up completely on the banks of the Niemen, and after that each acted and marched on his own account.

We had constantly travelled at the same rate as the second carriage, and we had gone some leagues beyond the slope of which I have spoken, when Pils, who noticed everything from his seat on the box, looked out for it in vain over the vast stretch of snow which we were crossing. We halted and waited. It was useless, nothing came in sight. There was nothing to be seen but the eternal snow, behind us, before, on every side. "Drive on," said the marshal. My heart seemed to split in two at the words. It seemed impossible to abandon my uncle. His wife, his children, all my family rose up before my eyes like threatening phantoms. On the other hand I felt that, before all, I must think of saving my husband. Between these two emotions I became like a madwoman.

Meantime it was growing late, and M. Le Tellier, unfailingly true to his post, came and told us that in order to make Antonovo, a small country-house which the marshal had appointed as our next resting-place, and fearing lest he should lose the way if we were overtaken by the darkness, he had taken a guide whom he had picked up in some ruined village. We discovered that it was a Jew, and I turned pale as death when I saw this man of ill-omen, clad in his long black gown, mounting our box and seating himself next to Pils. Soon, under his doubtful guidance, we turned off to the right, and thus lost from sight the slight traces which might still enable us to recognize the main road. It was almost dark, and we were trusting to this unknown wretch to guide us across that desert. I threw a last long look behind; there was no uncle to be seen, and no one to tell him of our change of road, if fortunately he were still following us.

The road was uneven, and we proceeded with difficulty. It became quite dark, and the guide, constantly questioned by Pils, continued to assure us that we were going right. I know not how long passed in this way.

At last M. Le Tellier exclaimed that we had arrived. He recognized our whereabouts, because the marshal had encamped there with his army corps at the commencement of the campaign. He and his staff had been harboured at the *château* by the Comtesse de ——, a zealous Lithuanian, and they had parted mutually charmed with one another. The carriage drew up, the door was opened, and by the light of many torches, I saw the mistress of the house appear. As she came forward the marshal said, from his carriage, "I have come to beg your hospitality once again."

"How pleased we should have been to receive you," she said, in excellent French, in a clear, soft voice, "if you had not come under such melancholy auspices."

We thought at first that these words referred to the marshal's wound, or perhaps to the general distress, of which the news had quickly spread. But there was a more pressing calamity. The household had been attacked by typhus; seven persons had already succumbed to it, both among members of the family and refugees whom they had sheltered. One of the ladies of the family was still extremely ill.

"What will you do?" asked the countess, after giving the marshal a brief account of the case. "I was bound to tell you the truth, and if it does not alarm you, your rooms are ready for you."

"I accept your hospitality," said the marshal.

Upon these words, the charming woman went to give her last orders, and to return to her patients. We had had to choose between the dread of contagion and an ice-cold night in the midst of that desert. What a position!

We were soon rejoined by Mme. de ——, who showed us to a room furnished simply, but in the French style, in which there were two good beds.

"I have put you as far away as possible from the epidemic," she said, "but I must return to it at once. Farewell, you shall not see me again."

I need hardly tell you what passed within me, at the sight of this tranquil courage. The countess gave me no time to express myself as I should have wished; but I hope that under such circumstances one's features are sufficiently expressive to convey all one wishes to. They soon brought us some provisions sent us by our kind hostess, but I could not eat. Our anguish had reached its climax, and for the first time I gave way beneath its weight.

I beheld your father resting under that infected roof; I feared on my uncle's behalf both the cold and the pursuit of the Cossacks; while with all my heart I shared the terrible troubles of our hosts. It was more than I was able to bear.

I had just assisted at the dressing of the wound by Pils, in the absence of the surgeon. The marshal, tired out, lay stretched on one of the two beds which had been prepared for us. I was about to seek some rest on the other, when suddenly a fierce jet of flame darted from the stove. It had been driven in by the wind, which was rising and blowing noisily. In an instant the room was filled with smoke. I rushed out terrified to call for help. But where was I to turn in this unknown and deserted house? At that moment a fresh noise made a diversion. It was Pils, sent by Providence; he had come to tell us that the second carriage had arrived. I will not seek to depict to you the contrast between the moments which ensued and those which had just passed. The fire, which had not had time to do much damage, was first put out, and soon the travellers, all suffering from cold, but safe and sound, were telling us of their adventure, due to a breakdown of their carriage, which it had taken several hours to repair.

We shortened as much as possible the sleepless night which followed that arduous day. Unable to afford any assistance to our hosts, we were naturally eager to leave them; and soon we were once more driving, at break of day, over the white, frozen country. I believe that our tracks of the night before were our only guide; for I do not remember seeing the Jew again. We resumed our journey along the main road, and after travelling as fast as our horses would go, we succeeded in reaching Wirbahlen before nightfall, and stopped before a deserted house.

An effort was made to call upon the authorities, whom we hoped to find still organized; but even if they were discovered, they were quite powerless, and we had scarcely a few logs of wood to burn. Our supper consisted of one grilled fish among our whole famished party. The temperature did not relax in vigour, and this night of cold and famine was one of the hardest we had had to pass.

Nevertheless, the morning found us all still alive; but the marshal declared that we must rest for a space at the first halting-place that should offer some resources. This was the town of Gumbinnen, where we arrived still frozen, on the evening of the 11th. I had noticed, on the journey out, the attractive aspect of this town, and it was still light enough to enable us to distinguish the clearly-marked streets. The cold prevented the inhabitants from going out, but the well-closed houses and pleasantly smoking chimneys made us very eager to enter one of these fortunate dwellings, fortunate because they were warm.

At Gumbinnen there was still some sort of French organization, and a good lodging was at once found for the marshal and the whole of his suite. And for the first time since leaving Wilna, we had a repast which did us good, since we partook of it in peace and warmth. Soup, followed by a beefsteak and potatoes—what a banquet, my children! But what completed our joy was the possibility of at last being able to change our clothes. You may have observed that, like the heroines of romance who, as a witty woman has said, never seem to think, nor to have the chance, of putting on a clean shift, I had kept on mine, together with all I possessed in the shape of winter garments huddled on my body, for the last ten days.

Well, I assure you that the little delicacies to which we were accustomed had soon been lost under our privations, and I was at last able to understand how those who are in want of a night's lodging and of bread cease to care for cleanliness. Till then, I had placed it first among the necessities of life, and when my heart rose involuntarily at the sight of the foul rags of poverty, I pitied the beggar more for his dirt than for his shivering or his hunger. I have learned to have sounder and fairer ideas since. But at Gumbinnen I was not yet sufficiently hardened to my calling as a canteen-woman's apprentice to be insensible to the luxuries of soap, combs, brushes, and clean linen.

Our stay at Gumbinnen had given my husband's staff the time to join him, and one morning he gathered them round his bed. It was a solemn occasion, and I regretted that I had not a room of my own to which to retire.

When all these young men were assembled in a semi circle around their chief, he said:

"Well, gentlemen, where are you going?"

They looked at one another without speaking.

The marshal resumed:

"What! You are unwounded, you are in good health, and you leave the army! Do you think I should be turning my back upon it, if I could be of any use to it at this time?"

The dismay reached its height. At last, M. Achille Delamarre took courage, and said, apparently in the name of them all, since nobody contradicted him:

"*Monsieur le Maréchal*, you are our leader, our 'governor;' we must follow your fortunes. Besides, there is nothing more to be done here, for the emperor has gone, and the army no longer exists."

These words, so constantly dinned into his ears, always infuriated your father. "In that case, gentlemen," he replied, "we shall reconstitute the army and bring it in the spring, with flags flying, to the Vistula. Wait for me there, and go and offer your services to the heads of corps who, more fortunate than I, are still able to be of use at their posts."

Not one of the gentlemen strove to argue against the marshal's opinion. They withdrew in silence, and their chief, after thus vigorously expressing his thoughts, did not return to the subject. He had the less excuse for doing so, as each succeeding day went more and more to prove the sad truth that there was no army left.

The next day, M. Le Tellier, who had so nobly taken care of us, took the road for France, accompanied by Messieurs Delamarre, de la Chaise, and the rest, while Messieurs Jacqueminot and de Bourcet, still enfeebled by their dysentery, accompanied the marshal, and travelled in the second carriage. After a time M. Jacqueminot procured a little sledge, and going ahead of us every morning, he bravely occupied himself, so long as we remained on foreign ground, in preparing lodgings for us.

All more or less restored by our rest, we left Gumbinnen to go to Wehlau, which was still in the hands of the French. But the principal authority of the town was absent on our arrival, and we were unable to obtain any comfort.

Our stay at Gumbinnen had enabled many of our companions in misfortune, deserters all, as the marshal called them, to precede or await us. They had all taken the road in the dress they had on at the time. Some were covered with furs, and looked like bears; others, who had lost all they had and were unable to buy anything in its stead, were clad in their full uniforms, as, for instance, General de Chasseloup of the artillery. He shivered beneath his gold lace, in his sleigh formed of four planks. Unable to keep his whole body warm, he had found a means of preserving his ears, and wore a cotton nightcap pulled down to meet the collar of his uniform, and over this another cap of grey taffeta. When he learned who we were, he arrived, accompanied by Colonel Bodson, of the same branch of the service, to call upon the marshal.

Neither of them thought of their personal appearance: a matter of small importance truly! The marshal was touched by their eagerness to pay their respects to him, and at first received them very well; but the scene changed when they started their litany of the misery we had left behind us, and of which they knew something, having left Wilna later than any of those who had caught us up as yet. When the general had finished, the colonel took up the thread. I do not know how long this would have gone on, if the marshal, irritated beyond endurance, had not suddenly exclaimed:

"My dear Bodson, do blow your nose!"

As a matter of fact, it had become very necessary; and while this operation was taking place, the marshal, bowing to the two gentlemen, closed the carriage-door, and we drove off. There was no laughter during this journey. But afterwards, when my husband and I have recalled this incident, we have often made merry over it.

To return to Wehlau, where we spent a night as cold as ice. We ought to have grown accustomed to it, perhaps, but we had not. Our meagre repast did not contribute to warm our blood, and we were starting at daybreak, shivering with cold, when we saw coming up to the carriage a young sub-commissary, looking very spruce, covered with gold lace, with a charming face and a great air of fashion. Contrasting with all this elegance was an enormous loaf of bread, with a hole in the middle, through which M. Solikoff (that was his name) had put his arm. After respectfully greeting the marshal, he turned to me, and presenting the loaf to me, said:

"It is all I am able to offer you, *Madame la duchesse*, as a poor compensation for the privations which you must have suffered in this place, from which I was absent yesterday. I shall find it very difficult to console myself for the inhospitality of which the marshal and you have been the victims in a spot where I am supposed to exercise some authority."

We thanked him as much as one can do when the north wind is cutting one in two. He bowed to us with an air of great emotion. ... I never saw this young man again, but later I met his brother in Paris. . . . He asked to be introduced to me, and I was happy to be able to tell him that I had not forgotten that loaf of bread which had been offered with such kindly grace and devotion. It was, as a matter of fact, a great help to us, and lasted us until we reached Königsberg on the evening of the same day.

Here we were, in a large and handsome hotel, in the centre of a capital. We thought we should now, by taking a few days' repose, be able to assure our welfare. Vain hope! The marshal suffered considerably; I found him irritated; I feared he was feverish, and was anxious that he should have calm and silence; but I foresaw some mishap. He was occupying a huge room, and the dinner-table was laid before his bed. During the meal he endeavoured to distract his attention from the clamour which he heard in the next room; but it became so great that he asked Mr Jacqueminot to go and find out what was happening. The latter returned with a gloomy face, and without categorically explaining himself, tried to prepare my husband for the indefinite prolongation of the noise in question.

Not caring to be further enlightened, the marshal dismissed us and sank back into his pillows. . . . I never learnt whether he slept. If he guessed the nature of the toasts which twenty or thirty Prussians in the next room were drinking to our disasters, he must have suffered cruel nightmares. I never ventured to ask him.

These inhabitants of Königsberg were under all the effervescence of the first news that had reached them. They knew of the emperor's departure and of all that followed. They had just begun their celebration when they were asked to moderate their cheering out of consideration for a wounded French general officer who had just arrived at the hotel. I do not know whether your father's name was mentioned; but they took no notice of the request, which even seemed to redouble their ardour. This savage conduct is an isolated instance in the marshal's life. Among his enemies, as well as among his friends, he was always an object of regard and delicate consideration.

From Königsberg onwards we had recourse to the post, and we arrived at Brandenburg on the evening of the 17th of December. Before reaching Dantzig, our next halting-place, the marshal wished to warm himself at Elbing. We had scarcely alighted at a hotel, which I can still picture in my mind, and where the door was opened to us with somewhat bad grace, when we received a visit from General, then Colonel, Farine, who was in command there, and who told us that he had all the difficulty in the world in preserving our military position, so hostile had Prussia become to us.

Proofs of the miseries of the retreat had already displayed themselves. The hospitals were crowded with sick, for the greatest part suffering from typhus. Poor General Pajol arrived a few hours after we had left, and he, who had so brilliantly endured both his wounds and his fatigues during this terrible campaign, was attacked by the reigning epidemic, and so severely that he would infallibly have succumbed if a French doctor had not devoted himself to him and fed and covered him with quinine. He powdered his body with it unceasingly, and saved him with the aid of this supreme remedy. But this treatment was not within reach of the generality of sufferers, who died in numbers of the contagion.

General Rapp,[2] who was in command at Dantzig when we arrived there, had left this important position, by order of the emperor, to go and fight in Russia. He had come back no less energetic and devoted than he had gone out, but broken down with fatigue and with both ears frozen. He had preceded us by a few days, on going to resume his

2. *Rapp: the Last Victor* by Jean Rapp also published by Leonaur.

command, and had declared to the marshal, when he met him, that he would get a lodging ready for him, and would force him, in spite of himself, to take his rest for some time within the ramparts under his command. Excellent man! what an amount of care and kindness he lavished upon us!

It was impossible to refuse the lavish and at the same time delicate hospitality of this generous heart. The general's position at Dantzig was that of a sort of viceroy. But while able long to enjoy the advantages of this position, he was none the less able valiantly to defend it in the bad days that followed.

Our stay gave time to a number of refugees from the great rout to catch us up in this fortress, where all of them, feeling themselves in a place of safety, seized a longer or shorter period of rest; and soon, as at Wilna, the marshal's rooms became at once a headquarters and a sort of ambulance where everyone arrived with his wounds, mental or physical.

One of the first who followed us to Dantzig was General Maison. Unfortunately he was not accompanied by his Chief of Staff, General de Lorencez, who had been left behind on the road, ill. His condition, when General Maison left him, had not yet attained the serious stage which it reached later. Nevertheless, the news saddened us greatly.

After a week's stay, we took a very affectionate leave of General Rapp, whom I was delighted to meet again later in France, and with whom we kept up excellent relations. I will abridge the details of our journey from Dantzig to Berlin, because the interest of a journey diminishes together with its danger. The temperature had become milder, and the snow, partly thawed, allowed us to catch glimpses of a landscape which was said to be rather pretty, although it was not possible to judge of it at the time. M. Jacqueminot, who acted as our advance-guard, had begun the journey in a sleigh, being unable as yet to ride his horse, he said. When the snow began to fail him, he nevertheless persisted in the use of his vehicle, to which he clung in spite of the thaw.

On the 31st of December, we slept at Zehden, on the banks of the Oder, which we had to cross the next morning, at break of day. There was no bridge, and the ferry was the ordinary means of crossing; but this was rendered impossible by the ice. On the other hand, they said that the ice was not strong enough to venture upon. It was a serious predicament. "Wait," said the inhabitants; "in a few days the ice will break and allow the ferry to work. This proposal had not the slightest success with the marshal, who ordered the postillions to drive on.

In a heavy carriage with six horses we undertook this terrible passage over the cracking ice, which seemed to give way beneath us. Again the fate of the second carriage increased my alarm. "Even if we escape," I thought, "we shall certainly have shaken the ice in such a manner as to double the danger of those behind." God watched over us yet once more and at last, on the 1st of January 1813, we entered Berlin. We alighted, at five o'clock in the evening, at the Hôtel de Russie in the Unter den Linden. There, as a New Year's surprise, we found the famous and ominous 29th Bulletin of the Grande Armée, which had crushed all France.

The marshal, who, as you know, would have liked to keep to himself the secret of our disasters, was dismayed and confounded on reading this bulletin, and, turning to us, expressed in energetic and eloquent gestures that there was nothing more to be done. The cup was rendered still more bitter to my husband because of the place in which we were made to drain it. Berlin, in which we had twice reigned, Berlin reading these deplorable avowals with us became really hateful to us. Nevertheless, the kindness of its sovereign was not withheld from us during the short time which we were obliged to spend there. From Potsdam, where he was still staying, he sent his brother-in-law, Prince Radziwill, to enquire after my husband's state of health.

It was at Berlin that I for the last time saw the Comte Louis de Narbonne. He had undergone all the miseries of the retreat from Moscow without losing, in appearance at any rate, his graceful and communicative gaiety. Nevertheless, the courageous old man's features bore the impress of his fatigues and privations.

Before leaving, we were joined by Victor, accompanied by M. de Thermes, with whom he had travelled from Wilna. They had, they told us, mutually saved each other's noses by throwing handfuls of snow at one another's faces when the dull pallor caused by the frost had threatened danger to that organ.

At Leipzig, M. Jacqueminot had prepared our lodging in one of the finest hotels I have ever seen. We arrived early, and if the weather had not been so wretched, I should have liked to go over the town. Victor, however, who, if not more inclined for sight-seeing, was more weather-proof than I, went out at once and did not return before night. He had not only inspected the public monuments, but also the more notable shops, which were full of English products, which were almost unknown to our young generation, and he brought me back a charming specimen of his discoveries. It was a muslin gown of the most marvellously fine network. The pattern was fluted, very rich, and in perfect taste. I was touched to the heart by this present bought with the savings of his pay as a lieutenant in the Imperial Guard. But there was one still more satisfied than I, and that was your father.

Before our return to civilized climes, I had taken no heed of our respective costumes, and it was only just about this time that I commenced to examine them. They were pitiful to look upon: we were really in rags and tatters. I shall always remember how I first made this discovery. It was a fine, sunny, winter's morning. The marshal, who was beginning to walk a little about his room, wanted to try the air outside, and leaning on Victor's arm, he slowly climbed a little slope. He was dressed in a dark-brown fur coat, with, on his head, a black astrakhan cap, dragged down over his ears; and he would have reminded me of a tame bear, if his legs had not been encased in a certain pair of boots, well lined with fur, but presenting to the outside view nothing save a blue and white striped ticking (the ticking of a feather-bed). These two striped legs emerging from under the fur coat had an indescribable effect. My uncle, when one did not look at him closely, had a brigand air which made me shed tears with laughter. My own fur pelisse was hanging down in rags.

As to our servants, they were frightful to look at. Their poor faces, especially Pils' and the cook's, still bore the traces of the frosts which they had faced on the box-seat of the carriage.

We slept successively at Weimar, Eisenach, Fuld, Hanau, and, at last, at Mayence, where we were all the more pleased to stay because at that time it was in France. We alighted at the Hôtel des Trois-Couronnes. Soon arrived good old Marshal Kellermann, with his suite of *aides-de-camp*, all his contemporaries. A number of visits followed, and M. de Bourcet sat down to the piano and sang! You can imagine how pleasant and sweet for us was this first return to civilization, this first sign of security. With what delight poor Dr. Campiomont enjoyed the good cheer of the Hôtel des Trois-Couronnes: ever since Wilna, he had been tormented by the craving which so often follows upon dysentery, and had suffered more than any of us from the privations of the journey. At the moment when the marshal was about to go to sleep, he was brought the password for the night: "Beresina, Reggio," a compliment of good Marshal Kellermann's, which proved the justice of his opinion of him who had saved the remnants of our army.

From Mayence we went on to Homburg, and from there to Metz.

Our friend Gouy hastened to our hotel. At sight of him, my husband displayed a delight and happiness which did everybody good to see.

At last I returned to Bar, after a very melancholy absence of four months. Assuredly, bringing back my husband almost restored to health; seeing once more my mother, who was awaiting me at my sister's; and restoring my uncle safe and sound to his family, I owed endless thanks to God, and I offered them from the very bottom of my heart.

Need I say that we were received with open arms? We divided our winter life between Bar and Jeand'heurs. It was cold wherever we went; but what was this temperature to us, compared to what we had lately gone through? Besides, we had not the slightest inclination to give our guests, who arrived from every side, an idea of what we had suffered from the temperature.

While your father was gradually completing his recovery, I began to pay my tribute, in the shape of an internal inflammation, to whose progress I refused to listen. Mme. de Lorencez, whom we found quite recovered, and carrying in her arms her little Victorine, set out to go and meet her husband, who was at last returning to France, having got over the serious illness which had overtaken him on the road. They came back so radiant with happiness that it was a delight to see.

While we were all seeking repose after our own fashion, the emperor was very differently employed. The French Public at last began to understand the reason for the truthful and crushing confession contained in the 29th Bulletin. Was it not necessary, in fact, to avow every loss and every disaster, so as to be entitled to demand every assistance? And must not our country, which seemed exhausted by the Russian war, attempt a new effort in order to face the Leipzig campaign? Assisted by England, the war in Spain was devouring us on the south, while Russia, now openly supported by Prussia, was advancing towards the Oder, where the Viceroy had succeeded in reconstructing a corps of about forty thousand men, the valiant remains of the Grande Armée.

Chapter 6

Journey to Paris

The emperor's measures advanced with such rapidity that it was hoped we should be able to enter into campaign in the course of April. In the middle of March, the marshal desired without further delay to go and show the emperor that he was in a fit condition to resume active service.

My mother had gone before to await us at Vitry, where the marshal, my sister and I arrived with the intention of spending a day with her. We knew that Enguerrand de Coucy had left Saint-Cyr with the grade of sub-lieutenant, but we were far from suspecting that, before being able to reach Hancourt, he had fallen ill at my mother's. We found all his relations in despair . . . But he was quite conscious, and wished to see us . . . The poor child showed us his epaulet, which he hid under his bolster so that it might not leave him, and bade us *au revoir* in a way that broke my heart . . . The death of this young man, who was a great favourite of the marshal's, was a deep-felt blow to all of us . . .

I myself was very ill, and it was under melancholy auspices that I made my first journey to Paris, which we entered the next day through the Faubourg Saint-Martin.

It was about four o'clock in the evening when we arrived; an icy rain obscured my view of the streets in what was at that time one of the dreariest quarters of the town. The faces, all new to me, of the servants attached to my husband's town-house looked to me like phantoms seen in my fever. I passed a bad night, and in the morning my distressed husband and sister sent to fetch the most famous doctors. Victor undertook the errand, and soon I was visited by Drs. Dubois and Roux. The inflammation from which I was suffering had reached its climax, and the two heads of their profession agreed that I should be ordered continual baths.

I spent in this way almost the whole of the first few days after my arrival. I was young and strong, and when my illness was once mastered, my convalescence proceeded quickly. It was well it did so, for our stay was necessarily limited owing to the new command which was being prepared for the marshal.

Nothing was spoken of but war, a melancholy subject for a convalescent patient; but I had to dominate myself to be able to cope with the present, which was so busy, and with the future, which was so deeply laden with clouds. While still on my bed of sickness I received a visit from the Maréchale Augereau, Duchesse de Castiglione. The beautiful Adele was just as charming, no more and no less, in all her luxurious finery as in the simple dress to which she had lent so much elegance at Vitry. We talked at length of our young past, of our brilliant future and of the present, and she gave me much information which the similarity of our positions caused to be very useful to me.

So soon as I had recovered part of my strength, my husband made me visit some of the marvels of Paris. I was astonished at all I saw; but although my youth inclined me to be delighted with everything, this visit was disturbed by many sad preoccupations.

In order to save my strength, the Marshal asked and obtained leave for both my presentations at the Tuileries to take place on the same day. The Duchesse de Bassano was to present me, and I went to fetch her in my carriage. Tall, beautiful and cold, the duchess overawed me, and her kindness to me, which was natural owing to our intimate relations with her husband, helped me but little; for, accustomed gradually to the lofty situation she occupied, she had either never experienced, or had long ago forgotten, the agony of timidity.

It must be granted that mine was very permissible under the circumstances. In fact, when I reflected that this great phantasmagoria which had so filled my imagination was about to be realized; that I was about to see and hear the emperor, and that I should have to reply to him, I quite lost my head. I could not understand my companion's calmness; she examined me tranquilly, without thinking that we were approaching the Tuileries, where we soon arrived. The emperor was at mass. We naturally waited for his return, but I cannot remember in which room: I took so little stock of my surroundings that during all the fifteen years of the Restoration I have looked for it in vain.

We sat down amid a number of people, and as any one presented for the first time is always an object of curiosity, I was much stared at. But nothing could increase my distress. I was absorbed by a single thought, and all the rest was but confusion. Everything seemed in a whirl in that *salon*, I felt ready to faint, and I turned so pale that one of the principal officers of the emperor's household (the Comte de Canouville, who was on duty that day) came and offered me a glass of *malaga* and a biscuit. I refused, with thanks, and almost at the same moment a significant tumult roused me from my lethargy. We all rose, and the emperor rapidly crossed the room in which we were.

The door was scarcely closed behind him when it opened again and our names were called out. I followed the Duchesse de Bassano and we entered the closet in which the emperor was awaiting us. He took a step in our direction, and nodding rather than bowing, said:

"Good-day, Madame la Duchesse de Bassano."

Then turning to me, he gave me the same nod, and without changing his form of speech or his tone, said:

"Good-day, Madame la Duchesse de Reggio."

I curtsied, for by this time I had recovered my wits. After a second's pause, the emperor enquired after the marshal, and then said:

"You are an old married woman, *Madame*."

He followed these words with an arch smile, which lit up his face like a ray. I replied that indeed I had been married fifteen months, but that circumstances had until then prevented my presentation.

"I know," replied the emperor, seriously, but with a shade of interest. "You have made a long journey, and," he added, earnestly, "a very cold one."

I bowed; he waited a moment, and then said:

"You come from Champagne."

When I had replied, he again asked after my husband, and turning towards my companion, he talked to her, I believe, of her children; he then bowed to us both and gave us the signal to leave.

It was thought that the emperor had received me very well. This was my impression too. It remained on my mind, and the remembrance of this short interview will never be effaced from it. I can still hear his voice and see that deep blue eye which one could no more look into than one can look into the sun, but which one felt was there, while instinctively and for all time realizing its power.

This was my only interview with the emperor. You can understand that everything must seem insipid to me after this reception; and I faced without any great emotion the brilliant circle of the Empress Marie Louise and the inquisitive gaze of her ladies. The empress, tall, stiff, shy, and very thin, came forward a step to meet us. She had learnt that my health had suffered seriously, and she addressed to me on this subject a few questions which were kindly worded, if insignificant in tone. This lasted two or three minutes, and my duties were over for that day. I found your father awaiting me impatiently; he was satisfied with the account I gave him, and according to custom, we went the same morning to thank the empress's Mistress of the Robes. This was the Comtesse de Montebello. She seemed to me to be worn out with her duties: that is all I remember of my visit.

A week later, the marshal was invited alone to the empress's circle. He either did not go, or else only just showed himself; and while I am on this subject, I will anticipate two months and finish it. Your father was walking by the emperor's side, in the environs of Dresden, when the latter suddenly asked after me.

"Sire," replied the marshal, "I did not think Your Majesty remembered I had a wife."

"What do you mean?" asked the emperor, sharply.

"Why, Sire, she was presented to you and to the empress, and Her Majesty has never invited her to her circle. I was very much hurt, because her rank entitles her to it."

"Why don't you make me responsible for all the blunders of a Mistress of the Robes?" said the emperor. "Look here, would you like your wife to have a place at the empress's court? This will prove to you, I hope, that I have not forgotten the Duchesse de Reggio."

The marshal thanked him, and soon events took upon themselves to solve this question. I return to Paris, to conclude the story of my other presentations.

I first went to the emperor's mother, who was visited, by her son's desire, with the most formal ceremony. She was very kind and obliging in the reception she gave me. I was next taken to Queen Julie, at the Petit Luxembourg, a kind and simple-minded princess, who endured, rather than sought, her momentary greatness. For that matter, she had only for a little while occupied the throne of Spain, where her husband, King Joseph, had enjoyed a short reign.

The other sovereigns belonging to the emperor's family were absent from Paris; but there remained a duty for me to fulfil at Malmaison, and it was with pleasant anticipations that I set out for there one morning with my husband, who had reserved to himself the exclusive right of presenting me to the Empress Josephine.[1]

1. *Napoleon's Letters to Josephine* by Henry Foljambe Hall also published by Leonaur.

The graciousness of her reception even surpassed my expectations. After making me sit down on the sofa by her side, she addressed to me that crowd of affectionate and obliging questions which the sight of a young and shy woman can suggest to a kind heart. She held in her hand a spray of white camellias, fresh from her magnificent hot-houses. She handed it to me with infinite grace. I was touched, and half rose to receive it, and the marshal, who followed all my movements with his eyes, told me afterwards that he was contented with the manner in which I had gone through this little piece of pantomime.

"Have you been presented?" asked Josephine; and I felt that I turned red as I answered:

"Yes, *Madame*."

"To the emperor and to . . . the empress?" she resumed.

And I felt that I blushed still more foolishly as I replied to this last question with a second, "Yes, *Madame*."

Soon after, the empress rose and went over to the marshal, who was talking at the further end of the drawing-room. She had not seen him for two years. He complimented her on her air of good health.

"Yes," she replied, in a voice of gentle resignation, and with a sad smile; "you see it agrees better with me not to be the reigning empress."

She asked us to dinner on the following Sunday, and I then for the first time met her daughter, Queen Hortense, who placed me next to her at table and captivated me with the very special charm of her conversation.

"Tell me," she said, "all about your marriage; I have always heard that the circumstances were particularly interesting."

From what she told me, I saw that her informants had made up, out of a few truths and a number of fables, quite a little drama. I told her the facts of the case, to which she listened with marked goodwill. The dinner seemed very quickly over.

The marshal next took me to pay a number of calls. We dined with some of the ministers, and notably with the Comte Regnaud de Saint-Jean d'Angely. This was one of my happiest days. My sister was among the guests; we met at the table of one of her husband's truest friends; and I also renewed my acquaintance with Aglaé and Blanche Buffaut, the minister's favourite nieces.

Meantime the days were slipping by, and we had little more than a week to spend in Paris before the marshal's departure for the campaign which was about to open. He had received the command of the

12th Corps of the Grande Armée; and while I was looking forward with dread to the period of agitation which was about to set in, two pieces of bad news came to add to the sadness of the last days of our stay. The first was the death of Enguerrand de Coucy. I have told you enough of this young man, the hope of our family, to make you appreciate the grief which my sister, my husband and I experienced at this loss. The second catastrophe also had its bitterness in another way. This was the burning of our house at Bar-le-Duc, which, although only just finished, and furnished with the greatest elegance, was reduced to ashes.

M. and Mme. de Lorencez were with us in Paris, but they had left their little daughter at Bar, and it was in consequence of the carelessness of the nurse that the fire had broken out in a room on the second floor which she occupied. What I most particularly regretted in this disaster was the superb collection of linen with which the marshal had presented me on my arrival at the house. He had had made in Holland all that the country could produce of the very finest linen. I heard afterwards that there were discovered in cinders whole piles of napkins which retained their folds until blown upon.

When the emperor heard of this disaster, he at once sent the marshal 100,000 *francs* from his privy purse; but gracious though this act of spontaneous generosity was, it only made up a part of our losses. Our charming house was quickly, but not so well, rebuilt. It was only refurnished in part; but what was this compared to the reverses of fortune which followed?

We returned to Jeand'heurs, where I took up my residence. The marshal there took leave of me, and recommended me to go often to Bar in order to survey the building-operations. Our separation was somewhat softened for me by a consoling hope which I entertained; but soon this vanished, after a series of cruel sufferings, and again I thought that I was destined never to see myself again in my children.

Meanwhile the campaign had opened brilliantly with the victory of Lutzen. I rejoiced in it, as a Frenchwoman, without having any fears on my own account, since the marshal had not arrived in time to take part in the action. For the moment I was moving to and fro between Jeand'heurs and Bar, suffering in body and mind, in spite of the precious cares lavished upon me by my mother, the members of my family who succeeded one another by my side, many old friends, and some of more recent date. Among the latter I may mention M. and Mme. de Saint-Aulaire.

The Comte de Saint-Aulaire had replaced M. le Comte Leclerc as *Prefect* of the Meuse. Although belonging to the *Ancien Régime*, he had frankly attached himself to the government of the Emperor, and had become a chamberlain of Marie Louise. His first appearance in public life dates from the Meuse, where his memory still lives. He was the widower of a princess connected with the Danish Royal Family, and the father of a little girl of twelve, who since became the Duchesse Decazes. His second wife, *née* Mlle, du Roure, was twenty-one years of age, and one of the prettiest and wittiest persons of her time. This delightful household soon won my heart, and in spite of the divergence in some of our ideas and in our political positions, we remained friends. They brought to Jeand'heurs the only movement which I allowed to be summoned there; but to tell the truth, nothing was able to divert my thoughts for long from the fixed idea that filled them.

The marshal, who regretfully learnt of the bad state of my health, agreed with my doctor that I should be sent to Plombières. At the end of my season there I made the acquaintance of some people of a very different kind. I had often observed the friendly looks which a whole family had bestowed upon me at each of our frequent meetings. This family consisted of the old Chevalier de Boufflers, famous for his literary productions and for his eminently witty and graceful conversation, of the Marquise de Sabran, whom he had married, and of her son Elzéar, whom he had, as it were, adopted. The latter was an elegant poet whom you will remember meeting as children.

I had confined myself almost entirely to my reading as a girl, and only knew of these gentlemen's celebrity by hearsay. I had never met any authors of whatever kind, and I felt a sort of elation, mingled with timidity, when one morning the amiable trio sent up their names to me.

"We have come to bring you a visit of gratitude," said the sympathetic old man, as he entered the room; "we wanted to meet you, and I do not know why we delayed our visit until today."

Touched with these words, and with the physiognomy of my three callers, I felt drawn towards them. The Chevalier de Boufflers continued:

> It is to your husband, *Madame*, that we owe the liberty of Elzéar. He is an intimate friend of Mme. de Staël's, and he redoubled the signs of his attachment during her exile. This was falsely interpreted into being of political import, and he was imprisoned at Vincennes. His mother grew more distressed the longer his

captivity lasted, until God sent me an inspiration, and without knowing Marshal Oudinot, except by reputation, and with no other claim upon him than our unhappiness, I succeeded in obtaining from him so ardent and immediate a support, that Elzéar was restored to us. I have not yet been able to assure the marshal verbally of our gratitude; I am impatiently awaiting the opportunity to do so: but meanwhile I bless that which has brought us into contact with his young wife.

I left Plombières improved in health but quite prepared to resume the condition of alarm which had been temporarily suspended by the armistice. I picked up dear little Stéphanie at Nancy, and soon after our arrival at Jeand'heurs our dear Auguste came home for the holidays: he was then thirteen. General de Lorencez had settled his wife in his place at Marbot, near Bar, before taking command of his division in the Grande Armée. Soon he received a grievous wound, and one of the painfullest moments in that fatal summer of 1813 was that in which I had to announce this sorrowful news to my daughter-in-law.

******

Meanwhile, the campaign of 1813 began. For the last time, our armies, already disorganized, were able to fight outside the old French soil. In spite of the treachery and desertion of some, in spite of the ill-will of others, in spite of the lassitude and disillusion of all, amid the universal disorder of men and things, Oudinot was one of a small number who never faltered, who uttered neither criticisms nor recriminations, and whose clear acceptation of their duties was never sullied with the smallest doubt. The patriot of 1792 was as he had been twenty years before, devoted, ardent, and unflinching.

Placed at the head of the 12th Corps, he went to take up his command at Bamberg, in Bavaria; and so soon as the victory of Lutzen (2 May) had made Napoleon master of the country between the Saale and the Elbe, the marshal, co-operating in the movement of concentration of the French forces, skirted the foot of the Bohemian mountains, and on the 10th reached the great rallying place at Dresden. They crossed the stream of the Elbe, behind which the coalesced Russians and Prussians were sheltering themselves, and advanced into the middle of Saxony, towards the upper valley of the Spree, which issues from the mountains in that region, and near which the enemy occupied a very strong position. The Duc de Reggio led the right.

At mid-day on the 20th of May, he received orders to cross the

Spree above the village of Bautzen, near Sinkwitz. Two of his infantry columns forded the river, scaled the opposite bank, which is very steep, and found themselves facing the Russians commanded by the same Wittgenstein who had been Oudinot's implacable adversary, the year before, upon the Dwina. Assailed without delay, they held firm, and gave the rest of the army time to arrive in its turn and, in spite of a very brisk fire, to take up an important position on the Tronberg. Macdonald, Marmont and Bertrand had also succeeded in crossing the Spree at other points, and by evening all were able to encamp upon the conquered bank.

But the Russians nevertheless preserved a very strong second line, stronger even than the first, among mountains and valleys. They commenced the attack the next morning, and Miloradowitch, their most brilliant general, who was known as the Russian Murat, made special efforts to recapture the Tronberg, which Oudinot had taken the night before. The marshal, although suffering enormous losses, obliged to give way at moments, but always returning, succeeded in maintaining his position through sheer force of energy, until at last Ney,[2] who had turned the position by re-ascending the Spree, made the enemy's position an impossible one. The victory remained with us, but unfortunately it was not a decisive one.

A fortnight later, the armistice of the 4th of June gave everyone a hope of definite peace, and the honourable proposals of the Powers, which recognized our occupation of our natural frontiers, seemed favourable to us; but the pride of the master was neither willing to yield nor to come to terms, and the struggle was resumed under more and more unequal conditions.

The emperor, maintaining himself in Saxony, on the Upper Elbe, entrusted sixty-four thousand men to Oudinot, with orders to march upon the Prussian capital and to give battle to the new King of Sweden, Bernadotte, who had become the adversary of his former brothers-in-arms. The Duc de Reggio in this way had under his orders in the first place the 12th Corps, then the 4th, commanded by General Bertrand, and lastly the 7th, commanded by General Reynier.

The reader must have no illusion concerning this imposing figure of sixty-four thousand men. As a matter of fact, the effective strength consisted, as to one half, of foreign troops, Italians moved by no feeling of patriotism, and Saxons fighting regretfully against their German

2. *Ney: General of Cavalry Volume 1* and *Ney: Marshal of France Volume 2* by Antoine Bulos also published by Leonaur.

kinsmen. As to the French, these were no longer the old invincible bands whom the deserts of Russia and Spain had swallowed up; they were brave and eager young soldiers, but inexperienced and liable to be promptly discouraged.

On the other hand, the country to be traversed before advancing upon Berlin from the south was as unfavourable as possible for manoeuvring: forests, rivers and marshes were interwoven in an inextricable net-work, in which the cannon-wheels sank deep into the clay, while our men exhausted themselves through the long circuitous roads they had to follow. Ground of this character, instead of facilitating the concentration of forces, rendered their dispersion almost inevitable, and the march was therefore an extremely dangerous one.

Bernadotte with his Swedes, the Russians and the Prussians, the latter prepared for every effort in order to cover their capital, was at the head of ninety thousand soldiers; our men therefore had to fight two against three.

Oudinot had represented to Napoleon all the difficulties arising from the lack of cohesion in the troops, their numerical inferiority, the nature of the ground, and also that adventurous position, so far removed from the main army and from the base of operations, which was Dresden. But he ran foul of a mind which was absolutely made up; the emperor refused to entertain his objections, and relied greatly upon the moral effect which would result, he said, from the occupation of Berlin. Oudinot made no reply, and accepted with much self-denial the accomplishment of his difficult task, whose unfortunate result he all too well foresaw.

On the 21st of August, the little town of Trebbin was captured in spite of the resistance of the Prussians, and the next day the army continued its uncertain march through those thickets, marshes and forests. They marched in three columns, Bertrand on the right, Reynier in the centre, and Oudinot on the left. On the 23rd, the marshal gave both his lieutenants the order to converge upon the village of Gross-Beeren, and there to await his arrival, so that the three united corps might all together attack Bernadotte, who occupied near there the position of Ruhlsdorff. These instructions having been clearly laid down, Bertrand advanced on the right by Blankensfeld, Reynier in the centre, and Oudinot himself on the left by Arensdorff.

Unfortunately, the desired accord, so necessary for this combination, which was a very wise one, was not realized. Bertrand, harassed by the Prussian corps under Tauenzien, was delayed by a fruitless cannonade which he kept up against the latter. Reynier, who was the first to debouch at Gross-Beeren, which is only thirty kilometres from Berlin, there met Bortsell's division, and dislodged it; but instead of halting, in accordance with his formal orders, he allowed himself to be drawn alone into pursuit of the enemy, with more courage than prudence, and soon found himself engaged against the main body of Bernadotte's forces. He at last saw his danger, but too late; and although he retired in order, he was unable completely to rally his Saxon division, which disbanded and lost two thousand prisoners. Oudinot, warned by the sound of the cannon, hastened up from Arensdorff in time to assist the troops to keep up a bold countenance, but not in time to prevent the retreat. Always as prudent in the conduct of an operation as he was impetuous under fire, he declined to persist, and in order wisely to limit his losses, he slowly retrograded upon the Elbe, and entrenched himself at Wittemberg on the 30th of August. The attempt upon Berlin had not succeeded; but at least the army corps was saved.

Napoleon, who at the time was much disappointed by this check, did justice later to Oudinot in his meditations at St Helena.

"As to the affair at Gross-Beeren," he said, "the Duc de Reggio managed it sufficiently well not to interfere with the emperor's favourite project. Had the operation only been delayed, it would have been all the more complete. The Duc de Reggio's attempt was useful as a military reconnaissance. It drew the enemy from his lines, dragged Bernadotte towards Wittemberg, and left open the line from Dresden to Berlin."

Oudinot, considering the operation more than ever impracticable now that he had experimented with it, asked to be relieved of his command-in-chief, which was handed to Ney; he himself remained at the head of the 12th Corps, and nobly consented to become the simple subordinate of his comrade-in arms.

Not only was Ney no more fortunate, but he lost a much more important battle than that of Gross-Beeren. Rashly venturing upon a flank march in order to reach Baruth, which the emperor had assigned to him, he divided his forces into three columns, which marched not in a parallel or concentric fashion, but one behind the other, and at a distance sufficiently removed to prevent them from easily assisting one another. Bertrand, who led the first, was unexpectedly attacked in the defile of Denneitz, and had to sustain an unequal combat against the main body of the German forces.

Reynier, who followed, succeeded with great difficulty in preventing the Prussians from taking up a position on our left. Finally, Oudinot, who brought up the rear, employed himself in a very efficacious manner in stopping forty thousand Russians and Swedes, who were threatening to outflank us on the same side. But summoned very inconveniently by Ney to support Bertrand on our right, he was compelled, owing to this dangerous conversion, to abandon to their own resources our wavering Allies, the Saxons. His departure was for them a signal of rout and for the army one of defeat (6 September). This time the road to Berlin was definitively lost, and it was necessary to fall back upon the Elbe, no longer at Wittemberg, but much further, at Torgau. The wind and dust had raged so furiously during that disastrous day that the combatants had hardly been able to see one another.

This check, combined with others sustained by several of Napoleon's lieutenants, compelled him to concentrate his troops, which he had dispersed too widely. Oudinot was summoned to take command of two divisions of the Young Guard. He took part with it in the supreme battle in which the fate of Europe was fought out on the fields of Leipzig. On the 16th of October, at mid-day, when, Napoleon decided to take the offensive with the centre, it was Oudinot who debouched from Wachau with Marshal Victor, and who, with irresistible impetus, repulsed Prince Eugène of Wurtemberg, drove him back upon Awenhayn, and destroyed the Russian *cuirassiers*, whose impetus broke against our lines. On the evening of the same day he also contributed to keeping Weissenwolff's grenadiers at bay. But these were brilliant rather than efficacious successes, the last pale smiles of fortune. Two days later, during the disastrous Battle of the Giants, Oudinot was only able to stand firm between Victor and Poniatowsky.

After the rout, it became incumbent upon him to lead the rear-guard, and to cover the retreat with his two divisions. After crossing the Saale, he heroically defended, at Freyburg, the two bridges over the Unstrutt, prevented General York from coming up, and killed some hundreds of his men in a stubborn fight; he himself was the last to cross (22 October). On the 26th, he kept Blücher in check, who attacked him at Eisenach.

His constant endeavours were directed to bringing up the laggards, starved and disarmed, who replied to their officers' reproaches:

"We prefer to let ourselves be taken prisoners; we have no bread; the Cossacks will give us bread."

Hard examples had not served them as a lesson.

Bringing up the march, he found the villages encumbered with sick, wounded and dying; every room, stable and barn was crammed with them. He was compelled to sleep at night outside the houses, in spite of the Cossacks at their backs, who howled ominously in the darkness:

"To Paris! To Paris!"

On the 28th he was attacked by typhus, which was devastating that poor remnant of the army, and he was unable to ride his horse. He was hoisted into a wretched *calash* and thus dragged, painfully jolted, in the centre of the artillery-park, with a shattered body, but brave in mind and with an impassive countenance. At Hanau, on the Mein, our former Allies, the Bavarians, who had abandoned us since our reverses, endeavoured with the Austrians to bar our retreat. He assisted in his *calash* at the battle which opened the road for us, and slept in his carriage, in the middle of a wood of fir-trees, with nothing by way of food save a little flour which a drummer brought him, and which was diluted in water. He did not know where he was, so great was the confusion. An officer, who knocked up against him without seeing him, recognized him and told him that the emperor's canteen was close at hand; he was then able to procure some relief.

★★★★★★

General and Mme. de Lorencez had come to spend a few days with me at Jeand'heurs. It was on the 7th of November, in the morning, that I saw M. Jacqueminot return, who had been sent out to meet the marshal. I did not remember until later the air of constraint and reserve with which he replied to the thousand questions which I put to him at once. He had told me to expect the marshal the same evening; I seized hold of this sole fact, and the young man lacked the courage to declare the whole truth to me. All I was able to get out of him was:

"The marshal is very tired and very much changed." Then, in order to evade my further inquiries, M. Jacqueminot re-entered his post carnage and drove off for Paris, saying to me once more, from the window:

"You will find him much altered; he will need all your care; courage!"

The day passed with no arrival and no news. I began to grow alarmed, and the general did not know how to calm me, for M. Jacqueminot had been more explicit with him than with me.

We had dined sadly, and we sat looking at the fire in the chimney of that big room number one, which I used at that time. We listened to every sound, but we heard nothing but the wind. . . . The general, taking pity on me, said:

"Come, let us have a game of chess."

I owed my instruction in this scientific game to my dear Auguste, who had taught it me during the holidays which he had spent with me; but we had hardly set out our pieces when the sound of a whip made us all start up. A carriage rolled under the archway which at that time closed in the great courtyard. I flew through the long galleries and down the stairs, and reached the carriage side.

The door was open, but nothing came out. A soft, icy rain was falling; the night was dark, and the silence complete. Torches were brought, and I climbed distraught into the carriage, where I vaguely perceived a man stretched out motionless. Then two voices in tones of emotion spoke to me at once in an urgent and mysterious manner. I understood nothing more, I was really out of my senses. They made me alight from the carriage; then six men together took the marshal (for, alas! it was he whom I had at last recognized, but who did not recognize me) and carried him to his room.

I mechanically followed the procession, and when my poor husband had been laid upon his bed, he opened his haggard eyes and distinctly spoke these words:

"I want a bath."

I had it got ready, and sent a carriage for Dr. Moreau. Soon the invalid was put into his bath; I held his hand, and he seemed to recognize me for a moment, and said, in a voice so weak that I could hardly distinguish his words:

"I feel better, but I am going to sleep."

And at the same moment he stretched himself out and slipped down under the water. I called out with all my might; he was taken out, but ice-cold and motionless. A great fire was lit, and we laid him on a mattress placed right inside the chimney; we rubbed his feet and hands; but his features remained livid, distorted and black, and putrid stains appeared upon his skin.

This was the condition of affairs when Dr. Moreau arrived. His brusque frankness never spared anybody; he thought the marshal lost, and took no trouble to conceal his thought. It would be impossible to describe what passed within me. . . . When I recovered from my first shock, I understood that the thing to do was not to despair, but to listen to the doctor and follow his directions. I clung to hope, and was alone in not weeping.

"*Madame*, what have you done," said the doctor, "and what induced you to put into a bath a man attacked with typhus?"

"But he asked me to," I replied.

"Is that a reason? You can see he is delirious."

And in fact, life had returned to him, but the fever too. Before long, the marshal was volubly talking, calling him-self a deserter, and saying he deserved to be shot for leaving his post during a battle. It was the battle of Hanau which had left him these last impressions.

The danger lasted five days, during which the marshal sometimes recognized me, without knowing where he was; more frequently he imagined himself with the army, called his generals to him by name, and so forth.

At last the fever abated, and the doctor said to me, as he entered my room on the sixth day:

"He is saved!"

"How can you tell, when you have scarcely seen him, and before you have even felt his pulse?"

"Merely by the way he holds himself in bed, *Madame*; he has always till now lain on his back, which was an alarming symptom; this morning, as you see, he is sleeping on his side. It is the beginning of his convalescence, but it will be a long and stormy one; do not relax your watching."

From that moment he gradually grew better. His fine constitution had recovered all its moral force in less than a fortnight after his arrival. His physical strength had not progressed so fast, and I remember that the first time that he was able to walk as far as my room, where he found a tall cheval-glass, he looked at himself in it and said:

"There's an ugly beggar for you!"

Events followed fast The passage of the Rhine by the allied armies was imminent, and the marshal was quivering with impatience to go to the emperor and show him once more that he was fit to resume his share in the campaign.

The enemy crossed the Rhine on the 20th of December 181 3. On receiving this news we started. We had no sooner left Jeand'heurs and reached the high-road between Saint-Dizier and Vitry than we found it already encumbered with our troops. We were able to shake hands with Victor, who was marching in the same direction. We breakfasted at Vitry, which was occupied by the Imperial Guard, and soon arrived in Paris, where I found my mother in very poor health.

Beginning with this period, one could remark in men's minds that general tendency towards selfishness which has nowadays become the almost universal rule. The enemy was advancing with great strides, and yet it must be admitted that our people were more occupied with mutual recriminations than with preparations for the common defence. It was clear that the army would have to act alone, without the assistance of the people, which was not yet aroused; and yet what should be more calculated to stimulate it than the heart-rending reflection that in fifteen months the allied armies had advanced from the banks of the Moscova and the Dwina to our own Rhine frontier?

Meanwhile, the Paris National Guard had been restored, and its officers, summoned in mass to the Tuileries before the emperor's departure, swore with enthusiasm that they would defend Paris to the death, together with the Regent and the King of Rome, who had been entrusted to their protection. And, indeed, the National Guard did, on the 31st of March, make a fine and honourable defence.

Marie Louise and her child were present at this scene. The child, who was then three years old was splendid. He had his father's head, and it was his presence which electrified the gathering much more than did the impassive features of the Regent.

My husband received the command of a portion of the Young Guard, and he prepared closely to follow the emperor.

CHAPTER 7

The French Campaign

I have already said that the enemy passed the Rhine, between Basle and Coblentz, on the 20th of December 1813. He continued his invasion by occupying Belgium about the 1st of January following.

To stand against the forces of allied Europe, the Emperor had, it was said, three hundred thousand men under arms, but divided as follows: about two-thirds were spread over our French garrisons and in the fortified places which were still in our occupation abroad; the remainder formed three armies: that of Italy, that of Spain, and, lastly, that which was to defend the territory, which was the only one that the Emperor could really oppose to the enemy. It consisted of about eighty thousand men, divided into small corps, placed under the orders of the marshals and commanded in chief by Napoleon.

The emperor's first operations carried him towards Saint Dizier. He left Paris on the 25th of December, slept at Châlons, and the next day at Vitry, where the marshal was awaiting him. The marshal stayed with my mother. How happy she was to surround him with her cares! Together with my mother and my aunt the canoness, he spent his last family evening during that disastrous winter. On the 27th took place at Saint-Dizier the first skirmish with the enemy, whom the emperor easily dislodged. Your father, who was at that moment in command of two divisions of the Young Guard, was carried forward, and thus came fighting, as a scout, right up to the gates of his native town. When they saw him approach, the inhabitants of Bar, regarding the names of Oudinot and Victory as synonymous, thought themselves saved; but, recalled by the emperor in the direction of Brienne, the marshal was compelled to leave at once and to put a stop to this illusion.

I should here tell you, my children, that the majority of the foreign generals who, in the course of this campaign, succeeded one another in the neighbourhood of Jeand'heurs and Bar, set safeguards upon your father's estates, a just and honourable acknowledgment of his conduct in the enemy's country.

Meantime the army commanded by the emperor reached Brienne on the 29th, and captured the castle and the town after a murderous combat, lit up till midnight by the flames of some burning houses. They fought at the point of the bayonet; the ground was strewn with dead and dying; your father, escaping his usual luck, was not wounded.

The emperor and his lieutenants did not sleep in the castle, which had become a field of carnage, but hurriedly partook of an improvised repast, during which the marshal received a message that two ladies, declaring themselves his relations, had been discovered in tears in the vaults. "Bring them here and let them share my supper," said the emperor. Thereupon appeared two of my cousins, Mmes. de Montangon and du Metz. The latter, who had just been married, was as beautiful as an angel; their husbands were absent from the Château de Crespy, situated at a league from Brienne, when public rumour forewarned them of the fighting which was about to commence. Thinking they would be in greater safety in the vast establishment at Brienne than in their little stronghold, they hastened to take refuge there, but had hardly time to install themselves in the vaults before the terrible shock took place over their heads. Not only my husband, but also the emperor, was full of kindness towards these young refugees, of whom one, Mme. du Metz, paid with her life, not long after, for this terrible experience.

Before going further, a word on the heroic share taken by your father in the combat at la Rothière. It was on the 31st of December; the marshal drove back the enemy, in a hand-to-hand fight, at night, under a terrific fire, captured the village, and fell back in good order upon Brienne, having thus marked his place in the history of that day, where thirty-two thousand men defended themselves against one hundred and sixty-six thousand.

I come to events which touch me more directly. After the Battle of la Rothière, my husband was almost constantly opposed to the Russians or the Austrians, in defending now the banks of the Seine, and now those of the Aube; on the latter he distinguished himself at Orsonval on the 27th of February, and was to return on the 21st of March to Arcis, on the same banks, and add a new jewel to his glorious crown; but in the interval he was recalled to the Seine to hold

Schwartzenberg in check. The two armies lay facing one another; and during a period of inaction that lasted some days he sent for me: it was on the 10th of March.

M. Verger, the commissary-at-war, and attached to the marshal's staff, was sent to come and fetch me. He arrived at nine in the morning, in a heavy snowstorm.

"I have come," he said, "on behalf of the marshal, to beg you to come at once to see him at Provins; he thinks he will be there long enough to be able to see you for a few hours."

"Well, then, send for horses, and let us go; my carriage is ready, come!"

"One moment," he resumed; "please first have the kindness to get together a few provisions. *M. le Maréchal* is dying of hunger."

I looked at him in amazement.

"It is literally true," he said; "remember that the most stubborn warfare has been devouring the same portion of France during six weeks. It is pitiful to have to beg for food, even by paying for it, of a population which is itself deprived of it; but, in a word, we are in need of everything."

The miseries of Russia returned to my memory: to think that they could reign within twenty leagues of Paris was as sad as it was surprising. I was not able to complete the loading of my carriage until four o'clock; the snow had ceased to fall; it covered the ground; but it was not thick enough to hide from my eyes the ravages of the battlefield through which I drove. One saw nothing but dismantled houses, trees cut down; and I clearly distinguished, not far from the high-road, a few dead bodies lying where they fell, and remains of combats recently delivered in the plains.

The night grew darker: M. Verger, silent and preoccupied, constantly threw anxious glances to left and right. He seemed to have lost all his usual gentle and serene temperament. We travelled at a rapid rate, and ended by falling into that species of torpor produced by the movement of the carriage and the darkness. We had arrived at a stage (it was Nangis), and I was inwardly hastening the putting-to of the horses, when a man came running up to my carriage, and asked, in a shivering voice:

"Is that the Duchesse de Reggio?"

"Yes," we replied together; and I recognized M. de Bourcet, my husband's *aide-de-camp.*

"You must go no further tonight, *Madame la duchesse. M. le maréchal,* knowing that parties of Cossacks have been infesting the; road since yesterday, sent me to meet you with all speed in order to make you suspend your journey. I don't know how I succeeded in escaping the Russian scouts who are spread all along the roads."

Imagine my distress at these terrible words. It was less my fear of the Cossacks, whom nevertheless I had been seeing as in a nightmare for weeks, than the annoyance of missing this so strongly desired interview.

"Do not lose courage," resumed M. de Bourcet. "Come, *Madame la maréchale*, and warm yourself inside the post-house. I will explain everything to you there."

I was obliged to submit. It was eleven o'clock in the evening, and we all sat round a half-extinguished fire in the post-house kitchen.

"All is not lost," said the *aide-de-camp*, on seeing my profound discouragement. "*M. le maréchal* is expecting a regiment tomorrow morning which will pass through here to-night; and he has recommended me to put your carriage into the ranks of that brave infantry. You will thus travel at its pace and in safety: it is only a delay of a few hours. Permit me, therefore, to have a bed got ready for you, where you will be able to sleep until the first roll of the drum."

I was cheered by these words, but refused the bed, and remained by the fire, which had been made up. Soon the gentlemen began to snore, while I sat watching the logs and reflecting on the singularity of my position and the strange resemblance which it presented to that in which I had found myself nearly two years before, at seven hundred leagues from Paris: and I was only fifteen leagues from it at present.

We did as was arranged, leaving Nangis with the regiment. At daybreak we had six leagues to travel: they took us six hours. We did not meet the shadow of a Cossack. These irregular troops feared our infantry too much to attack them on the march, even when in small numbers.

On approaching the town, the gentlemen made me leave the ranks to save me the spectacle of the wonderment of the town at the sight of my carriage entering to the beat of the drum. Soon I was able to embrace your father, whom I found in perfect health, in spite of his fatigues and his privations. He was far from considering the emperor's cause as lost; he admitted the chance of an occupation of Paris by the enemy, but he thought that the emperor, on crossing the Loire, would be able to continue sufficiently formidable to obtain acceptable conditions and save his crown. He hoped that the nation, demoralized at first, would end by awaking from a state of apathy which, until then, had left everything to the army, and that, weary at last of undergoing the hardships of war, the awakening of the country would be like that of a lion. In a word, he still had faith in the future.

My husband had smiled, not only upon seeing me, but at the unpacking of my carriage. I had sacked the shop of the famous Chevet, and soon pies, hams and fowls were triumphantly presented to the staff, who had been convoked to partake of these alms.

"I must send for a hungry neighbour of mine as well," said the marshal. "I mean Macdonald. Let us hope that Prince Schwartzenberg will let us dine quietly today."

He did; and five days passed in this way, during which the enemy held himself as dead, to the great astonishment of the army of the two marshals. This enabled me to prolong my stay at Provins, and I made a friend who remained faithful to me to the grave, in that excellent Marshal Macdonald, who came over from his quarters almost every day to share our dinner.

You can well imagine that my rich provisions were not able to feed for long the many starvelings whose appetites had been whetted by the first meal or two; and soon I was able to see for myself the scarcity into which the marshal was again about to fall, to my great distress. He enjoined upon me to follow at a distance the Government of the Regent, and to cross the Loire if that was the course taken, in which case it was arranged that I should go to my sister at Poitiers.

My fifth day at Provins had hardly commenced when the marshal, without waiting for the enemy to attack, decided upon my departure, without listening to any of my supplications to be allowed to stay. Prompted by a sort of foresight, he hurried my preparations, put M. de Bourcet on the box of my carriage, sent a company of cavalry to escort me for the first few leagues, and himself escorted me for half-an-hour, riding by the carriage side. Then, without telling me, and without taking his leave, he turned back, galloped off, and arrived just in time to hear that the enemy seemed to be preparing for a movement. During this time I was being rapidly carried towards Paris.

I arrived at the Rue de Bourgogne before it was quite dark, and I was able to distinguish in the courtyard a *calash* all covered with mud which had evidently, like myself, made a hurried journey.

"Who is it?" I asked of the concierge, excitedly.

He hesitated before replying.

"Well?"

"*M. le comte* has come back wounded."

M. le comte was Victor. I ran upstairs and reached the room in which he had been placed. He was quite calm, and began by reassuring me as to what had befallen him; a ball, he said, had entered his thigh and penetrated rather deeply, but without breaking anything. He had received this wound at the fierce affair at Craonne, where the Imperial Guard had charged with its ordinary impetuosity. So soon as I was assured that the wound was not dangerous, I surprised in myself a feeling of satisfaction, of which I gave no sign, at finding that it put one of us in shelter from the terrible hazards of the end of this campaign.

I was still with Victor, when another member of our family arrived in a mutilated condition. This was General Pajol, who had had a horse killed under him at the bridge of Montereau. His fall had opened his serious Leipzig wounds and had obliged him to return and get nursed in Paris. Although badly injured, he was able to move about, since he had only been hurt in his hand and arm. The general was accompanied by his wife.

I received no news of the marshal. I learnt vaguely that he had left the Seine in order to join the emperor on the Aube, where, on the 21st of March, had taken place the hard-fought combat of Arcis, of which I had no details.

After Arcis, the emperor, either because he had been for a moment deceived as to the march of a corps of the enemy (Wintzingerode's), or because he had an undefined idea of cutting off the Allies from the line of the Rhine, had returned to Saint-Dizier, where he arrived on the 28th; but hearing that the bulk of the army was massing upon Paris, he suddenly changed his plans and hastened to its assistance. It was therefore at Saint-Dizier that, resuming the thought of intercepting the line of the Rhine from the enemy, the marshal submitted the following proposal to the emperor: he asked to be charged with his unaided army corps, since he was not able to dispose of a greater force, to march upon the Rhine, taking from each of the fortified places he would pass on the way as many men and ammunitions as they could spare, without too greatly imperilling their safety, and to follow the same plan with regard to all the places which we still held beyond the Rhine in the direction of Vienna.

This scheme, which undoubtedly presented immense difficulties and a great uncertainty as to the result, had at least the advantage of temporarily disconcerting the enemy and perhaps preventing his march upon Paris, and might besides, by working upon the spirit of the population, induce it to rise in mass against the invasion. The emperor was for a moment struck with the idea; but, in addition to its being somewhat late in the day, he did not think that he would be able to dispense with the marshal's army corps. He asked him whether he would be willing to make the attempt with cavalry alone.

"No, Sire," replied the marshal; "it would then be a war of partisans. I could not accept that mission."

Meantime the hours sped by. They set out for Troyes by forced marches, and arrived on the 29th. Vain efforts! You know what happened on the 30th! France had long since been exhausted, not so much of money, for the countries conquered by us still supplied this, but of men. This last scarcity, which it was endeavoured to remedy by every kind of conscription, threw whole families into despair and want. They were really bled to the uttermost. The poor man had to give his last son and in him lost his support; and in the fields it was often the women and girls who led the plough. Husbandry suffered as much as individuals. And the same disasters occurred in the towns. Numbers of families condemned themselves perpetually to cripple their fortunes in order to save the young man whom other measures ended by reaching. Great names, great fortunes, in short, all that might have hoped for independence was compelled to assist at least in the recruiting of guards of honour.

In any case, the young man under the flag, whatever the feeling of repulsion with which his antecedents might inspire him for the government, saw nothing but honour before him, and served with courage and loyalty; but it was in the families that resentment was felt. The crape with which the Russian and Leipzig campaigns had covered France had not yet disappeared; bitter tears were still being shed. People realized that, by yielding a certain number of his conquests in preceding years, the Emperor might have saved France this invasion; that, a little later, the line of the Rhine would at least have been left to him; that, even at the very time we had reached, if he would only give the Duc de Vicence (his representative at the Congress of Châtillon) the latitude which that zealous functionary demanded, he would still obtain supportable conditions of peace. Peace! the cry was in every heart: for of glory, the everyday food of the country, France had had a sufficient share.

In Paris everything was assuming a more and more sombre aspect. Everyone was making final arrangements to ensure the safety of his possessions. The majority of those who held with the government, either from attachment or from the sense of duty, had decided, like myself, to follow the movements of the Regent. The Court of the Tuileries was spied upon from morning to night in order to obtain wind of the first preparations for departure. As for me, I was certain of being one of the first to be informed by the Sainte-Aulaire family, with whom I was to join forces, whatever happened, and I kept myself in readiness, although at the same time deploring the necessity in which I found myself of abandoning my two children at school and my husband's eldest son, who was still too ill to be moved.

At last, on the 29th of March, I was informed that the carriages and luggage-waggons of the empress were standing ready in the courtyard of the Tuileries, and that Blois was the probable destination of Marie Louise, the King of Rome and the Council of Regency. I at once made my arrangements with the Sainte-Aulaire family to set out the same evening.

While on this subject, I cannot keep back the reflection which I made later, as did many others, that the face of the whole world might have been changed if the Regent, using the power with which she was invested, and resisting the distracted heads which advised her, had decided to await events in Paris. Had they found at the seat of government the daughter of the Emperor of Austria, who among the Allied sovereigns would have wished to expel her, when they admitted that their sole resolve was to dethrone the emperor, without seeming to think of a successor? They would probably have maintained the Regent; but she threw up the game and thus lost it without hope of recovery.

I heard related with many details the resistance, which was thought instinctive, of the King of Rome, who uttered loud cries and clung to all the curtains of the Tuileries, so as not to go on what they represented to him as a walk. It was a natural whim on the part of a child of three, but it was turned into a presentiment.

It was known that the corps of marshals the Duc de Trévise and the Duc de Ragune alone were defending the line of Meaux from the heights of Romainville, while King Joseph acted as *generalissimo* in Paris. The Versailles road was free, and the Sainte-Aulaire family ready; we let the Empress, her suite and her escort set out, and at about four o'clock in the afternoon we ourselves departed for Versailles, which was to be our first halt.

It was almost dark when we arrived. We took possession of two adjacent rooms in an already crowded inn in the Rue de l'Orangerie.

During the whole night, an incessant and confused noise told us of the passage of a large number of men, horses and carriages, and soon the daylight revealed the most astonishing sight that human eyes perhaps have ever looked upon. We stood motionless at our windows; what we saw passing, my children, was . . . the Empire! The Empire, which was departing, with all its pomp and splendour; the ministers, all in their coaches and six, taking with them portfolio, wife, children, jewels, livery; the entire Council of State; the archives; the crown diamonds; the administrations. And instalments of power and magnificence were mingled on the road with humble households who had heaped up on a barrow all they had been able to carry away from the houses which they were abandoning, as they thought, to the pillage which was about to burst forth over the country. The cannon had begun to thunder at daybreak.

M. de Saint-Aulaire incessantly went to and fro. Sometimes he would stop some of those emblazoned carriages, containing people whom we knew; but they for the most part, gloomy and terrified, knew no more than we did.

They were fighting, they told us, at the gates of Paris. Alas! could we not hear it!

At about half-past four appeared the famous proclamation of King Joseph. M. de Sainte-Aulaire hastened to bring it to us; it was worded to encourage the defence, and ended with these words: "Parisians, I remain in your midst!" We had hardly finished reading this production when, amid the increasing tumult, we saw a numerous staff make way for itself with difficulty. It came slowly forward, and when within our range we distinguished . . . the emperor! At least so I thought. . . . I gave a loud cry of "Long live the emperor!" stretching out my arms, thinking I saw your father in each of the general officers who followed him. I must have lost my head to believe even for a moment that at that supreme moment I saw the emperor turn his back on Paris.

My travelling-companions, who had for a moment shared my illusion, recovered their presence of mind sooner than I did, and promptly convinced me of my error: it was not the emperor, but his brother Joseph, who was very like him, and who was abandoning the city almost in the same hour in which he had proclaimed his faithful presence. He left after saying to the inhabitants, "Fight!"

It was eight o'clock when we left the inn where he had spent so horrible a day and joined the interminable column of which I have spoken. The disorder on the road, in the complete darkness, was terrible. We reached Rambouillet at about two o'clock in the morning; it was necessary to give our horses a rest and some food if possible; but the crowd was so great that we could not recognise one another. However, M. de Sainte-Aulaire succeeded in elbowing his way to the castle, in order to enquire which of the retreating dignitaries had stopped there. He soon came back and told us that Queen Hortense had taken refuge there since the day before and was already preparing to leave; and he offered to take us to her at once. For want of another resting-place we would have been obliged to stay in our carriages, amid a compact crowd of people and horses. It was not without great difficulty that our guide made way for us; but at last we reached the gate of the castle, and, soon after, the princess's apartments.

I knew her but slightly, but under such circumstances one was above ceremony. We first entered the room of Mlle. Cochelet, her reader and confidant; she got out of bed and received us half dressed. We had hardly entered when she began to utter loud screams, provoked not only by the general situation, but also by certain particular acts, and notably the retreat of King Joseph.

"Would you believe," she said, "he quietly came and supped here! He wanted supper, after a day like that! "

We next went to the queen. She was less expansive than Mlle. Cochelet, but nevertheless allowed us to suspect all the fears, bitterness, and reproaches that filled her heart. Her two sons, aged four and six respectively, were already awake and dressed, and played about her. It was in order to remove them from the events in Paris that she had left the Empress Josephine, her mother, about whom she was exceedingly anxious, especially since she had learnt that, without giving her warning, they had blown up the bridge of Neuilly, in the interest of the defence of Paris. "And so she is alone at Malmaison!" cried the queen, in despair.

During this interview, which took place in a large room badly lighted by the dawn, which was only just breaking, and the candles, which were going out, we saw the maids, in tears, hastening the preparations for flight of this princess, whom I was never to see again.

We regained the town, not without difficulty. The day which had arisen brought to view the most tumultuous scene. Soon everyone resumed his journey. There was no *adieu* said; no *au revoir*: it was, alas, a rout! Each man for himself.

We arrived during the day at Liouville, an old *château* belonging to my travelling companions. That part of the Beauce in which it stood was not yet disturbed by any news of the events which I have described. We were received by the Comtesse Victor de Juigné, sister to Mme. de Sainte-Aulaire, who, although holding no political opinions, received us with exquisite, but cold, politeness. The fall of the Empire, it must be admitted, was for the time the object of every wish; but there was no necessity for explanations, and each kept his reserve. After a fish dinner (it was Holy Week), we retired to our rooms, worn out beneath the weight of the moral and physical fatigues we had undergone during the twenty-four hours that had just elapsed.

I was young: I slept long and soundly. No political news came to break the weariness of the next day. A few fugitives, friends or relations of the Sainte-Aulaire family, came to ask for shelter; but they knew no more than we did. It was impossible to prolong our stay at Liouville; we had given our horses a day's rest, and on the 1st of April our caravan took a cross road in order to reach the high road for Chartres.

We arrived in that town about the middle of the day, and were struck with astonishment at seeing all the doors and windows closed and a complete absence of people in the streets. Only a carters' tavern was open; our carriages rolled into the yard, and soon we were all gathered in a large room which I shall never forget. M. de Saint-Aulaire set out in search of information. They told us in the house that there was fighting going on at some little distance, and that soon they would be able to know how the troops were disposed, because there were people looking out from the cathedral belfry, which is a very tall one, as everyone knows. Our anxiety was great, but did not last long: it was a false alarm we heard, caused by the explosion of a convoy of powder, which had burst a few leagues off. The general terror had made a pitched battle of it.

My one desire was to place myself as soon as possible in the situation laid down for me by the marshal, that is to put the Loire behind me. I saw the Sainte-Aulaire family hesitating in its march, and for a thousand reasons I was distressed at parting from them; but the same evening I took my leave of them, and continued my journey to Tours. I travelled in fear and trembling, however; for I had no male attendant with me except my coachman, who had only been three months in my service.

About two o'clock, the coachman told me that the horses could go no further. We were in a village; I told him to knock at the first sign we came to. I was given a room of some sort, and I clambered on to a bed which almost touched the ceiling. I was ready to set out again at daybreak; but when I was asked to pay seventy -two francs for this short stay, I objected, and looking the old hag who wanted to fleece me in the face, I asked her for her bill in detail.

"There's no need for a bill; you can pay three *louis*, as the Princesse de Neuchâtel has just done."

"Possibly; but I am curious to know the price of things in your part of the country, and I want a bill. When I have got it, I will go and pay a little visit to your magistrate."

She thereupon brought me her bill, which amounted to twenty-seven *francs*; and I thought myself lucky to escape so cheaply, while recognizing that I was still being robbed.

To make up for this, I must tell you of my good Mme. Raymond, the hostess of the Trois Monarques at Châteaudun. I alighted at her house about mid-day, and as he unharnessed his horses, the coachman declared that they could not take another step that day. It was most discouraging; yet what should I have gained by killing them, when every other means of transport might fail me entirely? It was evident that I was the last fugitive who dared venture upon ground which they expected to see invaded at any moment by the Allies. All traffic seemed to have ceased since the preceding day.

"Oh dear," said I to the kind hostess, who, with her arms *akimbo*, was looking at me sadly, while giving me these details; "and suppose the enemy arrives while I am with you?"

"Well then, I will hide you; trust to me, little lady, and begin by handing me all those red boxes, which no one must be allowed to see."

She installed me in her best room, went and locked up my jewel-caskets, and returned to try and console me.

"I have seen a deal of sorrow since the last three days," she said; "whatever has delayed you so on this road?"

I then understood what a mistake I had made in spending twenty-four hours at Liouville; but if you think of my habits of life, always surrounded and watched over, you will perhaps understand how, in my ignorance of events, I hesitated to leave my Sainte-Aulaire friends and surrender myself alone, as I then was, to all the hazards of that flight.

The next morning I heard a great tumult beneath my windows; something had evidently happened, and soon I saw an officer of dragoons entering my room, visibly excited. I did not know him. His detachment, which had just entered Châteaudun, was galloping through the streets.

"I learnt a moment ago," said he, "that a section of the enemy was about to fall upon the town, and that the wife of Marshal Oudinot was alone and undefended in this inn. I have come to place myself at her disposal."

The frightful terror which had overpowered me was not so great as to paralyze my sense of gratitude; but the officer gave me no time to express it.

"If you will believe me, *Madame*," he said, "you will leave without delay; the road is still free in front of you, that is clear, and we shall be able to keep back the enemy here long enough to enable you to reach a safer retreat."

With this man's obligingness and devotion was mingled a sort of prodigious exaltation, which ended by bursting out in these words, pronounced with fury:

"Ah, *Madame la maréchale*, it's all up with the emperor and the army, and we are going to be governed by a king in petticoats."

I was stupefied, not knowing that an absurd rumour was about which thus clad Louis XVIII. in its imagination.

"But start, start!" cried the officer.

Half distraught, I stepped into my carriage, thanking him as best I could. I knew his name, and I have forgotten it. I am ashamed to have to make this avowal!

I reached Vendôme in the evening, and I was about to go to bed in an inn which seemed pretty quiet, when the Comte de Sainte-Aulaire forced my door and told me that the road which he had just followed behind me was still clear, and that my good dragoons had not been called upon to draw their swords. With an emotion which I fully shared, the traveller told me of the entry into Paris of the allied armies. Details were still wanting, but the name of the Bourbons had already been pronounced, and the emperor was known to be at Fontainebleau with his Guard. The alternative which resulted from these events was calculated to confuse a more experienced judgment than mine.

The emperor conquered and dethroned was enough to revolt my belief; the emperor in submission seemed still more impossible; and, from the chaos of my thoughts, what issued as most clear and most likely was still his retreat behind the Loire and consequently a defence with which I naturally associated the marshal. Accordingly I must continue my journey and cross to the other bank. My sister, with her husband's family, was expecting me at Poitiers; but I had resolved first of all to stop at Tours, there to await details. I arrived there the next day, and alighted at the Hôtel du Faisan, which stands in the middle of the Grande Rue.

It was very late, and I went to bed full of emotions, but I thought, with a sort of consolation, that at least for the moment there was to be no fighting. Yet this was only a conjecture, and my first course the next morning was to write to the *prefect*, who was at that time the Comte de Kergorlay, to ask him in confidence, although I did not know him, to communicate to me what I wanted to know. I implored him to take compassion on my anxiety concerning the marshal, and I received no reply.

The hotel at which I was staying presented the noise and movement of a beehive. I was sorrowfully listening to this humming when my maid came to tell me that a *chasseur*, covered with gold lace, had come to beg me to grant a short interview to his master. Who was this master? No one less than Fouché, whom I had never seen! Without having had time to prepare myself for this immediate meeting, I beheld him entering my room. What an astonishing face! Hair, eyebrows, complexion, eyes, all seemed to me to be of the same shade. So soon as he had sat down, he asked for news of my husband.

"Alas!" I replied, "I expect to hear news of him from everyone I meet, including yourself, *monsieur le duc*."

"What, *Madame!* you have just arrived and you know no more than all of us, who have been refuged here during the last two or three days."

I then explained to him the cause of my delay. He seemed overcome with his disappointment at finding that this newest arrival could tell him nothing. His strange glance wandered restlessly round my room. At last he spoke again, and asked me, with hesitation, what the marshal would do under the circumstances of the moment.

"Will he follow the emperor's fortunes, do you think, *Madame?* or, if the Empire goes down, will he attach himself to a new order of things?"

The question was hard, but the answer was very simple.

"Although I do not know what has happened," I replied, "and am unable to see into the future, I know that the marshal, as always, will let himself be guided solely by honour, duty, and the love of his country; that is all I can tell you."

Thereupon he made me a very deep bow and withdrew. I have never seen him since.

Meantime, I felt the necessity of communicating with the refugees who were in the same position as myself at Tours, and I called first upon the Maréchale Masséna, towards whom my husband had always told me to be very obliging as being so much my senior. She received me very affably, and groaned a great deal for me and especially for herself at the crisis of the moment. Then suddenly she said:

"Do you know, we may have to wander for whole months after the emperor and the army before the crisis is decided? I foresaw this, and have taken my precautions. How much money have you? I have sixty thousand *francs* in gold in the boot of my carriage."

I evaded the question, not thinking myself obliged to own that I only possessed just one year's interest on sixty thousand *francs*.

A long week was passed in this way, when suddenly the *prefect* sent out a cloud of newspapers, advantages which we had not known for a long time. They were printed under the Provisional Government and gave our eager minds the details of the events which had taken place since the 30th of March. When you read this period of our history, my children, after so many years' interval, you are astonished at the rapidity and importance of the catastrophes which it contains. You can imagine therefore of the impression produced by these revelations upon contemporaries and especially upon those whose dearest and directest interests were at stake!

Your father's name was not yet mentioned; but it seemed certain to me that his rallying to the new government would be the result of the freedom which was restored to him by the abdication of the emperor.

Amid this maze of surprises, regrets, and hopes of the realization of a peace so eagerly longed for, I remained confused and at a loss. My opinions hesitated between the traditional cult with which I had been inculcated as a child for the family of the Bourbons, and my enthusiasm as a young girl and young married woman for the Empire. Moreover, all my personal inclinations must give way before those of my husband; and my brain was on fire in presence of so many hesitations and uncertainties. The day was spent in this condition of moral fever. My want of experience paralyzed my power of taking any action on the spot; although I was not the only one who was in the same plight. I know not with what resolution I went to bed: I believe with none; but what I remember is that at break of day there came a loud knocking at my door, and before my maid had come, the following colloquy took place between the man in the passage and myself:

"Who are you?" I cried.

"Vergé," was the reply.

"Oh! Monsieur Vergé, where have you left my husband? Speak, speak!"

"*M. le maréchal* returned from Fontainebleau to Paris, after the Emperor's abdication. He has recognized the government of the Bourbons, represented by the Provisional Government. Peace is made and all is over. *M. le maréchal* is very anxious about you, *Madame*, and ordered me to follow this line, on which he supposed you to be, until I had the good fortune to find you."

I set out forthwith. On alighting from my carriage, all eagerness, in the Rue de Bourgogne, I was very disappointed at not finding my husband, who had gone to meet M. le Comte d'Artois. It was the 12th of April 1814.

This prince, the object of the adoration of his party, was, in the imagination of all those who composed it, like one of those heroes, great and beautiful, of romance and of fairytales. My mother and my aunts, although they had never seen him, had always spoken to me of him under this impression. They wept on pronouncing the names of Louis XVI., of Marie Antoinette[1], of the poor little *Dauphin*, of Madame Élisabeth; they praised all they knew of *monsieur* (since Louis XVIII.); but when they spoke of M. le Comte d'Artois, it was always to add to his name some gracious recollection. All these reminiscences, eclipsed for a time by the brilliant epoch which was coming to an end, now reawakened in me. I thought of the joy of my mother, of all my family; and I only awaited the Marshal with the more impatience, anxious as I was at last to satisfy myself as to his personal position and the manner in which he took it. He returned at last, charmed with him whom he loved sincerely and whom he served not only in deeds but as much as possible with his experience of French affairs.

Monsieur at once appointed your father a Minister of State, with a seat on the council. He spent much of his time at the Tuileries, and only returned to be assailed by interminable audiences; he was the central point of a large number of various interests which he strove to serve. These were those of the army, the Royalist party and the emigrants. The latter addressed themselves to him with a confidence based upon a very honourable past. In the victories of the Republican army over the army of Condé, your father, while acting according to his duty, had not forgotten that he was fighting against Frenchmen,

1. *Marie Antoinette and the Downfall of the French Monarchy* by Imbert de Saint-Amand also published by Leonaur.

and had softened, perhaps by exceptional proceedings, the hardships of the situation.

Events and obligations accumulated for my household. It was a question of visiting the Lieutenant-General of the Kingdom, *monsieur*, at the Tuileries. The prince had declared that he would receive all the ladies; and this was taken so literally that confusion inconceivable reigned at this assembly, where I was told that even the Montansier was seen, she who gave her name to one of the small theatres of that period.

The Marquise du Roure confided to us that, anticipating the interview which was about to take place, she had gone with some of her friends and placed herself somewhere where *monsieur* would have to pass, and that, struck with their demonstration of loyalty, he had greeted them with his usual graciousness: so much so that each one said, "He recognizes me." On the evening of *monsieur's* reception, she successfully piloted the troop of young married women who had placed themselves under her guidance. As for myself, I felt moved; I thought much of my mother . . .

The excitement of the Royalist ladies surpassed description, and would have been touching if, by the side of their joy, they had not allowed to transpire occasional acrimony against the beaten party; but Mmes. du Roure and de Sainte-Aulaire were not among those who acted like this. Meantime the heat, the noise, and the agitation seemed to have reached their height, when a redoubled clamour informed us that the prince was approaching. I stood on tiptoe, and perceived his very noble head gracefully and unceasingly bowing. At last he stood before us. He was exceedingly amiable to Mme. du Roure, who presented me to him. At the sound of my name, he made a quick movement of interest, eagerly stepped towards me, and said so many kind things bearing upon the marshal's reputation that my voice, filled with tears, could hardly be heard in reply.

But the kind prince understood, and he has often since told me that my emotion added to the favourable impression which the mention of this new name, so renowned and so unblemished, had produced upon him. Myself, I at once felt for Charles X. the commencement of that veneration and confidence which grew naturally from the acquaintance which I afterwards made with his character, when I had to fill my important office about the person of his daughter-in-law. Among the duties which arose, in complicated fashion, at that time was one which a very regrettable death left me only just time to fulfil.

I wished to see the Empress Josephine, who had remained at Malmaison, where she had been respected amid all the tumult. I called one morning with Mme. de Sainte-Aulaire. We were shown into the drawing-room next to the gallery where the princess was closeted, we were told, with Mme. de Staël. The emperor's personal enemy had probably thought it in good taste to put in an appearance at that time at Malmaison. The action was kindly enough in itself, if the woman of genius had not been so eager to exploit it in favour of her study of the human heart, as perhaps you will agree when you read what follows.

When the empress and Mme. de Staël appeared, the former wore an air of great excitement and emotion. Mme. de Staël rapidly crossed the room, bowed, and went out. I must tell you that during the conference there had been shown into the drawing-room, in addition to Mme. de Sainte-Aulaire and myself, the Countess Waleska, the Polish woman to whom the emperor was said to have attached himself so fondly during the campaign of 1806. These two women, of whom one had detested the emperor whom the other had perhaps too well loved, drawn by the same impulse towards the repudiated consort, formed, you will agree, a strange contrast. Josephine, however, gave us no time to reflect upon this singular meeting; after responding to Mme. de Staël's farewell courtesy, she quickly came up to the chimney, where we were all standing in silence, and said, without any preamble:

> I have just finished a very painful interview. Would you believe that, among other questions which Mme. de Staël thought fit to put to me, she asked me whether I still loved the Emperor? She seemed to wish to analyze my heart in presence of this great misfortune. I, who have never ceased to love the emperor in the midst of his greatness . . . did she think that I should now grow cold towards him?

The empress was already very ill. Her head was wrapped in a large English shawl; she was flushed, her breathing was oppressed, and she complained of catarrh. One could see that she was suffering in both body and soul. She conducted almost the whole of the conversation, talking with a freedom inspired probably by the sympathy which she saw imprinted upon Mme. de Sainte-Aulaire's features and mine; and when she withdrew, she made us promise to return and dine with her the next Sunday. Alas! before then she was dead! . . . She was followed by many regrets. I have heard King Charles X., who went to pay her a visit, say that he would have been very happy to continue on intimate terms with this excellent princess.

Impressions of every kind succeeded one another without interruption. Not many days afterwards, the marshal came home one evening and told me to prepare to receive the *Czar* of Russia the next day. My agitation was great at this news. My husband summoned his staff and all the cripples of the war whom he was able to collect among his intimates; and in fact nearly all those who gathered round him at the top of the staircase to receive the emperor were more or less mutilated. Since Montereau, General Pajol wore his arm in a sling; since Craonne, Victor walked upon crutches; M. de Xaintrailles was bent in two as the result of a lance-thrust in the loins; M. Jacqueminot still limped badly, as did General Pactold: in a word the gathering was a striking one, and did not fail to produce its effect.

With the exquisite grace which never left him, the *Czar* gave me his hand to lead me to the drawing-room, where all our cripples followed us. They formed themselves in a circle, and the marshal mentioned their names one after the other. Each was plied with questions in detail, full of a visible interest.

"Gentlemen," said the *Czar*, when he had finished, "you have been very badly treated by this war; but if on our side we have gained a certain skill, to whom do we owe it? Why, the terrible lessons you used to give us have ended by turning to our advantage."

As he pronounced these charming words, the *Czar* sat down, and invited everyone to do the same. He continued in the same tone, taking us back to the last campaigns, always allowing us a large share in the glory, and fascinating us to such a degree with his conversation, so elegant and chivalrous at the same time, that we, the vanquished and mutilated, fell beneath the charm of the conqueror. This was because Alexander was both magnanimous and sincere, and the perfect harmony between his language and his fine physiognomy and the inflection of his voice carried conviction to every mind.

This memorable visit, which was prolonged for about an hour, left in all of us a precious remembrance. When the emperor rose to go, he found for his escort a company of cavalry which the marshal had requested of the first military division; the marshal's principal *aide-de-camp* had orders to command it and to ride by the *Czar's* carriage-door.

The Bourbons really appeared in the guise of a pledge of peace; and it was as such that they were accepted by the generality of the population, who, while not knowing them, received them as the olive-branch, the symbol which removed all idea of war. By the minority they were received with the enthusiasm of hearts which had religiously preserved the memory of the past. But the graciousness of the lieutenant-general, of which I have already spoken, was beginning to incline all minds in their favour, without distinction of party. The rumour soon spread of a charter which Louis XVIII. had long meditated, based upon the British Constitution. From that moment, all ideas, combinations and hopes were turned in his direction, and the arrival of the king was anxiously awaited. The approaching entry of M. le Duc de Berry was also announced. He preceded the king his uncle, and had disembarked at Cherbourg, whence he travelled by short journeys, receiving the homage of the population on the way.

General de Lorencez was in command at Cherbourg, and was the first military authority to welcome the prince. He accompanied him to Paris, and seemed quite impressed with the candour, the kindness, the wit and even the extreme vivacity of M. le Duc de Berry, who on his side had refused to be separated from the general during the whole journey. They had travelled from *fête* to *fête*; the prince's head was really turned with happiness; and no pre-sentiment cast its shadow over that confiding heart, which was to be pierced by an assassin's dagger not many years later. My husband soon made the acquaintance of M. le Duc de Berry, and they conceived for each other a mutual affection, the outcome of their frank and winning natures.

Meantime the king had disembarked at Calais with Mme. la Duchesse d'Angoulême. The liberal intentions (for the word Liberalism now first came into fashion) attributed to the new monarch had attenuated, although perhaps not in the army, the hostile rumours which had at first been spread with respect to him. Everyone agreed in saying that he was full of experience, enlightenment and erudition. As to the princess, although nothing was known of her appearance or her habits, she aroused great interest; and as one likes to give a shape to people one has never seen, it was settled that Louis XVI.'s orphan, the august prisoner of the Temple, was shy, sad and gentle, and that she had a pale countenance, a supple form, and a weak, soft voice.

Let me say at once that upon her apparition the Princess gave the lie to all these conjectures; and she was never forgiven for it. Mme. la Duchesse d'Angoulême, in fact, was strongly built, with a high colour; her eyes had been inflamed by the tears of her youth, but her keen, quick, frank glance was not at all cast down. Her voice, which was, it was said, her father's, was a little masculine, abrupt and positive. Her movements were almost always sudden; there was no deliberateness about her whole person, any more than about that noble heart, which had never anything to conceal.

One of the king's first acts was to promulgate the Constitutional Charter. The king had turned the senate of the Empire into a House of Peers, after adding to the list some names selected by himself, of whom my husband formed one. The solemn sitting for the reading of the charter was held in the hall of the Legislative Body. I was present with a host of other ladies, all eager to witness the reception accorded to the important words which were about to be read. After the customary ceremonial, the Comte Dabray, the Chancellor of France, read this important act in a very loud voice, and it was passed with enthusiasm before the House rose. If there were any dissentients, they did not show themselves then.

Soon the time came to be presented to the king and to his august niece. The day was appointed, and the discussion on the costume to be worn commenced forthwith. We must have court mantles, said one. No, said the others, the court properly so-called is not yet organised. The great question was decided in favour of gowns with long trains; and the *fleurs-de-lys* were revived. The king's reception was, like the preceding one, very numerously attended and very agitated. His Majesty, who at that time used still to stand up, made one forget, by his amiable and dignified address, the enormousness of his size. He received me with extreme graciousness, but I confess that I always felt a little timid in his presence.

I have not yet spoken of M. le Duc d'Angoulême, that misjudged prince, a very type of virtue, whom God alone will have rewarded. Although somewhat resembling the prince his father, he could not be described as good-looking. His figure was frail, his movements sudden, and he was very short-sighted. This *ensemble* did not predispose one in his favour; but when you saw him in a drawing-room, the expression of his loyal and kindly face captivated you before long. Of an exemplary piety, M. le Duc d'Angoulême was, and remained until the end, the slave of his duties as a husband, a son, and a subject. If he always insisted upon the prerogatives due to his rank, this was because he regarded himself as their depositary; for personally he set no price upon them.

His innate courage was further supported by his perfect resignation to the events which might follow from duties accomplished. He was inflexible upon subjects that he considered just, and nothing then could make him change his resolution. In one word, he was the gentleman of olden time, in his faith, his loyalty, and perhaps even in the abruptness of his speech.

Together with the Royal Family, there returned successively to France all the Princes of the Blood. One of the best known of them, through his name and his influence upon the emigration, was M. le Prince de Condé. This august chief of the army to which he had given his name had lost part of his intellectual faculties at the time of his return to France, although this did not prevent a multitude of people from calling upon him. He received with extreme politeness. The old names were always present in his recollection; but he was not always able to remember the period of events which had happened, and he once replied to a lady who came to ask a favour of him, "I will mention the matter to Mme. de Polignac, who will explain your business to the queen," thus passing over the whole terrible period which at moments escaped from his weary head.

When my husband was presented to him, struck with the name, he said:

"Oudinot! Ah, that is my antagonist at Constance."

His recollection then became more lucid for a time, and after exchanging a few words with my husband upon that military event:

"You are a brave man," he said, "and I will talk to the king so that he may make you a general."

I remember a dinner to which he invited us at the Palais-Bourbon, to which he had returned. Victor was one of the party. He had just been appointed Colonel of the King's Hussars (4th Regiment), and sat facing the old prince, who had placed me by his side, while the Princesse de Wagram sat on the other. The prince was almost blind and very deaf. Soon a laboured conversation was started. He mixed up his two neighbours and their husbands, and there was nothing but interrupted remarks and explanations, which were the more confusing inasmuch as it was necessary to shout them out amid an immense table at which all the guests maintained a silence full of respect for the august old man. I was half dead with the effort; but after an interval, during which I had taken time to breathe, the prince looked across at my stepson.

"Who," he asked, "is that Austrian officer!"

"Why, *Monseigneur*, it's my stepson."

"Your son?"

He turned round and looked at me: I was twenty-two.

"But at what age were you married then?"

"But, *Monseigneur*, he is my stepson."

"Ah, I understand, his mother. . . . Where is his property?"

In those days Victor's property, my children, was somewhat indefinite; but as I did not want to give a full explanation of our position before all the witnesses who were listening to us, I replied:

"At Bar-sur-Ornain, *Monseigneur*."

"Where is that?" asked the prince. "I don't know the name."

Utterly nonplussed, I replied:

"Bar-le-Duc."

"Why are you not more explicit, *Madame*: now I know where you mean."

Why indeed had I called by its revolutionary name the capital of the Ducs de Bar? Great beads of perspiration stood on my forehead after this tough conversation.

We also visited the princesses: the Dowager Mme. la Duchesse d'Orléans, *née* Penthièvre, mother of Louis-Philippe, and Mme. la Duchesse de Bourbon, mother of M. le Duc d'Enghien. M. le Duc d'Orléans, his wife, a daughter of the King of Naples, his sister, Mlle. d'Orléans, and two or three of his children, still very young, returned a little later than the Royal Family. I must not forget M. le Duc de Bourbon. He was tall, distinguished, and sad-looking. There was something about his whole appearance which seemed well-suited to the father of the Duc d'Enghien.

The private events and general interests in which my husband took part kept us constantly occupied. A serious question came up for debate before the Council of Ministers, at which your father assisted in his quality as Minister of State without portfolio. This was to define the position of the ex-Imperial Guard. Your father endeavoured in vain, in the interest both of the dynasty and of those picked troops, to use all his credit in order to have only one word changed, and to have all these brave soldiers made into a Royal Guard. He met with keen sympathy among the princes and also among the minority of the Council of Ministers, including M. l'Abbé de Montesquiou, the Minister of the Interior; but they were opposed and unfortunately defeated by men whose devotion to the cause of the Bourbons was estimable because of its fidelity, but very regrettable in its results.

These carried the day, and the infantry of the Imperial Guard was divided into Royal Grenadiers and Royal Chasseurs. Their command-in-chief was given to Marshal Oudinot, with instructions to establish these troops, who had lost their high pay, in two garrisons far removed from Paris, where they had always performed a confidential service. Metz was assigned to the grenadiers and Nancy to the *chasseurs*. Unable to obtain any of the advantages of the past for these magnificent regiments, the marshal asked and obtained that at least one of the princes should come with him and review them before they were removed from Fontainebleau. Yes, it was in this spot, still resounding with the emperor's last farewells, that his Guard had been left for several months.

It was decided that M. le Duc de Berry should fulfil this mission. In order to make it as fruitful as he could, the marshal went on ahead, and worked so hard and so well that he did not fear to urge the prince to hurry his visit. By showing these whiskered veterans his well-known face, the marshal had disposed them as favourably as was to be expected. On his side, M. le Duc de Berry put so much graciousness into his words and his actions that the marshal could only congratulate him and ask him always to continue in the same road.

The prince returned to Paris charmed with the ex-Imperial Guard, too much charmed perhaps, for he looked upon it from that moment as won over to his cause; whereas it was not by such a trifle that so great a conquest could be made! The marshal knew this, and repeatedly said so; but M. le Duc de Berry, quick and impressionable, and still possessing at thirty-six all the illusions, tastes and ardour of youth, had taken everything in confidence since the first day of his return to France. If he had been the master, the opinions of the marshal would probably have been adopted. It would have been the best means of gaining the nation. But generally only half-measures were taken, and soon dull discontent and ill-restrained murmurs began to be heard. They issued from both camps.

I often felt very sad. I thought that everybody was in the right or that everybody was in the wrong, as you prefer. I should have liked to work to conciliate everybody, as my husband did. In fact, idolized by the army, and respected by the emigrants for having supported them on certain unfortunate occasions, the marshal spent his life in lecturing the one, in consoling the other, in pleading for the interests of all, now with the princes, to whom he had access at all times, now with the ministers. His life was so greatly divided among all these divers interests that I scarcely ever saw him.

The city of Paris gave a *fête* to the king. Now the city of Paris is a great and puissant lady, and when she puts herself out, it is to some purpose, I promise you. I was almost not taking part in this function, for I had just undergone a fresh deception in my maternal expectations. However, my strong constitution soon restored my health sufficiently to enable me to content the marshal, who very much wished to take me to this fete. It commenced as early as two o'clock in the afternoon.

Seven immense rooms had been prepared at the Hôtel de Ville, in each of which a different entertainment was to be provided, from two until nine in the evening. Seven sets of tickets had been distributed, upon which all Paris threw itself with the avidity which distinguishes it and which always will distinguish it on occasions of this kind. The marshals and their wives were asked to the whole series. I cannot give you a very exact account of this splendid fete, first because my fatigue prevented me from taking note of everything, and then because I have seen so many since that this one grows confused with the rest. There were, in short, speeches, replies, *cantatas*, interludes befitting the occasion, music, sumptuous repasts, magnificent illuminations, and finally, balls consisting of official quadrilles of which I did not stay for the end of even the first

At this first banquet of the Hôtel de Ville, as at all those that I have attended since, what struck me was to see the twelve mayors of the town, dressed in their uniforms, standing behind the king's chair and waiting upon him at table, while all of us who formed part of his suite received our plates from the hands of *messieurs* the members of the Municipal Council, all wearing their uniforms.

It was at this dinner that I more specially made the acquaintance of the Maréchale Duchesse d'Albuféra. How pretty she was, and how perfectly happy! Our husbands were intimate with one another, our positions were analogous, and from that time onward we were great friends.

Soon after, M. le Duc de Berry gave a *fête* at Bagatelle. I have omitted as yet to depict to you the character and appearance of this prince. He was short and a little cramped of stature, and had at the first glance nothing that told very much in his favour; but his physiognomy was delicate and gracious. His desire to please was seconded by a charming wit. Very well educated, he spoke several languages with ease, loved all the arts, and encouraged them with generosity and discernment. He was good-natured and sincere, but sometimes hasty to the pitch of passion. This last weakness was greatly to be regretted; because princes, always placed in full view of the people, are obliged to play a part from an early date. It is therefore the duty of those who train them to accustom them to self-constraint (not to be confused with hypocrisy), and to exercise over themselves the empire necessary to their duty as princes. M. le Duc de Berry, brought up in exile from 1791 to 1814, had been left to his own nature, which was sometimes violent, more often generous, and which became sublime when his last hour had struck.

There was talk of a journey of M. le Duc de Berry in the East. In September, the marshal received orders to go and prepare the way, and it was to this that I owed the happiness of being at last able to revisit my mother and my family. A short-lived joy, for every minute was apportioned. However, one can say and hear much even in a few moments, and I gathered many details on the terrible months which had been spent. We had no more time to delay at Jeand'heurs and at Bar than at Vitry, being bound with all possible despatch to reach Metz, Nancy and Thionville, for the marshal had much to do in all these places.

Our excellent friend M. Gouy, who lived at Metz, was of great help to me. He drove me round this charming country while my husband's military expeditions took him to this side and that. The last of these was to Thionville, I believe; but what is certain is that he returned with the prince, and then commenced the turmoil of all the bewildering *fêtes*. In a fortified town, containing a garrison of ten or twelve thousand men of all arms, all under the command of Marshal Oudinot, so active and eager, there were bound to be plenty of military displays. In the morning it was reviews, sham fights: at night, performances at the theatre, balls, fireworks. I remember that once, during a display of the latter, we were standing on the balcony of the *Prefecture*, among a great many people, when we were assailed by the falling rockets. The prince, taking off his helmet (he always wore a *chasseur* uniform), came and held it over my head to protect me, which I would not allow; but you will agree that it was a chivalrous intention!

I suffered during the whole time from the unpleasantness of occupying the place of honour. This was the inevitable consequence of the rank of my husband. I did not dance, and remained with a large number of ladies in the boxes of the theatre, where the ball was given. The sight was animated and charming; and when M. le Duc de Berry started to walk round the room, the officers, with a spontaneous movement, placed themselves in two rows, drew their swords, and crossed them above the prince's head, he passing beneath this vault of steel with a quick feeling of happiness, eagerly displayed.

From Metz, the prince went to Nancy, where the marshal preceded him. My husband and I stayed with Mgr. d'Osmond, a prelate who was both witty and gracious: this without prejudice to his Episcopal qualities. The honours of the Episcopal palace were admirably done by the Comtesse d'Argout, the bishop's sister. We spent a day at Nancy and then went on to Bar, the prince having intimated to the marshal that he would end his journey by a visit to the chief town of the department of the Meuse, and that he would stay beneath our roof.

Unfortunately, this roof was only just rebuilt, and everything was still wanting in the inner arrangement of the house. The furniture, or what remained of it, was not sufficient to furnish the two storeys, which had been ravaged by the fire, and we were barely able to make good the deficiency during the two days which we had beforehand. Luckily, the furniture of the bedroom and drawing-room known as the emperor's was only somewhat faded. We were therefore certain of being able properly to accommodate the prince during the twenty-four hours he promised us.

The marshal had invited my mother, my Aunt Clotilde de Coucy, and her daughter Zoëlie (who has since became Mme. de Beaufort) to be with us against the prince's arrival. The thought of beholding a Bourbon and of assisting me to receive him under our roof had turned the heads of my three dear Royalists.

The streets were full of movement, which overflowed into the courtyard and the house itself. There were the authorities; there were the young ladies with baskets of flowers, of course escorted by their parents; there was my family; there were our friends; there were the Grenadiers, keeping order; and last of all there were the old emigrants, the Knights of Saint Louis, seeking to dispute with the last the honour of guarding *Monseigneur*.

They had swarmed from every side, these poor old men; they had put on uniform as far as they were able, and, encouraged by the marshal, had met in his house. Certainly, there was something very legitimate and very touching in the eagerness of these fine old gentlemen, and yet one could hardly restrain a smile on seeing their attitudes as, with their bare swords at their shoulders, they drew themselves up at the outer door of the drawing-room to guard, as they said, their prince. Those old rusty blades, those superannuated uniforms, those antiquated faces, mingled and confused with the hundred grenadiers of the Old Guard, the brilliant *aides-de-camp* of the marshal, the no less elegant of M. le Duc de Berry (including General de Montélégier and the Prince de Leon) and a large number of officers who had come up from the neighbouring garrisons, personified this period of transition, which was perhaps unique in our history.

The prince, who had made his entry between four and five o'clock, amid the movement of which I have spoken, at once received with great graciousness all those who filled the house. We then sat down to a dinner to which all the leading authorities had been invited. At night, the marshal asked *Monseigneur* to come outside and see the illuminations from the doorstep, which, together with all the other arrangements, were in the expert hands of M. Jacqueminot.

The next day we were to go to Jeand'heurs, where tables were laid along each of the four sides of the grand courtyard, and spread with wines, joints, and hams in profusion. This was in honour of the detachment of grenadiers who had preceded the prince, and who were to resume in the country the service which they had rendered in the town the day before. We arrived at about eleven o'clock in the morning, and breakfast was served at once both in the *château* and the courtyard. A joyous tumult reigned. When he had finished, the prince had a charming idea: accompanied by the marshal and his staff he left the table, and standing on the step, amid the tables of the grenadiers, he lifted his glass and drank to their healths. There issues from those formidable voices a "Hurrah!" which seemed to us to be of good augury.

A fine autumn sun lit up the park, which was radiant. The boats, all dressed with bunting, were drawn up before the oak; the rowers were at their posts, and we embarked at once. *Monseigneur*, on the principal boat, took all the ladies with him, M. Jacqueminot steering. The second boat contained the marshal, the *prefect*, and so forth. The five others followed, filled with people. The cannon, the music, all contributed to animate the scene; but it was soon disturbed by an incident which filled us with affright.

M. Jacqueminot, with a movement quick as thought, left the rudder, took off his sword and, taking no account of his uniform, leapt from the barge into the river, while at the same time my stepson Auguste did the same from his father's barge. The scarlet uniform of the Chevau-Légers shone out beneath the water, and in no way impeded your brother's movements; he gracefully executed all the evolutions of a consummate swimmer, paying no heed to, or not hearing, the stentorian words of M. le Duc de Berry, who shouted to both the rash young men:

"I order you to get back on board""

But one of them was no longer in a condition to obey. M. Jacqueminot, seized with the cold, painfully and in a feeble voice cried:

"Give me an oar, I am sinking!"

Frozen with terror, we who were in the barge almost capsized it, owing to the spontaneous movement which carried us all towards the side of the drowning man. Only one of us retained his presence of mind and made us resume our seats, and that was M. le Duc de Berry. He held out an oar to M. Jacqueminot, who had hardly the strength left to seize it, pulled him up to the barge, and taking him by the collar, thanks to the strength of his two vigorous wrists, hoisted him into the barge, where he lay for dead.

Auguste had climbed back, on his side, full of life and animation; he did not become aware of the terror which he had occasioned until he saw the distress upon his father's face. We were rowed back at quick speed, and soon a warm bed and proper care restored the only one of the two who had suffered, so much so that two hours later he was able to take leave of the prince, together with his comrades, at the carriage-door.

The catastrophe of the immersions, which had upset us all, put an end to our water-party; moreover, time was passing, and *Monseigneur* had still to distribute among the officers who had come up from every side several Crosses of Saint-Louis and of the Legion of Honour. He knighted them beneath the fine vaulted ceiling of the drawing-room at Jeand'heurs; it was an imposing sight, and one not easily forgotten. General de Castelbajac, one of the knights, could never speak calmly of this solemnity, which well suited his fine and noble figure. My uncle, who was at that time *sous-prefet* of Vitry, was also decorated, and received under the eyes of his family. I was very pleased at this.

A few weeks later, we returned to Paris, and this winter was my real *début* in society. Visits, engagements, fetes simply rained down upon us. The marshal used to accompany me at first, but he soon grew tired of it, and wished me to present myself everywhere alone. I had no one to consult, and could only rely upon my good intentions and upon the principles and examples which my good mother had instilled into me. But what was also a powerful aid to me was my pride at being the wife of your father, who bore so well and so proudly his baton as a Marshal of France! I was proud too of my title taken from a foreign duchy, and won abroad at the sword's point. I thought that Reggio figured well among the Montmorencies, the Crillons, the Noailles, and the Perigords. Imbued with these reflections, I gradually learnt to occupy the place due to your father's wife in this new and brilliant world, and this position, which preceded that which I held a little later at court, has, I believe, never left me.

Eugénie de Coucy
Maréchale Oudinot, Duchesse De Reggio

Chapter 8

Oudinot's Attitude

In midwinter 1814, Marshal Soult, Duc de Dalmatie, who was then Minister at War, ordered all the governors to go and reside in the centre of their respective commands. Your father's, which had Metz for its principal town, was one of the most important, both because of its geographical position, and because of the presence of the ex-Imperial Guard, which was garrisoned at Metz and Nancy. We were hardly given time to pack up in Paris and to make our arrangements at Metz.

We took up our quarters at Metz at the large Hôtel de la Princerie, which we were told was destined for the commanders-in-chief, and which did not contain a single chair until hasty arrangements had been made by M. Gouy. The marshal desired at once to receive the inhabitants, the garrison and the whole province, and I cannot describe to you the trouble we were put to, since everything was unfinished or in ruins. However, by making many purchases, and hiring the rest, we were able to keep open table almost immediately after our installation.

Apart from the uniforms, which naturally swarmed at our receptions, there were local authorities and notabilities without end. I had already met the *prefect*, M. de Vaublanc, and his wife. My intimacy with M. and Mme. Gouy increased; and they were very useful in initiating me into the details of Metz society. I did not know whether we were there for a long or a short while, and my continual receptions during this provisional period were really bewildering. The remainder of February and the first few days of March were spent in this way. The marshal determined to give a great ball, which redoubled my occupations as hostess.

The day for it had arrived, and I was giving a last glance at the preparations, and was going to dress, when I heard some unexpected news. The emperor, they said, had just disembarked at Cannes, and was marching upon Paris with the nucleus of his Elban Guard, which had grown like a snow-ball, and was already developing into a positive force. I still doubted the truth of the rumour, when the marshal came to my room and confirmed all this news, which he had just received by an express from the War Office. An express! when the telegraph might have been employed to inform him twenty-four hours earlier! And meantime the hour for the ball had come!

"You shall dance tonight, my dear," said the marshal. "You must keep a good countenance, know nothing, and allow nobody else to know anything. I want the ball to be very animated, for while it lasts I shall be holding an extraordinary council in my room, consisting of the generals and colonels of the garrison and the notables of the country."

Among the colonels was your brother Victor, who formed part of the garrison with his fine regiment of the 1st Hussars.

Guests came in crowds, and the music and dancing never ceased. Refreshments of every kind were handed round without stopping. The marshal had his wish, the ball was very animated, and it did not finish till well into the night.

Greatly agitated because the marshal had not returned to the ball-room, very tired, worn out in body, soul and mind, I went to bed without knowing what had happened downstairs. There was no time for your father to give me long details, for he had received very tardy but very definite orders as to the course to pursue He was told to march a portion of the Royal Grenadiers and *chasseurs* to Langres, in order to oppose the progress of the emperor, who had arrived at Grenoble in triumph, and was marching at full speed in the direction of Paris.

The marshal had no illusions as to the feeling and intentions of the troops. Nevertheless, he at once took his measures, both as to what he was to leave at Metz, the most important of our frontier places, and for his march of the next day. Though the first news of the emperor's landing had come late, the news of his triumphal march followed rapidly enough. With the ministers, anxiety and dread had succeeded to the sort of presumptuous security which had greeted the first announcement of the return from Elba. And the orders transmitted bore evident signs of this perturbation.

It was, I believe, on this same day that my husband received a letter from Marshal Ney which he was glad to be able to produce at a later date, on the occasion of the latter's distressing trial. I do not know it by heart, but I can still, as it were, read these words:

"Let us unite our efforts," he wrote to Marshal Oudinot, "against the attempts of the common enemy."

If this is not the exact text, it is at least the sense of the message, which was dated from Franche-Comté on the eve of the day when Ney turned, at the head of his troops, from the king to the emperor.

Meantime, unspeakable tumult reigned at the Princerie. While the marshal was despatching to Toul a column of his grenadiers, whom he was to join the same evening, and multiplying his arrangements as to what was to be done and left undone within the walls of Metz, I gave my keys to Mme. Gouy, unreservedly surrendering to her the care of my house, and prepared to accompany the marshal, who was to put me down at Bar in passing.

As we were stepping into our carriage, a Royal Express came up and handed my husband an urgent message. This was an autograph letter from Mgr. le Duc de Berry, authorizing the marshal, in the name of His Majesty, to proclaim the Royal Grenadiers and Chasseurs as a Royal Guard from that moment, a tardy and useless measure, which the marshal had solicited in vain at a more opportune time.

"Drive to Toul," said the marshal.

It was night when we arrived at an hotel in the Place d'Armes in that town. It was full of officers; the principal room had been reserved for us, but it was only one room, without a corner for me to retire to. Soon, the generals arrived by command. Without exactly explaining what he might have to say to the troops, my husband asked these gentlemen how they would be likely to receive an address ending with a "Long live the King!"

"Try, and see, *monsieur le maréchal*," said General Roguet; "try, and see."

The others made no reply.

"Well, then, give my orders," said the marshal. "I will hold a review at daybreak tomorrow and speak to them."

They had hardly gone out, when General Trommelin returned alone. He had seen and heard the emperor's emissaries in the *cafés* of the town, and had gathered unequivocal proofs of the intentions of the officers of all ranks.

"But how about my review of tomorrow!" said your father. "And my cry of 'Long live the King!' which I don't want to compromise.

Look here, I must clear up this question directly and without delay. Go and tell the generals to send me all the officers, from sub-lieutenant to colonel: I must speak to them and have done with this position."

Not long after, a treble row of officers was crammed in our room, forming a circle with the marshal in the centre. He waited until they had all taken their places in silence, and then expressed himself more or less in the following words:

"Gentlemen, in the circumstances in which we are placed I wish to make an appeal to your loyalty. We are marching under the white cockade. I am to review you tomorrow before our departure: with what cry will you and your men reply to my 'Long live the King?'"

These words were followed by absolute silence. Nothing so striking ever passed before my eyes. I was hidden behind a curtain, and had remained a forced witness of this unparalleled scene. Two hotel candles lighted it sufficiently to prevent me from losing any of it; but their pale reflection on those manly and gloomy faces produced an indescribable effect. This silence, expressive though it was, could not be accepted by the marshal as a reply. I saw the storm about to break forth; each second was a century. . . . At last the marshal said:

"Well, gentlemen?"

Then a young officer of inferior rank stepped forward, and said:

"*Monsieur le maréchal,* I am bound to tell you, and no one here will contradict me: when you cry, 'Long live the King!' our men and we will answer, 'Long live the Emperor!'"

"I thank you, gentlemen," replied the marshal. Then he bowed to them, and the last of them filed out without another word.

That same day the marshal drove to Jeand'heurs, where he set me down, and the next day he followed his troops, who still wore the same colours as himself; for although insurrection was undoubtedly in every heart, not a single outward sign or breach of discipline had as yet given the commander-in-chief the right to believe his soldiers to belong to the opposite camp. The crisis burst at Chaumont. It was there, at the *prefect's*, where my husband had just received the news and the positive details of Marshal Ney's defection, that his grenadiers, who had arrived before him, sent in word to say that although, from personal respect for himself, they had till then retained the white cockade, they must warn him that they were about to hoist the tricolour and march towards the emperor under those colours, not to fight him, but to support him. They besought him not to leave them, and so forth.

The marshal's only reply was to take post to Jean-d'heurs, where he picked me up, and without stopping took me to Metz. Immediately upon his arrival, he declared the place in state of siege. The seat of the deliberations was naturally the Princerie, where the marshal was surrounded by the *prefect*, the generals, the superior officers, and all the leading men of the country. The proclamation declaring the city in state of siege was in the king's name, and was posted at every corner. Part of the town and garrison was seething. What a life I led during those hours which corresponded with the emperor's entry into Paris!

My rooms were on the first floor, overlooking the Place d'Armes, the whole of the ground-floor belonging to the marshal and his service. I only came down for meals, and even then I hardly took time to finish them, so tumultuous were they and interrupted. I had gone back to my room on the evening of the second day after our arrival, and was sitting by the fire reflecting sadly upon the events of the day and of those which were to ensue, when a vague noise was heard outside, increasing to such an extent, as it drew nearer, that I went to my window and saw the whole of the Place d'Armes literally covered with people. Distracted with fear, I went down to my husband, whom I found receiving the reports of a number of terrified people, who announced a most decided disturbance.

"Well," said the marshal, "what do they think? What do they want?"

"Some say that M. le Duc de Berry is here, and that you have declared the city in state of siege in order to keep a refuge for him; others say that you mean to open the gates to the Prussians."

These words were received with cold disdain; and the marshal only said to me:

"Go back, my dear, and stay in your room."

With my face glued to my window and my ears pricked up, I saw and listened to the riot, which rose like the surge of the sea. They threatened to force the gates of the house. The marshal went down and mingled with the crowd; he spoke, and was listened to. During this time, an attempt was made to divide the crowd and make it separate peacefully; but how difficult it was to persuade the troops to put down a clamour which expressed their own sentiments!

Colonel Oudinot's regiment, a model of discipline, was still perfectly obedient to its chief, and took a large part in the allaying of the riot. Their measures were partly seconded by the lateness of the hour and the badness of the weather. The marshal's guard was trebled, and he spent the whole night in receiving all kinds of reports and giving endless orders.

When the morning came, the town was still disturbed, but seemed less threatening. I did not leave my window. Towards mid-day I heard an increased noise, but this time they were shouts of joy; all heads were upraised, and following their direction, I saw that they were hoisting in front of me, upon the topmost tower of the cathedral, the tricolour flag. . . . All was over! The marshal's authority was disowned; there was nothing left for him to do but go away. Moreover, the king had abandoned the seat of government without giving any directions, of whatever kind, to your father. Since the tardy and futile letter of the Duc de Berry, relating to the grenadiers, he had not received a single order emanating from the Bourbons. In all that he had done he had been prompted solely by his duty towards them; and this duty he had loyally fulfilled. And thus, when he saw with his eyes those three colours which had once been so dear to him, and which he could not now salute, he gave orders for his immediate departure. We left that evening, escorted from the town by Colonel Oudinot's Hussars. No hostile demonstration came, to our knowledge, to add to the sadness of this fresh journey.

It was a strange and contradictory position in which your father found himself placed, obliged to withdraw before the glorious flag for which he had fought victoriously for twenty years of his life. Ah, how cruel it was! But he had been relieved by the emperor's first abdication from his oath to the three colours; and as he had accepted the command of Metz under the white flag, he was bound not to leave under any other emblem."

******

On leaving Metz, Oudinot wrote the following letter to the new Minister for War, his old comrade Marshal Davout:

> Metz, March 1815.
>
> Unable and unwilling to play a double part, I am leaving Metz in order to repair to Bar-sur-Ornain, my residence. I will leave General Duruth in command of the 3rd Division. This general officer will fill the post capably and trustworthily.
>
> I only ask one thing of you, my dear minister, and that is not to enquire into my means of existence. I will sell the little I possess to pay the more delicate portion of my debts. Prevent anyone from spying into my mode of life, and tell them that

Oudinot, in the midst of his unhappiness, is incapable of an act of perfidy.

Your friend,

(Signed) Marshal Oudinot.

This letter probably crossed the following appeal from Davout:

War Office,
Paris, 21 March 1815.

My dear marshal,

You must know and have learnt from published documents the nature of recent events and their results.

All Frenchmen must rally to prevent civil war and drive back the foreigner. There is no need to recall these sentiments to the heart of an Oudinot. I am informed by a general whom we both hold in esteem that, when separated from the Guard at Chaumont, your one plan was to bring back to the frontier places already threatened and coveted from abroad the troops which you had set in movement in another direction. In this resolution not under any pretext to suffer an invasion of French territory, I recognized your devotion to the common interests of the country. The orders which I shall transmit to you from the Emperor will have no other motive or object. I long, both as your friend and as a minister, to give, or rather to repeat to you this assurance.

Kind regards.

(Signed) Marshal Prince d'Eckmühl.

Oudinot replied to this appeal:

Metz, March 1815.

My dear marshal,

You were right in believing that in returning to my strongholds I had no other object than that of preserving France and employing every means to prevent the foreigner from entering, even in small numbers. His threats on the frontier have led me to declare them in state of siege, after taking the advice of the civil and military notables, who have unanimously decided, in assembly, that there was a case of urgency.

I am thus hedged in amidst parties, and in a position difficult to sustain owing to the divergence of opinions. Providence and their confidence will save me, I hope, from this pass. As to my principles, you know them, my friend, and you will never compromise yourself by answering for them; for they are as pure as the actions of my whole life.

Speaking of this, I have received a curious letter from General Loison: he informs me, among other things, that the emperor, remembering my old and loyal services, forgets the past.

Ah! I ask myself what the emperor can have to reproach me with; for, besides my whole conduct during his reign, my constant fidelity can have left him nothing to desire from me. Since then, I am faithful to my new master. There is therefore no occasion to hint at a pardon which, for that matter, I would never wish for, had I been for an instant guilty. My existence would be a burden to me if it were stained with one dishonourable fault. On the other hand, my friend, I will never commit a baseness to recover an esteem which is due to me. Remember this; and should I have to drag the remainder of my life in misery, I shall always be Grenadier Oudinot, a title which will never cease to delight me.

In any case, my dear minister, write to me and believe that, whatever the events which the future may have in store for me, I shall know how to die as I have lived.

Your old friend,

(Signed) Marshal Oudinot.

★★★★★★

We travelled all night in the direction of Paris, where the marshal wished to go without delay to explain his position to the emperor, and to beg him to understand it and leave him, in good faith, to the repose of his fields. We had passed la Ferté-sous-Jouarre, when we saw a general officer, mounted on a post-nag, ride up to our carriage, which pulled up.

"Ah, is that you, Trommelin?" asked the marshal.

"Yes, *monseigneur*; I bring you a despatch from the Imperial Minister for War."

"Davout?"

"I asked to be allowed to bring it."

"Is it an order of exile?" asked the marshal.

"Yes, and it is that I might explain the motive to you and put it to you in a less harsh light, that I begged and obtained leave to be the bearer."

A shed stood by the roadside. "Let us get down here," said the marshal, and in a few moments we were listening to the comments of poor General Trommelin, who was unable to make any change in the principal fact, which was that an order to withdraw to his estates had been addressed to the marshal in the name of the emperor by the Minister for War.

******

Here is the text of the letter written by Davout:

War Office,
Paris, 26 March 1815.
Monsieur le maréchal,
I am commanded to express to you the emperor's dissatisfaction at all that was done at Metz to-prevent the inhabitants from knowing what was happening in France, and to suppress the patriotic ardour of the people and the soldiery, and also at your permitting the Prefect to publish declarations of the Congress throughout the town.
"His Majesty desires that you should retire to your estates in Lorraine until new orders.
I have the honour, &c,
(Signed) Marshal Prince d'Eckmühl,
Minister for War.

******

"He is very angry with me, no doubt?" asked the marshal.

"Yes, yes, but he will calm down."

"He has anticipated me, for I was going to tell him that I asked nothing of him," replied your father. "No matter; goodbye, Trommelin; drive on."

The postillions faced about, we took a few hours' rest at la Ferté-sous-Jouarre, and the next day we were at Jean-d'heurs. As in all the trials of his life, my husband had shown, during these first moments, the most remarkable moral force and correctness of judgment; but it did not take long to see that this new position of a suspect to the powers that ruled his country would be a difficult one for him to undergo. Sadness was not familiar to him; if a few passing clouds came and obscured his brow, he soon accepted distraction, and everybody resumed his serenity when he had recovered his. But this time he remained bent beneath the weight of his preoccupations, and this burden which

I bore with him, without delivering him from it, was very heavy upon me too.

Meanwhile France was in a ferment. The king, *monsieur* and M. le Duc de Berry had gone to Belgium, after disbanding their Military Households. M. le Duc d'Angoulême was valiantly striving to defend his cause in the province from which he took his title. But in the east they swore only by the emperor. The majority had fallen absolutely under the influence of the prestige attached to his name; but our district, which was entirely a military one and naturally Imperialist, did not give a fair idea of the opinion of the mass of the population, which caught a new glimpse of a foreign war. The Congress of Vienna was still sitting. We were represented at it by M. le Prince de Talleyrand; and surely he, the intermediary of the Bourbons in 1814, was not likely to attenuate the demands of the Allies upon the emperor in 1815.

However, five or six days after the marshal's exile to Jeand'heurs, M. Jacqueminot came travelling express. He had left Metz as the marshal's *aide-de-camp*, and returned a week later with the appointment from the emperor as colonel of a regiment of lancers. Let us hasten to add, however, that his first thought in this new situation had carried him towards his former chief, and that, knowing that the emperor desired to see him, he had begged to be allowed to carry the order of recall, which for the time he regarded as a great happiness.

The marshal left for Paris, leaving me provisionally at Jeand'heurs with his son Auguste. Many casualties had already impeded his youthful career. Destined to be a page of the emperor, this plan was upset in 1814. In 1815 he had entered the Chevau-Légers, and had just seen his company disbanded. For the moment he had no other reminder of his status than an Imperial order of exile against all that composed the King's Household, which was not to approach within thirty leagues of Paris.

My husband sent us his news. A few moments after his arrival in the Rue de Bourgogne, he received a visit from General Bertrand, who had come to fetch him from the emperor. The latter, on seeing your father, went up to him and said, in a tone that was half ironical and half severe:

"Well, Monsieur le Duc de Reggio! and what have the Bourbons done more for you than I, to make you want to defend them so finely against my approach?"

The marshal's reply was ready to hand; he had nothing to deny and nothing to excuse; and it was received favourably as a request for inaction of which the reason was well understood.

"I will serve no one, since I shall not serve you, Sire," said the marshal. "I shall remain in my retirement; but pray have sufficient confidence in me not to have me spied on by your police. I could not endure that."

With this the interview ended. A few days later the marshal dined with the emperor, but they did not see each other again alone.

Meantime everything was assuming a fierce aspect, and even in our peaceful valley of the Saulx the population were becoming both suspicious and hostile. I besought the marshal to let Auguste and me come to him; he consented, and after taking some measures of safety for our houses at Bar and Jeand'heurs, we set out for Paris. The excitement was great all along our road, which was covered with the extraordinary levies which the emperor was urging on. I dared not face that movement at night, nor was I much easier in my room at an inn. The appearance of Paris did not tend to calm me. The federals from the suburbs had been reviewed that morning by the emperor, and this had increased the general ferment

We found the marshal in company with Victor, who had been replaced in command of the 1st Hussars. Thus my husband and his two sons found themselves in a state of forced inaction at a time when all were under arms! For men of their temperament this was a bitter trial. And then what divisions in parties and even families! General Comte Pajol had embraced the side of the Empire. General Comte de Lorencez had remained faithful to the Restoration, like the marshal and his sons.

We decided to hire a small place in the valley of Montmorency. We had need of air and silence; these preparations, these rumours of war, of a war threatening our native soil, which seemed on the other side to be destined to be torn by civil war in the west, were more than the three Oudinots could endure. The present was almost insupportable, and the future offered no probable compensation. In spite of the reforms in our household, the sale of our carriages, part of my diamonds, and so on, we had hardly enough to suffice for the needs of the moment.

We went about almost the whole day, mostly on foot, sometimes on donkeys. This mode of locomotion was a novelty for the marshal, and sometimes provoked a smile from him. It was cherry-time; and we often went and robbed the fine trees of the valley, although never omitting to pay for our depredations. We were all young, and this life possessed a charm for all of us during the first few days.

Meantime the emperor had set out to take command of the army which he had so promptly organized. The first blow was to be struck in Belgium; and so soon as we were able to calculate that the time for this blow had come, our anxiety resumed the upper hand. We eagerly awaited the news of the fighting. This was at first favourable, having reference to the engagement at Fleurus. Two days passed by, and on the third, as we were sitting down to breakfast, we saw first M. de Bourcet and then M. du Plessy come up, who told us in a few words the story of Waterloo!

The terrible consequences of this event at once presented themselves to the marshal, who, without yet making up his mind as to what he should do, set out immediately for Paris with his two sons and his officers, leaving to me the care of settling our accounts and moving. It was night when I returned to Paris, a night in June. Nothing seemed to augment the usual movement of the town at this season, and I learnt on my arrival in the Rue de Bourgogne that the excitement had centred round the Chamber of Deputies, which had declared its sitting permanent. I also learnt that the emperor had arrived not at the Tuileries but at the Élysée-Bourbon; that he was talking of a new abdication, but this time in favour of the King of Rome, asking for himself the command as general-in-chief of the remnants of the army which would have to be opposed without delay to the victorious enemy advancing upon Paris.

The emperor cannot have long retained his illusions on the chances of power which remained to him; because in 1815 it was much less the wish of the nation than of the army that had brought him back from Elba.

During the days of excitement which preceded the return of the king, the marshal had sent Victor to Belgium. His errand was to learn from the king if the proposal made in the Chamber of Deputies to give Marshal Oudinot the command of the National Guard of the Seine was agreeable to His Majesty. This proposal was accepted, but it was not put into execution until October. It was these wise and devoted troops which alone maintained order and dignity in Paris during the influx of the invading armies. It had much to do, notably at the Clichy barriers, which the more zealous among the Royalists desired to force in order to go to Saint-Denis during the king's stay there, a stay devoted to treating peacefully, if possible.

Auguste, in his capacity as a Chevau-Léger, had succeeded, with some difficulty, in reaching Saint-Denis and presenting himself to the king. With my husband's consent I took the same step, together with the Marquise du Roure, and soon Louis XVIII. received us with truly paternal affability. All his circle welcomed me with the greatest kindness. The marshal had paid his visit to Saint-Denis earlier. The king had awarded him the most flattering reception; and this was only justice.

The 8th of July was fixed for the king's fresh entry into Paris. At noon, the marshal in uniform, followed by his *aides-de-camp*, set out on horseback from the Rue de Bourgogne for Saint-Denis. During the long drive, there reigned a sort of gloomy tranquillity which gave food for reflection at the moment of a significant event, occurring in Paris, always so full of life. The marshal has since told me that he was not free from anxiety respecting the march of the procession. When the king appeared, all were able to see that he showed himself calm and smiling as in the past. In the evening there were public *fêtes*.

The emperor had retired to Malmaison, where he lived disarmed and powerless, from the force of things. How great must his moral sufferings have been! But it must be admitted that at this moment of reaction, when all personal interests were at stake, the general attention was for a while turned away from him. His departure, his journey, and even his embarkation upon the English ship, the *Bellerophon*, did not at first attract public attention. It was not until later, when people had heard of his magnificent letter to the British government, and had seen the manner in which that government had abused the confidence placed in them by a disarmed enemy, that the remembrance of many and the sympathy of some returned to the illustrious exile.

The Allies entered Paris shortly after the king, and laid hands upon the military command of the place as in time of war. I have seen a bivouac of Prussians in the Carrousel; I have seen the English in the Champs-Élysées and in the Bois de Boulogne, which was in part destroyed to keep up their bivouac fires. There was not a French uniform to be seen in Paris. The National Guard alone did duty, conjointly with the foreign troops.

The marshal resumed his place as Minister of State, and his office continued to be besieged every morning by those who were occupied with him in the interests of government and those who came to him with requests or complaints. My mother, who had joined us at the commencement of the second invasion, had since settled at Versailles with the Guérivière children.

It was at this time that the Chamber of Deputies was revived. Your father was appointed chairman of the electoral college of the Meuse. What sometimes gave us great sorrow, in the midst of our personal satisfaction, was the state of minds, which seemed to grow excited rather than calmer since the restoration of the Royal Government. I doubt whether the unhappy Colonel de la Bédoyère was paler than I was, when I heard of his condemnation. I knew that he left behind him a young wife whom he adored, a child in the cradle, and a family in despair. I learnt later that, when he reached the place of execution, he gave the order to fire, and ordered them to aim at his heart, on which spot was later found the shattered portrait of his wife.

On his return from the elections, the marshal resumed his busy life in Paris. He endeavoured to bring his influence to bear upon the princes in favour of clemency; he always found an echo in their hearts, but too many diverse elements mingled in the government for the marshal's work always to bear fruit. No one has ever known or ever will know all that your father has said, particularly in favour of the army; but God knows it, and that is a great consolation. It was with profound sorrow that he saw the lists of proscriptions following upon one another.

Towards the end of the summer, the armies of the Allies were removed from Paris and ordered to different parts of the country. In this distribution, our poor Lorraine was not spared. It bore this enormous charge for about three years. Each day the Allies gave fresh proofs of their ill-will. They despoiled our museums; they sought means to destroy the monuments which commemorated our victories over them. One day, among others, I saw the marshal return from the council in a state of great excitement. I do not know what fly more spiteful than usual had bitten the ferocious Blücher, who was commanding-in-chief in Paris; but the king was suddenly interrupted in the midst of his work, and told that the Prussian general was preparing on his own authority to blow up the Pont d'Iéna.

"Go and tell him," replied Louis XVIII., "that I only beg him to give me time to come and place myself upon that monument before he destroys it."

The bridge was respected.

A second visit which the Czar Alexander paid us enabled us to judge that, although he had had reserved the same feelings for the marshal as in the preceding year, he looked at France in a very different light. Oh, how cold he had grown concerning the interests of our poor country! And yet it was to him that the country was indebted in that it was not still worse treated and even perhaps divided. . . . He had not announced his visit this time, and he found the Marshal and me alone. It was during this intimate and unconstrained interview that he impressed us with the opinions which I have uttered above.

About the middle of October, there called upon us, in the Rue de Bourgogne, M. de Vaublanc, the former *Prefect* of Metz, who had since become Minister of the Interior. After a short conversation in the drawing-room, he asked to speak to the marshal alone in his study. He entered and came out again without laying aside a certain solemnity of which I soon possessed the enigma. The minister had come in the king's name to offer your father the command-in-chief of the National Guard of Paris and the surrounding districts. Your father hesitated; the post did not seem to agree with his tastes and habits; and yet the position was a splendid one.

In the end, and after much urging on the part of the king, the ministers and his own friends, the marshal yielded, and towards the end of October we bade goodbye for ever to our dear little house in the Rue de Bourgogne, in order to install ourselves in the staff-offices of the National Guard, in the Rue Grange-Batelière, which had formerly been the town-house of the Duc de Choiseul, Louis XV.'s minister. It was a vast and superbly furnished mansion. A numerous establishment, kept up like all the rest at the expense of the city of Paris, filled the entrance-halls (there were two entrances) in their capacity as concierges, ushers, office-messengers, and so on, while the drawing-rooms were made brilliant by a numerous staff, which was always on service by turns. Guard-posts enlivened the courtyards by day and night. One of these posts was for the principal entrance, the other for the Rue le Pelletier. They communicated, for the performance of the service both by day and night, by an underground passage which ran beneath my private apartments. There was a perpetual movement.

All who were able to rally usefully to the exclusive service of the National Guard had hastened to us. The marshal numbered on his staff, and among the *aides-de-camp* wearing this uniform, celebrated names of every kind. Those of the Faubourg Saint-Germain constituted the majority. Among the twelve legions of infantry were several commanded by a Montmorency, a La Rochefoucauld, and so on. The cavalry had at its head the proud and noble Duc de Fitz-James, one of the king's most devoted and enlightened servants. He had under his orders such names as Caumont, Boisgelin, and kindred families.

So soon as we were installed, the Marshal issued a permanent invitation to his table for breakfast and dinner to the officers in command of the guard-posts, and this independently of the *aides-de-camp* and so forth. Eleven years were spent by me in this company; and this is not said by way of complaint, because, apart from the good worked by this incessant fusion, I thus met at my table a vast number of personalities whom it was interesting to know. Magistrates, financiers, artists, authors, poets, celebrated actors, all Paris of that time passed in review before my eyes; and as on the whole I had never been accustomed to domestic *tête-à-têtes*, this overflow of guests, of which the marshal seemed never to weary, inconvenienced me in no way.

There was much question of establishing a Royal Guard. The first elements were to be taken from the brave old remnants which had been so disastrously exiled behind the Loire at the commencement of the first Restoration. The marshal was to receive one of the four commands which it was proposed to create, and which were to succeed each other every quarter, of these picked troops. The holders were soon appointed: they were Marshals Oudinot, Macdonald, Victor and Marmont.

But while the government very properly tried to reorganize itself on a strong footing, very regrettable facts continued to take place and to be foreshadowed. No day passed without its political trial! I went to bed one night heart-broken at the sentence of death passed upon the Comte de La Valette, who was to be guillotined the next day upon the Place de Grève for having actively worked against the Restoration and delivered state secrets to the Elban conspirators. I did not know him at all, but I thought of his wife and children. How great was my relief when I learnt in the morning that he had made good his escape!

We were less fortunate in the matter of Marshal Ney, that ever deplorable affair. I have told you of the letter which he wrote to the marshal, on the eve of his defection. Though the terms in which it was couched proved his fickleness, they justified him at least against any charge of premeditation. Full of confidence in the usefulness of this document for the purposes of the trial, my husband had hastened to hand it to the *maréchale*, and heartily congratulated himself upon in this way becoming a witness for the defence of his unfortunate companion-in-arms. The length of the trial was an agony to the marshal. The last of these unhappy days arrived and passed without any news coming from the Luxembourg; the verdict was not pronounced until night: a sleepless night, alas! We still hoped in the royal clemency; but before daybreak, Victor came to share his grief with us and to tell us that all would soon be over, and that the marshal was to be shot on the Place de l'Observatoire.

It seems hardly credible, my children! But among a large number of well-intentioned people, who had till then been always humane and kind, there had arisen a fatal agreement to do violence to the king's inclinations and to persuade him that his crown depended upon his showing no mercy this time . . . And yet an act of clemency would have been the most politic act of this renewal of the reign, and in my family we did not wait for long years to pass before taking this view.

I wish I could wipe out from my memory the remarks I heard uttered, both on this event, the most notable of all, and on many others that occurred about this time. Women, women especially, who took so great a part, unfortunately, in the politics of the time, often uttered ferocious phrases. These roused my indignation and pained me to the core; and it was from this period that dated my horror of all party spirit.

The king had promised the marshal to be the godfather of the child we were expecting. The Duc de Choiseul, who was then Chief of Staff of the National Guard of the Seine, under my husband's orders, on learning this news, said to me, as he was dining with me one day:

"That is excellent, *Madame*: but you should have the whole city of Paris for godmother, that is clear. Do not laugh, *Madame la duchesse*; it would be both becoming and charming."

This led to no result, however, and the choice which the king made of Mme. la Duchesse d'Angoulême for godmother left me no cause for regret. The baptism of Louise was celebrated in the chapel of the Tuileries, where her royal godfather, Louis XVIII., and her saintly godmother, Mme. la Duchesse d'Angoulême, attended in person. The administration of the sacrament was entrusted to the Grand Almoner of France, His Eminence Cardinal de Talleyrand-Périgord.

The Duc de Choiseul was succeeded as Chief of Staff by the Duc de Mortemart, a brave and worthy friend, whose noble heart beat with all the honour which befitted his lofty birth. He became closely attached, in thought and friendship, to the marshal, for whom he always kept up, and still keeps up, a real cult.

Meanwhile, the projected Royal Guard came to be realized. It was decided during the winter that the king should hold a review in the

Carrousel and in the courtyard of the Tuileries, and it was considered that the National Guard, which had till then executed the service of Paris since the final occupation by the enemy, ought also to receive from the sovereign, on the same day, a mark of gratitude and remembrance.

We reached the end of March. I had gone one evening to my husband's study and, alone with him, I was enjoying one of those opportunities for unrestrained conversation which were so precious to both of us, and which the multitude of our occupations caused to become so rare. Suddenly the door was opened by two of our intimates, the Duc de Fitz-James and the Comte de la Ferronnays. The latter, so soon as he entered, took my husband by his arm and led him to his room, while the other, sitting down by my side before the fire, began to jest on all sorts of subjects, as was usual with him. I was laughing heartily when the others returned.

"You will never guess," said my husband, "what M. de la Ferronnays has just come and proposed for you."

"All that comes from him must be good to accept," I replied, without being in the least able to guess what they wanted of me.

"Tell her all," said M. de la Ferronnays.

Thereupon they both went away.

"Well," said my husband, "M. le Duc de Berry, who is to marry a princess of Naples, seventeen years of age, offers you the post of Mistress of the Robes."

I was taken aback, and wept.

"But reflect," said the marshal, "that at your age it is a fine thing, it is an exceptional thing, to receive such a mark of confidence and esteem."

"What more have I to wish for, to satisfy all my pride, than to be your wife?" I cried. "I confess I look with dread at the idea of our freedom being fettered, our home abandoned. I see before me a gilded slavery, but a slavery nevertheless. However, my friend, does it suit you?"

"Impossible to refuse," said my husband.

I accepted, therefore, since I had to. The marshal wished me to go at once and thank the king.

"I have approved this appointment," said His Majesty, "but it was not I who made it; my nephew selected his bride's household himself. It is a great business to be a Mistress of the Robes," he continued.

I looked at the king; he had an air of being so penetrated with the importance of my functions that he set the climax to my flutter. It was in this condition that I went downstairs to M. le Duc de Berry. He thanked me effusively for accepting. His expressions were filled with gratitude and were almost respectful. I asked him when he expected the princess.

"Alas!" he said, "I have only two months more of liberty."

I looked at him in surprise.

"Do not be astonished at my melancholy, *Madame la duchesse*," he said. "I am only marrying from a sense of obligation; I only know my betrothed by a portrait which makes her look very ugly. No matter, the die is cast, and the dear child shall never know what it costs me to submit to the yoke."

I had to receive the successive visits of the persons who composed with me the young princess's household. Here is the list, in hierarchical order. I am bound to place myself first:

Mistress of the Robes, the Maréchale Duchesse de Reggio; First Lady of the Bedchamber, the Comtesse de la Ferronays; six ladies-in-waiting: the Vicomtesse de Gontaut-Biron, the Comtesse Francois de Bouille; the Marquise de Béthisy; the Comtesse d'Hautefort; the Marquise de Gourgues; the Comtesse de Lauriston.

Then came the gentlemen:

The Duc de Lévis (author of the *Maximes*, &c), First Lord-in-Waiting; the Comte de Mesnard, First Groom j the Marquis de Sassenay, private secretary.

First Bedchamber-Woman, Mme. de Wathaire. I will not mention the names of the bedchamber-women-in-ordinary, nor of the rest of the establishment of the third class.

In accordance with the ceremonial which was adopted at the time of the marriage of Mme. la Duchesse de Bourgogne, the general impulse was supposed to be given to the princess's household by the Mistress of the Robes, the responsible editor, as it were, of all public ceremonial. This is what the king had wished to convey to me when he looked me between the eyes on the occasion of my recent audience and said, "It is a great business to be a Mistress of the Robes."

Soon after, the Marquis de Dreux-Bréze, Grand Master of the Ceremonies, sent me a long chart containing my instructions, drawn up by himself, and confirming the extent and the multiplicity of details of my task. To my great regret, I have been quite unable to find this very curious official document, from which, on my own responsibility, I struck out a number of superannuated items, which it would have been worse than useless to keep up in our day; but there remained quite enough to keep me occupied in the essential part, of which I omitted nothing.

I was recommended, and I thought it in good taste, to go and visit Mme. la Duchesse de Duras, who had been Mistress of the Robes to Queen Marie Leczinska. Her great age kept her away from society. She received me very well. Very tall, and wearing a great black head-dress, she cast upon me a not unkindly, but very searching glance. She gave me many hints on the powers and attributes of a mistress of the robes, things which have since been modified by time; as did also Mme. la Duchesse de Vauguyon, who had been attached to the service of Madame Élisabeth.

The young princess was married by procuration at Naples, her paternal uncle, the Prince of Salerno, representing the bridegroom; and the time was drawing near for her departure for Marseilles, where we were to arrive in time for her landing and for what was known as the remise, that is to say the handing over of the princess by the Neapolitan Ambassador to the French Ambassador, who would fulfil his mission at our head.

A number of the household were sent on in advance: Mmes. de la Ferronays, de Gontaut and de Bouillé; Messrs de Levis and de Mesnard; two officers of the Gardes du Corps; a master of the ceremonies; an almoner. All these were to wait indefinitely at Marseilles. They came to take leave of me before starting. I also had orders to give to all the waiting-women who followed each other in my apartments, which were crowded with a multitude of tradespeople, who brought me articles of the toilet with which I was obliged to supply myself in order that every-thing might be ready when, at the last moment, I too should have to set out.

For the first time in my life I was about to undertake, far from my husband and without his assistance or advice, an entirely new life, one depending upon my sheer initiative, and strewn with pitfalls. I was about to endeavour to subject to my will, to my advice, an un-known personality, who on her side would perhaps display certain caprices to which I should be unable to yield; and it was to these possibilities that I was sacrificing my domestic joys, which had been so greatly increased a few weeks ago by the birth of my youngest child! But it was inevitable; and on the 11th of May 1816, my husband put me into my carriage. I was all in tears. With me was good Mme. Cossa, my new maid; two of our domestics rode on the box, and in front of the carriage rode a courier in the Royal livery, to order post-horses. I was too nervous, and still too weak after my confinement, to be able to travel at night.

I was compelled therefore to sleep at an hotel each night; but this was my only delay, with the exception of an excursion which I made at Vaucluse, whence I drove with the *prefect*, the Comte de Saint-Chamans, and his sister, the Comtesse de Lambertye, to visit the Castle of the Popes at Avignon. Nevertheless, to my great regret and annoyance, this was sufficient to make me late at my journey's end. I had just passed Aix when I saw dashing up a courier all covered with white ribands. He was smacking his whip, and seemed bathed in perspiration. He stopped before my carriage and told me that he had come to announce the landing of Mme. la Duchesse de Berry[1], who had come into port safely, and had been received at the Lazaretto. Full of disappointment, I hastened on at full speed to Marseilles. M. le Comte de Villeneuve, the eldest of the five brothers bearing the name, came to receive me and to show me to the room which was prepared for me. It was adjacent to that which the princess was to occupy on her arrival at the *prefect's*. He confirmed what the courier had told me.

"We received Her Royal Highness," he added, "as nearly as the inexorable rules of quarantine would permit. Our boats rowed out to the frigate in which she made the voyage, and escorted her to the foot of the Lazaretto stairs. She took up her abode there with none but her Neapolitan suite, with the sole exception of Mme. la Comtesse de la Ferronnays, who has been locked up with her."

"But," I asked, "cannot I also be admitted into the Lazaretto?"

"It is too late, *Madame*," replied the *prefect*; "you would be obliged to remain twenty-four hours after the others had gone, since the rule is that everyone must complete the prescribed ten days."

I must needs wait; and the next morning I sent in my name to the young princess, who soon appeared behind the grating which separated the two rooms in which we were. We were each of us watched by warders belonging to the Lazaretto service. Their sombre faces and gloomy costumes reminded me of the pictures of the plague of 1720 and 1721. This recollection contrasted strangely with the joyful mission which I had to fulfil; but soon recovering myself, I was about to place in the hands of the young bride, who seemed to me charmingly white and pink, the letters which the French Royal Family had given

1. *The Rebellious Duchess*, the adventures of the Duchess of Berri and her attempt to overthrow French Monarchy, by Paul F. S. Dermoncourt also published by Leonaur.

me for her, when I was suddenly stopped by one of the severe guardians of whom I have spoken, and obliged to deposit my despatches upon a table on the other side of the grating, where the princess came and took them. This was to avoid any personal contact between her and me.

Mme. la Duchesse de Berry was not pretty, but there was an air of extreme youth about her whole person which disposed one in her favour. She was only seventeen, and did not look more than fifteen. This explained, in the eyes of the French population which she had to pass through, the timid silence with which she accepted the harangues and demonstration with which she was received along the journey from Marseilles to Paris.

We arranged for my daily visits to the Lazaretto, and the time which was left to me at the *prefect's* was devoted to the thousand preliminaries connected with my duties. At last the day came for the *remise*. Clad in a rich court-dress, followed by Mmes. de Gontaut and de Bouillé, preceded by the Duc d'Havré, the King of France's ambassador, the Duc de Lévis, the Comte de Mesnard, the Marquis de Rochefort, &c, I set out in a gala-carriage to drive from the *prefect's* to the Hôtel-de-Ville, while the princess, her Neapolitan suite and the ambassador of the king her grandfather arrived from the Lazaretto by sea. The population of Marseilles, in its enthusiasm, had divided itself into two to welcome the Royal bride. Part followed her progress in boats, the other crowded the approaches to the Hôtel-de-Ville and the streets through which the procession would have to pass.

Installed in its place at the appointed time, in the principal hall of the Hôtel-de-Ville, the French court, with the ambassador at its head, silently awaited the entrance of the Neapolitan Court. In the middle of the hall stood an enormous table, destined to hold the documents which were to be signed by the two diplomatists. As I have said, the ceremonial was based upon that which was followed at the wedding of the Duchesse de Bourgogne. It was therefore a sort of unrehearsed performance which was not without its terrors for the boldest of us.

At last the folding-doors opposite us opened wide, and admitted the Prince de Scylla, who accompanied his princess, while the Duc d'Havré stepped forward and stated the mission which he had received both from the king his master and from her Royal consort. The Neapolitan Ambassador, increasing the embarrassment of the position, replied forthwith; and his words were immediately followed by this curious pantomime: the Duc d'Havré, by strength of the ratifications which had been exchanged, led over to our side her whom he had just greeted as Duchesse de Berry, and while the Neapolitan Court remained motionless in its place, we, as had been arranged beforehand, each assumed our respective functions. Mine consisted in first having myself officially presented, with my names and titles, by the Duc d'Havré; but so soon as this formality was completed, the latter became as it were the subordinate of myself as Mistress of the Robes, and from that moment he was not allowed to do anything without my knowledge and participation.

Approaching Mme. la Duchesse de Berry, I presented to her in my turn all the small French court, commencing with the Duc d'Havré, who, now that his duties as ambassador were accomplished, simply ranked as one of ourselves. None of the spectators of these different movements can have understood much about them. I myself thought them strange, but I was following a programme, and as a rule I made it a point to depart from precedent as little as possible, and only when I considered certain portions to be too superannuated.

Soon the First Lady of the Bedchamber, the Comtesse de la Ferronnays, assuming her personal functions, took Mme. la Duchesse de Berry to a room where all her French garments were prepared. She was made to take off, down to her shift, all those in which she was dressed. This over, she reappeared in the hall of the Hôtel-de-Ville, where all the civil and military authorities awaited her.

Her timidity prevented her from replying to all the addresses presented to her, although if all these serious and pompous speeches had resembled that of the Comte de Bastard, who received her at Lyons, she would have avoided all necessity for reply of any sort.

"Daughter of St. Louis," he said, after bowing profoundly before her, "give us sons who resemble you."

There was no answer possible to a command of this description.

The journey was a long triumphal progress. Reception succeeded reception, *fête* followed upon *fête* at the different towns we halted at, until at last we reached the little town of Nemours, the last stage at which we were to pass the night before arriving at Fontainebleau, where the king, the bridegroom and the whole court awaited the Royal traveller.

Chapter 9

Death of Napoleon

The latter part of the day spent at Nemours was devoted to meditation. Her Royal Highness had been accompanied by her almoner along the whole journey, and at this moment was more fully occupied with him than ever. She was naturally much excited at the thought of the coming interview.

The next morning, after Mass, at which Her Highness partook of Holy Communion, and after a private breakfast, we all assumed court dress, for it was in this attire that we were to travel the six leagues which separated us from Fontainebleau.

The meeting-place was at the cross-roads at St. Hérem's Cross, which stands in the middle of the forest. The carriages of the king and the bride were to arrive at the same time from opposite directions upon this vast expanse of lawn, which was easily able to contain all the carriages and their horses and those of the escort. Signals had been arranged along both roads, in order to hasten or slacken the respective speed of the carriages, so as to enable them, as prescribed by the ceremonial, to arrive simultaneously.

We followed our princess, to whom the king, who had alighted on his side, stretched out his arms in order to prevent her from kneeling to him, as was also prescribed by the order of ceremonies. Without waiting to read the letters from the King of Naples presented to him by the princess, the king re-entered with her the Royal chariot, which was all of glass and of a dimension to carry the whole family. We followed in our own carriage, and in this way made our entrance into Fontainebleau.

In spite of the frigid solemnity of the etiquette followed on this occasion, there was a certain display of sentiment, and M. le Duc de Berry had seized an opportunity to say to Mme. de la Ferronays and myself:

"Ah, you bring me some one incomparably more attractive than I had imagined."

He seemed delivered from a nightmare, and in his joy he thanked us as though we had moulded the young arrival with our own hands.

There was a solemn dinner, finished by a solemn evening. A game of *loto-dauphin*, over which the king presided, formed part of the programme, and I found it a very imposing task, I can assure you, to have to call out the numbers in my turn, amid profound silence. When I had finished this duty, I thought that was all; but the king, looking me straight in the face, asked:

"Have you finished, *Madame la duchesse?*"

"Yes, Sire, the blanks are all filled."

"But at the last number you ought to say 'and,' which explains to all of us that you have finished calling out the numbers."

I remembered it for the future.

We retired early, and the next morning we drove to Paris, where an official entry was made.

Next came the day of the marriage ceremony at Notre Dame. The procession and the religious service were very imposing and fine. All the State bodies were represented. The entire garrison under arms and the National Guard had difficulty in restraining the flood of the population, which rolled in billows from the Tuileries to the cathedral. The weather was magnificent.

The whole programme, which dated back to the days of Louis XIV., was followed out to its last limits; and after the fete which ended the evening of the wedding, the king, followed by all the court, men and women, conducted the bride and bridegroom to their room, and when they were in bed, bid them goodnight in public. After taking part in this strange ceremony, I was at last able to return home. Need I describe my joy on meeting my dear ones again, or my delight at being able to take my little daughter upon my knees!

My duties as Mistress of the Robes, which were encumbered with a multiplicity of details, did not compel me to follow up the whole of the service out-of-doors, which was divided among the eight young ladies-in-waiting whom I have named to you. I organized their services, and strictly speaking, I was only obliged to do mine on Sundays, for the king's Mass, the receptions of ambassadors, which took place periodically, and the presentation of distinguished foreigners to Her Royal Highness, which could only be performed by myself; and under some other exceptional circumstances. But it would have been very ungracious of me to harden myself against the affectionate appeals which were made to me outside my obligations, especially when I observed the price which was put upon my presence and the care bestowed on the selection of occasions which would be the least irksome and the most agreeable to me.

Among the excursions in which I took part at this time, I consider that to Chantilly one of the most interesting. I have told you how the old Prince de Condé, who spent the last two or three years of his life there, had no longer the complete use of his faculties; but the Royal couple's wedding-visit seemed to restore them to him. Of the magnificent residence of the Grand Condé, nothing remained save the stables and offices of the *château*. It was in this latter part of the buildings that the prince had made himself a very comfortable summer residence. He received the prince and princess, followed by their little court, with exquisite politeness.

It was a pleasant sight, and at the same time touching. The old man supported his tottering steps upon the vigorous arm of the prince, who at that time seemed the most solid pillar of the Royal dynasty. We passed through a number of rooms decorated with historical paintings, having for the most part the great deeds of the Grand Condé for their subject. One of them depicted his victory over the Royalist troops. The august family had not wished to lose any of the military triumphs of this great man; but a figure had been painted in the corner of the picture to represent History. In her hand she held a book, from which many leaves had been torn, and upon these you read distinctly the details of this battle, which was guilty in principle, but glorious as a deed of arms.

Mme. la Duchesse de Berry was also upon very good terms with her aunt, Mme. la Duchesse d'Orléans, who lived at Neuilly with her husband, her numerous family, and Mlle. d'Orléans. It was also a great pleasure to meet the Dowager Duchesse d'Orléans, who had a little private court of her own. She was Egalité's widow, and *née* Penthiévre. Her reputation for perfect goodness was so well established that opinions, however diverse, had never any but sympathetic words to utter towards this princess. She had happened to break her thigh when the emperor returned to Paris on the 20th of March. He hastened, I was told, to send her a safeguard, accompanied by words expressing his deep interest. In the summer she lived in a very simple little country-house at Ivry. We often dined there informally; and she exchanged plants, bushes, and water-fowl with the marshal. This conformity in their tastes had brought them together.

The court spent the summer at Saint-Cloud, and in the autumn a short stay was generally made in one of the other royal residences, such as Fontainebleau, Compiègne and Rambouillet. Nothing could well be less country-like than the invariably official life in these palaces, with the exception that all the services of what was called the "great posts" breakfasted with the king, who retired for dinner into the bosom of his family, while we took this meal at the table of the Lord Steward, a favourite office which was filled in all the courts of the Restoration first by M. le Duc de Cars, and after his death by M. le Comte de Cossé-Brissac. Their charming wives admirably did the honours of this table, which was in every way perfectly served. In Paris we had the honour of breakfasting with the king three times a year. This was on the 1st of January, on his saint's day, and on the anniversary of his restoration.

When Mme. la Duchesse de Berry began to entertain hopes of motherhood, I received full instructions as to my duties in this connection from the Grand Master of Ceremonies. It was the rule that the mother of the children of France should give birth to them in public. It was a select public, I admit, consisting of the king, the royal family, the princes of the blood, the ministers, the chancellor of France, in a word, the government. And all these were to be summoned by me at a certain moment, that is to say, not long before and certainly not after the decisive moment. All this seemed a very formidable business to me; but before reaching the precise time concerning Her Royal Highness, I had to occupy myself on my own account with the birth of my second daughter, Caroline. *Monsieur*, the king's brother, and Mme. la Duchesse de Berry personally held this child over the baptismal font. She arrived brimming with health in bright sunshine on the 2nd of June 1817, and was the marshal's sixth daughter.

I was keeping myself prepared for eventualities when, some months after this birth, I was summoned in all haste to the Élysée-Bourbon. Already Louis XVIII. and many members of the government had been warned and were at their posts. I sent out as quickly as possible the notices which had been delayed, and only after these formalities had been carried out was I allowed to go to my poor young princess, whose screams could be heard in all these rooms filled with people in full dress.

Her Royal Highness gave birth to a daughter who seemed very

healthy, but whose sex was a great disappointment to her family. Nevertheless, I went home in the evening much relieved, if not satisfied; I went out again very early the next morning, and did not expect, when I reached the Élysée, to find the palace in a turmoil. The child had been attacked with internal convulsions which threatened its days. The faculty exerted itself in vain; in a very little while the poor babe was dead.

The young mother accepted this sorrow with a Christian resignation which edified me greatly. A consolation seemed about to follow before a year was passed, only to result in renewed disappointment. Mme. la Duchesse de Berry gave birth to a boy, but he came prematurely, and only lived long enough to be privately baptized, like his sister.

We thus came to the year 1819. I brought my son Charles into the world; and this arrival of a boy brought joy into our household. A third confinement came to console the Tuileries and the Élysée-Bourbon, and on the 27th of September was born, amid the ceremonial I have already described, Louise of France, who was known by the title of *Mademoiselle*. I well remember the strange feeling I experienced on seeing Mme. la Duchesse de Gontaut, who had been appointed governess to the children of France, pass by, carrying on an immense pillow the little girl, weighing less than three pounds, who was about to be installed in the immense apartments prepared for her; and on seeing the crowd of courtiers rise in a body at the cry of "*Mademoiselle*" uttered by the gentleman-usher. Will she live? I asked myself. Will it be in France? What has the future in store for that little being? What influence will it be able to exercise if God preserves its delicate life?

The child grew up to become the worthy and noble Duchess of Parma, whose virtues and whose pure and magnanimous character were admired by all Europe.

M. le Duc de Berry gave many entertainments at the Élysée-Bourbon. It was, I believe, early in January 1820 that during the preparations for one of these, the upholsterers and all the staff were seized with alarm at the fall of a whole panel full of mirrors which occupied one of the sides of the long gallery of the palace. There was nothing to explain this catastrophe, which caused only a temporary annoyance at the time, for it was quickly repaired, but not long afterwards it gave cause to superstitious people to regard it as a sinister omen of what followed.

Nothing notable occurred during the ensuing weeks to delay my mention of the terrible event which I will now describe to you.

On Friday the 11th of February 1820, I was not on duty and had gone to a supper given by the Grand *Referendary*, the Marquis de Sémonville, at the Luxembourg. Several of the guests had come on from a masked ball which the Comtesse Greffulhe was giving the same evening, and told me that they had recognized M. le Duc and Mme. la Duchesse de Berry there beneath their *dominoes*. They all agreed that the ball had been charming. The next day I asked Her Royal Highness if she had taken much part in it.

"I enjoyed myself immensely," she replied; "there were so many different and ingenious disguises, and we were particularly amused by the Duc de Fitz-James made up as Potier in the part of the sly old father in the *Petites Danaïdes*."

This play was drawing all Paris to the Porte Saint-Martin. It was a parody of the grand opera of the *Danaides*, which was much in vogue at that time.

"Oh, how funny the duke was," resumed the princess, "ferociously sharpening all the fifty little knives which he drew from his pockets. His imperturbable face in the midst of this occupation, which he continued through all the ball-rooms, was exquisitely comical."

Alas, this zealous servant of the dynasty little suspected that at that moment a real knife was being sharpened in the courtyard of the Hôtel Greffulhe, and that, but for a shower which upset all the assassin's plans, he would have put into execution that same night one which he had long been meditating. Yes, the rain caused Louvel to postpone the crime on which his mind was gloating.

In order to finish with the Greffulhe ball, I will add that, upon my asking Mme. la Duchesse de Berry why she had not danced, she replied, in a whisper:

"In confidence, I have fresh hopes; but they are so vague, dear duchesse, that I do not talk about them."

You can imagine with what satisfaction I received these words.

At last rose the sad day of Sunday the 13th of February 1820. I went, as usual, to breakfast at the Élysée-Bourbon. These breakfasts were always gay. We were called, not without reason, the young court. Our princess was only twenty years old; none of her ladies, excepting perhaps the Duchesse de Gontaut, was as much as thirty, and some of us were much less. M. le Duc de Berry, who was thirty-nine, had selected the greater part of his *aides-de-camp* from among the young heroes who had figured in the last wars of the Empire; and if, among this world full of life, there were to be found some few devoted old emigrants, they spoilt nothing, because not only was the right of their presence naturally recognized, but they were generally both gay and amiable. At their head was the Duc de Lévis, who was welcomed wherever he went.

Monseigneur amused himself, as he often did, in testing the dexterity of his most elegant officers by throwing new-laid eggs to them across the table, which, had they failed to catch them, would have broken over their brilliant uniforms. But we had reached the last of all these breakfasts. On this 13th of February we rose hurriedly from table, fearing lest we should be late for the king's Mass. Wrapped in furs, the prince, his wife and I stepped into the carriage, and driving across the frozen streets of Paris, we arrived at the Tuileries just in time.

I had taken leave of the royal couple from the Élysée, when I remembered that Mme. de Sainte-Aulaire had written to me that morning asking me to obtain M. le Duc de Berry's box at the Variétés for her for that evening. She wrote that she was dying to see *L'Ours et la Pacha*, and that there was not a seat to be had. I ran after the prince, and caught him up at the end of the gallery.

"Your box at the Variétés, *Monseigneur?*" I asked.

"Whom for?"

I hesitated, with a smile; the Sainte-Aulaire family had been playing a little at opposition since the famous Toulouse proclamation had caused them to be somewhat severely judged. I did not wish to deceive the prince, and I mentioned their name. He smiled in his turn, and after an instant's hesitation, he said, "Yes." It was the last word he ever spoke to me. With that, it was an act of graciousness, and that is the reason why I have entered into all these minute details.

I made use of my complete liberty of that evening to take my stepdaughter Elisa to my friend the Duchesse d'Albuféra's ball. It was very brilliant, and I was amusing myself, and talking gaily with a friend, when I suddenly observed two gentlemen evidently preoccupied and whispering together with their looks turned in my direction. It was Casimir Périer and General Pamphile de la Croix. One of them left the other, came straight up to me, and bending over to my ear, said:

"We have made up our minds that it is our duty to inform you of a melancholy event. M. le Duc de Berry has been stabbed with a dagger, at the Opera."

"Ah God!"

"The assassin has been arrested," resumed the general, "and the wound has not been pronounced mortal."

"Please, general, find my stepdaughter, who is dancing in the next room, and put us into our carriage."

The Hôtel d'Albuféra was next to the Élysée-Bourbon, and I at once entered the courtyard, which was already filling with other carriages. When I reached the first lobby, a frightened woman flew up to me, crying:

"Where do you come from? What do you know?"

I had difficulty in recognizing in her the Duchesse de Gontaut. Several people joined us, men and women of our circle, some in silk gowns, others in *dominoes*, all arriving from the different entertainments which are always given on Shrove Tuesday. It was not till then that I learnt that the prince was unable to be moved, and was lying at the spot where the crime had been committed. "To the Opera!" I cried to my coachman. Two gentlemen stepped into the carriage with me: General Comte Belliard and the Comte de Saint-Cricq. "We will not leave you alone at such a moment as this," said the former; "one never knows what may still be in store." I had sent my stepdaughter to my room at the Élysée.

We arrived without hindrance in the Rue Rameau, which was destroyed together with the opera-house. We got out beneath the little portico which afforded a private entrance to Their Royal Highnesses' box. I hastened up a steep, narrow staircase, crowded with people, of whom one alone was seated on the stairs, the last one, I believe, touching the fatal door. In spite of the feebleness of the light which barely made the surroundings visible, I thought I recognized in this person Mme. la Duchesse d'Orléans. It was she, in fact. She had come hurriedly, with her family; and without entering the room, she was close at hand, so as to receive the first news of the victim.

"Go in, go in," she said, making room for me to pass; "your place is there," pointing to the door. I opened it, and went in. . . .

The victim lay stretched on some mattresses brought together in haste. His face and lips were livid. Already the shadow of death was upon his forehead, and yet his dying eyes were astonishingly full of expression. By his side was his wife, wrapped in a blood-stained dressing-gown which had replaced the silk gown, also soaked with blood, which she had put off. She held the prince's hand in one of hers; with the other she beckoned to me to approach.

"Speak low," she said, in a sort of wandering voice, "for he hears everything."

I did not speak, low or otherwise; none spoke but Dupuytren alone, who declared that he was going to enlarge the wound, which had stopped bleeding. In fact, the streams of blood which we saw with dismayed eyes came from a heap of leeches, which had been thrown by handfuls upon that broad uncovered bosom; but the wound proper, caused by a very fine blade, seemed closed, and internal haemorrhage threatened to set in.

But this conscientious and indispensable operation added terribly to the wounded prince's martyrdom, and he uttered such cries of pain that I fell upon my knees, and leaning against Madame de Noailles, who was in the same attitude as myself, I stopped my ears and felt as though paralysed with horror. If anyone could have saved M. le Duc de Berry, it would have been Dupuytren. As it was, this expert surgeon, unable to do more, had obtained a temporary improvement, which restored to the dying man the faculties which he employed in sanctifying the last moments of his life.

The first use the prince made of the power of speech which had been restored to him by the flow of blood was to ask for a priest, the object of his first cry. Mgr. de Latil, the archbishop of Rheims, was there; bending his ear over the dying man's lips, he received a confession which we were all in danger of hearing, the words being jerked out in hiccoughs. At last, with every possible precaution, the mattress was laid upon the floor, in order that the archbishop, almost lying over the sick man, should have a greater chance of hearing alone. In consequence of the prince's constant vomiting, it was impossible to administer the *viaticum*; but immediately after the absolution, the prince cried in a loud voice:

"I should like to see all my children—"

Until that moment, we knew of no child except *mademoiselle*, who was four months old.

"Heavens! what is he saying?" whispered Mme. la Duchesse d'Angoulême to me, seizing my hand. This princess knew of the English connexion, as did all the royal family. A general stupor ensued; but the prince, guessing and understanding everything, spoke again, and looking towards Mme. le Duchesse de Berry, said:

"My dear, I confess to you, I have several children!"

"Charles," she replied, "why did you not tell me before? I should have adopted them. Let them be sent for;" and then, turning to the Duc de Coigny, one of the prince's *aides-de-camp*, she said, "Go also and fetch my daughter."

The two little English girls arrived before the royal child. They approached the bed, knelt down, and in tears received the blessing of their father, who spoke to them in English. The unhappy princess embraced them; but the minutes were numbered, and her own child did not come. Dupuytren did not leave go of the prince's pulse, and the latter said to him:

"Do not deceive me, give me fair warning, I have more to do down here."

At last the Duchesse de Gontaut brought the august little babe in swaddling clothes, who also received that precious blessing. Giving way before all this emotion, the princess threw herself on her knees beside the bed. "Take care," said her husband, then, "think of the child you carry." At this solemn revelation, whose importance escaped none of us, we were all profoundly impressed. Meantime the prince's strength was rapidly sinking. He had several times begged for the presence of the king.

"It is especially to ask for pardon for the *man*," said the prince, for he never described the assassin by any other term. The constant reply was, "The king is coming." It was not that His Majesty lacked the will, but his growing infirmities made it very difficult for him to rise and be moved at night. We asked ourselves how it would be possible to bring him up to the top of the sort of ladder which we had mounted. He arrived nevertheless.

But meantime the long wait was not wasted. With his eyes fixed on his father, the dying prince recommended all his servants to him; then turning to M. le Duc d'Angoulême, he whispered a few words which were piously received by the latter. When all these duties were accomplished, the unfortunate Prince suddenly asked himself what he could have done to bring this treatment upon himself; and then, as though to expiate this accusing thought, he said:

"Perhaps I had unintentionally offended him."

It struck half-past five, and the pale dawn became visible through the candle-light of the death chamber. The prince's chest became obstructed, his words came fewer and fewer, and a mortal stupor was weighing upon the numerous witnesses of this dying agony, when the sufferer seemed to revive at the sound of a faint noise which he was the first to hear, and in a loud voice, he said:

"There is the king's escort!"

Soon we heard the painful efforts by means of which the king was brought from the bottom to the topmost step of the staircase.

His Majesty stood before the death-bed of the heir of his race, but yesterday so full of the hope of life; and the dying man did not waste one of the few seconds which remained to him in which to attain his object:

"Sire," he said in a voice of entreaty, "I was waiting for you to beg you to grant me, as one last favour in this world, the life of the man—"

And when the king's emotion prevented him from replying at once:

"Ah! uncle, quick, quick, the life of the man!—"

"Let us speak of yourself, my son," said His Majesty.

A third entreaty in the same words came from the lips which were growing paler and paler; but that was all we heard, for at that moment Mme. la Duchesse de Berry was seized with a nervous attack, and had to be carried away. I followed her, but I had neither the power nor the wish to keep her from returning, and then . . . all was over . . .

The lifeless head of the defunct was supported by Dupuytren, who with the other hand held a mirror before the mouth from which the last breath had issued. The king, the unhappy father, the brother, the sister, all the heartbroken spectators at first restrained their feelings, and the silence of death hung over the room. But when the young widow approached the motionless corpse, amidst this silent scene, she flung herself upon her knees and with all the effervescence of her age and her Italian nationality, exclaimed:

"Charles is dead, I want to return home. Sire, let me go back to my country."

These vehement words were received with profound and tender pity; and during the exhaustion which followed upon them, His Majesty signed to us to remove the unhappy princess in a carriage which brought us back to the Élysée-Bourbon.

So soon as she arrived, the princess rushed in despair to her husband's room, and then returning to her own, without at first occupying herself with her poor little child, she was seen to take up a great pair of scissors from her toilet-table and cut off the two long tresses of fair hair which the prince, she said, had loved so well.

"One shall be for him," she added, "and must be placed in his coffin; the other I will keep for my daughter."

We succeeded at last in persuading the bereaved young princess to go to bed. This was only after we had reminded her of the expectations with which her future and that of the royal family and of France were bound up. It was at this moment that the marshal sent for me to go to my room in the Élysée, where I joined him in that ball-dress which added, if possible, to the impressiveness of the situation.

I had but little time in which to discuss with your father the terrible event that had taken place and its uncertain influence upon our future. The marshal, awakened at the first news of the catastrophe, had at once put on his uniform and hastened to the scene of the crime. With horror and distress he followed the agony of the prince and the interrogatory of the assassin. I caught glimpses of him all through the night.

The two dramas were only separated by a partition-wall; and to explain this fact to you, I will leave Mme. la Duchesse de Berry for the moment, and return to the murderer and his affairs.

On the Friday, after giving up the idea of killing the prince at the Hôtel Greffulhe, Louvel decided to carry out his project on the Sunday evening, not doubting but that his victim would go to the opera, for he had been studying his habits for some months. He therefore took up his post at eight o'clock in the evening on the pavement of the Rue Rameau, walking up and down so as not to attract attention. He only stopped for a moment near the portico of which I have already spoken, in order to catch the order given to the coachman. "At eleven o'clock," the prince said; and then he entered with his wife, the Marquise de Béthisy, the Comte de Mesnard, the Comte César de Choiseul and the Comte de Clermont-Lodève.

The prince never permitted the six grenadiers who composed the guard of the private entrance to turn out either at his arrival or his departure; the sentry alone stood outside and presented arms; and Louvel, who knew this, went towards the side to which he knew that the sentry turned his back. Towards the time appointed, he came up from the Rue Richelieu and waited, walking to and fro, for the carriage to drive up; and its owners came out soon after. The party from the box crossed the pavement, and while the sentry presented arms, turning his back to the murderer, the two footmen, in the same position, let down the carriage-step, the prince took leave of his wife as he handed her into the carriage, and the three officers saluted.

In an instant, agile as a panther, the assassin, springing behind the six men, roughly seized the seventh by the right shoulder, and drove a long, fine blade to the hilt into his heart. With another bound he at once removed himself from the witnesses of this scene, which was so quick that for a moment no one quite realized it. A dull moan from the prince suddenly caused the Comte de Mesnard to ask him:

"Have you been struck?"

"I am killed," he replied, himself drawing the dagger from the wound.

Then another cry issued from the carriage, and the unhappy young wife, who had guessed all, sprang out. She reached the prince as they were laying him on the bench of the guard-room and began to assist the witnesses of this horrible scene, some of whom hurriedly undid the garments which covered the chest of the prince, already stifling and almost swooning away, while the others rushed into the streets in pursuit of the assassin.

"Send for a priest, my dear—" were the first words the wounded man uttered.

"A doctor," was added on every side.

The material succour was the first to arrive. Dr. Blanheton was within reach, and made the first examination, without being able to conceal the gravity of the situation from the palpitating hearts which were awaiting his pronouncement.

"The wound does not bleed sufficiently," he said.

Dr. Bougon, *monsieur's* Physician-in-Ordinary, arrived as these words were spoken, and said:

"I will suck the wound."

"Take care, Bougon," said the victim, "it may be poisoned."

The faithful servant took no notice of this, but his courageous endeavours were of no avail.

Doctors, apothecaries, people with mattresses came from every side. At last it was decided, for want of a better resort, to carry the prince into the actors' room where the tragedy was completed. The heartbroken family and friends and devoted servants of every kind had hastened up and filled the room when I arrived, almost immediately after Dupuytren. All the practitioners had made way for him, and you have seen how he stayed by the illustrious victim's side until the end.

To return to the murderer, he ran towards the Arcade Colbert, hoping that if he succeeded in reaching it, he would be able to disappear in the darkness before he was caught up. This plan might have succeeded but for an accident which delayed him for a few seconds. He came into violent collision with a waiter coming in the opposite direction and carrying a dishful of ices. The fall of this young man with his load caused a noise with which was mingled the shout of the sentry, who had thrown aside his musket in order to run more easily, and who had outstripped the other grenadiers, constantly repeating his cry of "Stop him! stop the murderer!" It was during the struggle with the waiter, who had seized Louvel while he was trying to rise, that the sentry came up with him and caught him by the collar. His comrades came to his assistance, and the man was brought back, bound hand and foot, to the scene of the crime.

For want of another room, he was placed in a sort of closet leading out of the death-chamber. From there, he distinctly heard all that went on, and when, in the course of the examination, which was proceeded with as quickly as possible, the chancellor or the ministers asked him if the cries of his victim did not trouble him, he replied:

"No; I was only touched by the cry of his wife."

His fierce composure never flinched during the long hours of the investigation, which lasted almost as long as the life of the prince. In vain was it sought to discover whether he had any accomplices; and nothing occurred during the five months that elapsed before the trial to give the lie to his denials.

The man's physiognomy was, I was told, most repulsive. One of my companions during that night of terror and sorrow whispered to me:

"Would you not like to see the assassin? He is just through that door."

She took no heed of my refusal, and went alone, returning shocked by his hideous image.

A second dagger was found on Louvel, but no hint was to be obtained as to the use he intended to make of it. He kept to his invariable reply:

"I only killed M. le Duc de Berry as being destined to propagate a family which I desired to destroy. Personally, I have no hatred for him or any of his; but their reign over my country did not agree with my ideas."

Someone said to him:

"A word uttered by *Monseigneur* has revealed that perhaps your crime will have failed to advance your project of destroying the royal race."

These words seemed particularly to fix his attention, and he replied:

"I am sorry that I was not aware of that fact."

He persistently refused to explain this speech.

During a few moments he turned livid with pallor. They thought it was remorse, but when he was questioned on the subject, he simply said:

"The handcuffs are too tight."

These were loosened and his pallor disappeared.

I must not omit to mention one of the most striking contrasts of that tragic night. M. le Duc de Berry had only come out in order to hand his wife into her carriage, intending himself to return and enjoy the last act of the beautiful ballet, *Le Carnaval de Venise*, which was to last half-an-hour longer. As a matter of fact, the performance continued. Nothing within the opera-house pointed to the tragedy which was taking place outside, and it was to the sound of the most joyous and captivating music that the sad scenes which I have described to you were enacted. An early rumour reached the Orleans princes as they were leaving their box, and you have read how they lined both sides of the staircase when I myself arrived; but generally speaking, the news was not known in Paris until the morning of the 14th.

I now return to the Élysée-Bourbon, where the royal family had arrived, in addition to a constant flow of visitors belonging to the court and the government. I never left the side of my dear princess, except to attend to such details as came within my special province. I knew that the family were deliberating as to the residence which was to be provisionally allotted to the young widow. It was at once decided that she should leave the Élysée-Bourbon, which had become impossible for her, the same night. Orders were given at Saint-Cloud, and our mournful procession arrived there at nightfall amid an icy coldness. The princess was carried to the largest and most comfortable apartment in the Royal *château*. I had my bed placed near hers, and lost none of her sobs during this second terrible night.

Before leaving the Élysée, I had heard from a trust-worthy source that the deliberation concerning Her Royal Highness's permanent residence, had fixed it, as I had hoped, at the palace of the Tuileries. Our stay at Saint-Cloud was only to last so long as was required to prepare the Pavilion de Marsan, the whole ground-floor of which was to be given up to the use of Mme. la Duchesse and *Mademoiselle*.

After the funeral, we returned with the young widow to the Pavilion de Marsan, where we found the rooms hung from floor to ceiling with black cloth. Not a mirror, not a corner of gilding visible! This was the etiquette under these circumstances. The many tall windows of these immense rooms gave hardly sufficient light, in the middle of the day, for the usual occupations of one's life, such was the gloom produced by these hangings. It was worse still at night. Candles were lighted here and there to little purpose; we lived in a tomb none the less. As a concession, Her Royal Highness's bedroom had been hung with grey cloth only. The mourning of the whole household was carried out with the greatest strictness; thus, besides having to wear stuff dresses for more than a year, I had to have my carriage draped, that is to say, the panels were covered with cloth, which even concealed the armorial designs. My servants also were dressed in deep mourning.

In spite of the melancholy conditions under which I beheld Mme. la Duchesse de Berry return to the Tuileries, I felt an immense relief when I saw her installed under that protecting roof. I was then able to return for a time to my husband and my children, whom I had completely neglected since the catastrophe of the 13th. My presence was the more necessary in that the marriage of my stepson Victor with Mlle. Eulalie Minguet had been decided upon in the early part of February. I had told the poor prince of it on the Sunday morning—.

When the widow's pregnancy was officially announced, the rigidity of her situation had to be relaxed, now that the princess possessed a chance of offering an heir to the throne. She showed herself little, but sufficiently to assure everyone of her condition. During this time, the preparations were continuing for the assassin's trial. He refused to employ an advocate, insisting upon defending himself. He talked at great length to little purpose, and was executed on the Place de Grève in the course of June 1820. I slept at the Tuileries, scarcely ever leaving the palace except, at rare intervals, to go and see my husband and children.

On the 28th of September, we breakfasted with Her Royal Highness in a little summer-house, which was concealed amid the shrubberies at the end of the water-terrace giving on the Place Louis XV. The princess's features bore an air of repose; if they did not denote gaiety, at least there was in the atmosphere, that morning, a sort of serenity. She walked briskly along the terrace, following with interest the movements of a regiment which was passing at the same time along the quay beneath. She made no complaint during the day, and when, at eleven o'clock at night, her *accoucheur*, M. Deneux, who was staying at the *château*, came as usual to enquire after her health before retiring to bed, she sent him away quietly, and bade us all goodnight. I went up to my room, which was above *monsieur's*; it was on the second floor, but I had nevertheless about a hundred steps to climb.

I had been suffering during the day from a violent headache, and I had just fallen asleep with the soundness which usually follows after such a day, when I was precipitately awakened by three violent knocks at my door, through which a footman shouted to me to come down to Her Royal Highness without delay. I slipped on a skirt, threw a large shawl over my shoulders, and ran down the huge staircase, on which reigned an unaccustomed movement; it was two o'clock in the morning. This movement grew into a block as I drew near to the bedroom, and I had difficulty in entering. Among others who disputed the passage with me was the Duchesse de Gontaut, in her dressing-gown and night-cap, dragging a young National Guard by the hand.

"Come," she said to him, "let us lose no time."

I followed her, stupefied. I saw confusedly a number of other people moving around the bed of Mlle, la Duchesse de Berry, who was sitting up, barely leaning upon one of her elbows, and when she caught sight of me, cried:

"It's a Henry—look!"

She showed me a newborn child lying against her upon the coverlet. I turned a look aghast upon the surrounding persons; there was not an official person among them.

"Where are the witnesses, *Madame?*" I exclaimed. "Where are the king and the royal family?"

"There was no time to warn people," she said; "I only had two pains: at the first I called for my maid, and at the second she received my child. But nothing is finished yet between him and myself, and I shall await the witnesses appointed by the king; they will come in addition to all those you see around me."

I did not waste time rejoicing over the event, realizing as I did the importance of making it as public and official as possible. In an instant I was at *monsieur's* door. The Baron de Saint-Aubin, his First Groom of the Chambers, was in uniform, and seemed to expect somebody.

"Tell *monsieur,*" I said to him, "that Mme. la Duchesse de Berry has given birth to a boy: quick, quick, quick! "

"But, *Madame,* I have no right to enter *monsieur's* room at this time; all I could do was to send for his First Lord, the Duc de Maille, who will be here in a moment."

"Don't wait for anybody," I said; "if you will not tell *monsieur,* let me pass, and I will tell him myself: it is urgent."

I spoke with authority; he went in front, and there we stood before the bed of the good prince, who was sleeping soundly.

"Wake the prince," I said to M. de Saint-Aubin, who thereupon began to shout:

"*Monsieur, monsieur!*"

No result.

"Well then, shake the prince," I said, losing my patience with the worthy servant, who dared not lay his hand upon his master. He ended, however, by taking him by the shoulder and continuing to shout:

"*Monsieur, monsieur!*"

The prince then sat up with a bound, and rubbing his eyes, looked at me with a startled air. I told him of the facts.

"What!" he said. "You come and tell me when all is over!"

"The *accoucheur* himself was not there, *Monseigneur*," I replied.

At that moment the Duc de Maille entered the room.

"And what were you doing all this time?" asked *Monseigneur*. "We are late, go and tell the king at once from me."

Without any further explanation, the Duc de Maille rushed to Louis XVIII., who was being dressed. He had the door opened in *monsieur's* name, and told the king that he had come to inform him that Mme. la Duchesse de Berry was in labour, for that was all the good duke had understood. Louis XVIIL, who knew more than he, received this announcement with a sly smile, and said:

"I am happy to be the first to inform you that my niece has been safely delivered of a boy, and that mother and child are doing well."

On returning to the princess's bedroom, I found the official witnesses, Marshal Duc de Coigny and Marshal Duc d'Albuféra, who, together with a number of others whom chance, or rather providence, had brought there, had come in time to assist at Her Royal Highness's delivery. The king, *monsieur*, M. le Duc and Mme. la Duchesse d'Angoulême arrived in the room, which was crowded to suffocation. An alarming pallor had succeeded the first animation on the princess's features. The *accoucheur* grew alarmed, and entreated everybody to go out. Fresh air and care restored life to the courageous princess, for whom I had really for an instant trembled.

During this painful moment, of which I was the only observer, if I except the *accoucheur* and the nurse (Mme. Lemoine), all, commencing with the king, had eagerly surrounded the newborn prince, who was small, but very lively. The Orleans princes, who had been quickly summoned, formed part of the group surrounding the child when I, in my turn, went to look at him, and gave him my silent blessing for having at last arrived safely in port after so many storms!

During the rest of that night the Tuileries were full of people. The first rays of daylight lit up a state of joy which seemed universal. The hundred-and-one-salvoes of cannon which announced the newborn's sex explained the turbulent delight of the great city. My husband was on duty, as Major-General of the National Guard. Desiring the troops which he commanded to make a display of their feelings, he distributed to the soldiers a number of cartridges, each of which was to shoot out its rocket. Mme. la Duchesse de Berry, hearing of this arrangement, which was to take place the same evening in the gardens of the Tuileries, had her bed moved to the windows, so that she might take part in the sight. This showed that, thanks be to God, her condition had become satisfactory.

I have mentioned a young National Guard whom the Duchesse de Gontaut led into Mme. la Duchesse de Berry's room. To explain this incident and some other particulars of the memorable hour which witnessed the birth of M. le Duc de Bordeaux, I must return to the first pangs which awakened his mother soon after she had gone to sleep and made her call out for the waiting-woman on duty, who was sleeping near her. Mme. Bourgeois rushed to the bed, and at the second cry she received the child . . . It was necessary at the same time to call for help. What a position! But Her Royal Highness's energy made everything easy. A single summons from the footman sleeping in the ante-chamber to the Groom of the Chambers near at hand, soon spread, first over the *château*, and then through the different posts of the Gardes du Corps, the Royal Guard and the National Guard.

I do not know what inspired M. Sauton with the happy thought to ask the sentry of the National Guard to hand him his musket, while he, the National Guard, went to fulfil an important mission in Her Royal Highness's apartments. It was at this moment that the Duchesse de Gontaut, hearing of this opportunity and eagerly seizing it, hastened the steps of the young man, who thus became one of the legal witnesses of the prince's birth, together with myself. M. Laisne, as he was called, thus placed his signature near those of the two marshals of France above-named. I am almost sure that a grenadier of the same company arrived at the same time as M. Laisne, and was the fourth signatory; but I am not quite certain of this fact, and I do not remember the last one's name.

For that matter, the room, when I entered it, was full of a number of different persons whom I did not take time, as you know, to distinguish; but I since learnt from Her Royal Highness that she employed them all without distinction of rank upon the various things to be done. "Light the candles," she said to one; to another, "Please unfasten my dog and send him out of the room." This referred to a large spaniel who slept at the foot of her bed; he was white as snow, with curly hair; his name was Chicorée.

Mme. la Duchesse de Berry had made a vow during her pregnancy to visit Notre-Dame de Liesse after her recovery, but this plan was postponed until after the baptism, which took place at Notre-Dame with all possible pomp in May 1821. The court and the town of Paris indulged in brilliant festivities, and all passed off well. Mme. la Duchesse had laid aside her mourning on the joyful occasion of this birth of an heir to the throne.

I was very tired at that time, and not at all well. I obtained a month's leave, but upon condition that I should first accompany Her Royal Highness upon the pilgrimage of which I have spoken. After the touching ceremony, and *Madame's* communion at Liesse, we made several excursions in the department of the Aisne. Soon after, my health becoming worse rather than improving, I obtained a longer leave than I had at first hoped for, and we all went to Jeand'heurs for the best part of the summer. It was there that we learnt the death of the emperor.

Being absent from Paris, we did not hear many details concerning the reception of the news in the capital. General Rapp, formerly an *aide-de-camp* of the emperor's, although devoted to his memory, had nevertheless accepted a place at the Court of Louis XVIII. He was in attendance upon His Majesty when the latter received the news. The king heard a cry of regret, and turning round, saw Rapp's manly features covered with tears.

"Weep without restraint, my dear general," said the king; "I understand and pity your natural sorrow."

The political position of Mme. la Duchesse assumed a growing importance in the measure that her son prospered and she herself became better known. Good-hearted, easy-going, affable, loving the arts, she revealed qualities which inspired general sympathy. I had first been allowed one secretary, and soon I required two. I had chosen the first in my husband's offices: he was the son of Mme Morel, the lady's maid who had followed me to Russia, and to whom we had given the post of housekeeper in Paris. Her son had received a very good education; he was intelligent, and full of delicacy and tact, qualities exceptionally suitable for the functions which he had to fulfil, for I often brought him into contact with Her Royal Highness; and particularly during my short absences, he was called upon to work with her direct. This work was divided into different parts: first the accounts of the budget which the Mistress of the Robes disposed of; next, the correspondence, which covered every subject, since people applied to Her Royal Highness to try and obtain every kind of benefit and favour of which the French are so greedy.

I broke the seals of between ten and fifteen letters a day. I had grown accustomed to the petitionary style, and learnt to appreciate the leading point of the question. If it was a request for private assistance, except when it represented some special interest, I sent it to the First Almoner, the Bishop of Amiens, or else to the private secretary, the Marquis de Sassenay. If it was a request for help for a church or other public institution, I placed it in my day-to-day portfolio, which contained all the other requests of lesser or greater importance.

I made out a list of all these, and took it to the Tuileries on the days appointed for this work. I returned with the princess's verbal replies; these I immediately noted on the corner of the letters, and then, summoning M. Morel, I added the necessary explanations, and instructed him to bring me the replies which he had written from my notes. I never signed these replies without first attentively reading them, and yet I had very rarely to correct his work, in spite of the delicacy of treatment required, which I would not have met with in every secretary.

On the 3rd of February 1822, I gave birth to my son Henry. This birth of a fourth son was received with rapture. My husband went off to the Tuileries to announce his paternal satisfaction, and brought me, on his return, the news of the kind phrases with which the news had been received. About the same time I lost my dear Aunt Clotilde de Coucy, and shortly after, I suffered a yet crueller affliction: my beloved and saintly mother was taken from me. She died in my arms on All Saints' Day 1822, surrounded and mourned by my husband and all her family. On our return to Paris we received the most touching marks of sympathy from the Royal Family, and I only partly resumed my duties, owing to my deep mourning.

In the winter of 1822, there arose a prospect of war between France and Spain, where the revolutionaries were becoming formidable. The Cortès had removed to Cadiz, where they kept Ferdinand VII. in their power. At first there was a great political question in dispute. Opinions were violently divided on this principal point. This was the first time that the French army had been mobilized since it had hoisted the white flag. All our minds were greatly agitated. I foresaw that a command would be offered to the marshal, from whom I expected to be separated for an indefinite period. I recalled the struggle of the Spaniards in 1808, and this recollection did not tend to raise my spirits. All was promptly decided. Various army corps, commanded by the Marshals of France, were organised during the course of the winter. M. le Duc d'Angoulême was appointed *generalissimo*, and my husband received orders to march upon Madrid at the head of the 1st Corps. He reorganized his staff, which he selected both from among his old officers and those who came in crowds to beg to be chosen for this service, which brought them into personal contact with him.

Still saddened by my recent loss and distressed at this separation, I was profoundly discouraged when my husband set out on the 12th of March 1823. But the campaign was purely a political one for your father. He was not wounded, for he did not fight; but although he was physically spared, he had much to suffer morally, in consequence of the difficult mission which was entrusted to him. To keep order in a capital deserted by the government, in a country where political passion runs so high, was a task worthy of his genius. More than any other analogous occasion, it offered opportunities to the marshal to display his habitual tact and to exercise his well-known humanity. He had much to think of, and much to do; but his labour was not lost, and moreover his spirit of conciliation and generosity was supported by the will and inclinations of the prince *generalissimo*. The place of honour had been reserved for the latter, that place where the fighting was expected; he had demanded it, and with justice.

And indeed it was he who, by attacking the Trocadero, delivered the King of Spain from the tyranny of his chambers. I will not go into the question whether or not Ferdinand VII. made a good use of the power which we restored to him; but what I will say is that the French prince, after valiantly and humanely fulfilling the task which the king his uncle had laid upon him, did not wait to receive the thanks of the sovereign whom he had saved, and returned to France without seeing Ferdinand VII.

Our army, which had preserved admirable discipline, was brought back promptly and in good order by all its chiefs. Your father returned about the beginning of November, and he seemed delivered of a great weight.

The headquarters of the National Guard had been transferred to the fine mansion belonging to the Duke of Padua, who had let it to the city of Paris. I had taken up my residence there during the marshal's absence. We had given particular care to the decoration of his private apartments, and he seemed vastly satisfied with his new-quarters; but I was not there when he alighted from his carriage. He had omitted to announce the time of his arrival, and I was sent for to the Tuileries, where I spent the evenings daily.

Not long after, Élisa was married to M. Chevalier, Baron de Caunan. He had long been *Prefect* of the Var. The wedding was celebrated in the chapel of the Élysée-Bourbon by M. l'Abbé Feutrier, who later became Minister of Public Worship. About the same time my brother Gustave de Coucy married the charming Mlle, de la Bigne.

But I had not much time to devote to the joys of the family. Madame la Duchesse de Berry had obtained permission from the king to visit part of Normandy, ending with Dieppe, where she was to take sea baths. Her Royal Highness did not leave Saint-Cloud without some anxiety about the health of the king, who, in spite of his courage, seemed to have been growing weaker for some time. However, we set out, and our first halt was at Rouen, where we were to make a solemn entry.

At the last posting-house, Her Royal Highness changed her travelling carriage for an open landau; she was thus able to see the people and to show herself to them. The crowd became innumerable as we approached the town, and even if the order had not been given to proceed at a walking pace, we should have been compelled to do so. Before long the carriage was drawn along by men who had unharnessed the horses. It was impossible to prevent this demonstration, which in my opinion is always a dangerous one.

Two days of receptions, of petitions, of evening fetes, composed the short programme of our stay at Rouen. I will take you straight on to Dieppe, where the princess was received as one receives a ray of hope. And in fact she brought for the time being endless prosperity to that watering-place, which till then had been much neglected. She encouraged the manufacture of ivory and of rough lace by her purchases and orders, and she attracted a number of fashionable visitors. The sea-baths which we took together proved very beneficial to both of us, and our stay would have been both satisfactory and agreeable if the news of the king's health had not been of such a nature as to hurry our return to Paris, where it had been thought prudent also to bring His Majesty, so that he might be within reach of all the physicians.

The king, therefore, had returned from Saint-Cloud to Paris. The feast of St. Louis was drawing near, and we asked ourselves whether

His Majesty would appear. His attendants wished to save him the fatigue of this day, but Louis XVIII. replied:

"I will keep up to the end. A sovereign can die, but he must never be ill."

And in fact he did appear. I had not seen him for a long time, and when he was rolled in his chair into the dining-room, where we were all standing and awaiting him, according to the rule on this occasion, I was painfully struck at seeing how thin he had grown. His coat had become too wide for him, his epaulettes hung from his shrunk shoulders, his whole appearance filled one with alarm. At the king's entrance, the trumpets of the *Gardes du Corps* burst into a joyish flourish. Our court dresses, embroidered with gold and silver, the brilliant uniforms worn by those who, together with ourselves, had been admitted that day to the king's table, the flowers heaped up on every side and the dazzling sun formed a festive whole which rendered all the more striking the threat of a speedy dissolution that was to be read on the brow which evidently bent beneath the weight of the crown.

We sat down amid a profound silence; the music only was still heard. After bowing to the company in general, the king took his place, as usual, at the centre of the table; but instead of offering to each in turn the choice between the two dishes which he had before him, and that with the good grace which would have served as an example to every host, he gave way beneath the effort which he had made, his head fell heavily upon the table, and in this position the king remained perfectly motionless, while the music, which had not been countermanded, went on playing!

Try and picture the scene, my children. I was seated on the right of *monsieur*, the king's brother and heir to the throne, which he was so little eager to ascend.

"Look," said he, with ill-restrained terror, "see what that forebodes!"

I was unable to reply.

Meantime the king, rousing himself from this drowsiness or weakness, whichever you prefer to call it, gradually rose, and was taken back to his room without any further accident. I never saw him again out of bed. Nevertheless he continued to work with his ministers, and this went on more or less regularly until the week preceding his decease.

During these final days I rarely left my princess, who even expressed the wish that I should sleep at the Tuileries. We led a sad life, as you can well believe. Frequent bulletins were distributed among the people of Paris, who crowded incessantly into the Place du Carrousel. It was, I believe, on the 16th of September that I returned to my room for a moment after breakfasting with Her Royal Highness, but was hurriedly summoned to accompany her to the king, who was about to receive the Last Sacraments.

I entered his bedroom, as was my duty and my right, and while his family knelt down before his bedside within sight of him, I knelt at the foot, behind the green taffeta curtain which partly screened him from my view; but I lost nothing of the solemn and imposing scene which was accomplished before my eyes. The king, who had prepared himself, received Extreme Unction at the hands of the Grand Almoner of France, and replied in a distinct voice to all that the obligations of the sacrament require. Nothing was heard in the great room but the voices of the priest and the king.

"Now," said he to his successor, who was weeping bitterly, "come near me, brother, with your children."

At these words, all withdrew. After this final and intimate interview, of which no one had the right or dreamt of collecting the details, it was known that the king had said to his family:

"Now that my earthly mission is over, I bid you farewell; leave me to my duties towards Heaven."

They all went out overcome with emotion, and remained, like ourselves, at the Tuileries, amid a perpetual going to and fro. The doctors and personal attendants alone remained in the king's room, which was never quitted by the First Lord of the Chambers, the Duc de Duras, whose service it was. The death agony commenced towards the evening. Consciousness and power of speech had disappeared. Then the royal family returned to the bedside of the dying monarch. The door closed upon the great *Galerie de Diane*, in which were gathered all the households of the king and the princes, which made up a great number of persons; but nothing interrupted the gloomy silence. The whole evening was spent in this way, and part of the night.

About two o'clock in the morning the door leading to the king's bedroom was opened to give passage to a footman, who returned almost immediately carrying a large crucifix; then all once again became silence and immobility. It was not until about four o'clock that the door opened again, this time noisily and precipitately, and we beheld the Duc de Duras coming forth in tears, who in a loud voice pronounced the sacramental words:

"Gentlemen, the King is dead. . . . Long live the King!"

A shudder followed the first words, but immediately there was a general shout of "Long live the King!" At the same moment the new king came out from the death chamber. His face was bathed in tears. He made an expressive gesture that the cheer which he had just heard was not to be repeated, and hastily proceeding towards the Pavilion Marsan, taking no notice of our crowd who followed him, he went to his own apartments.

A few hours later, orders were given by him who was thenceforth to be known as Charles X. Dating from that day, M. le Duc d'Angoulême bore the title of *Dauphin*, Mme. le Duchesse d'Angoulême that of *Dauphiness*, and *Mme. la Duchesse* became Madame, Duchesse De Berry. It was decided that the king, his family and the entire household should leave in the morning for Saint-Cloud. The marshal was on duty for the Royal Guard; he consequently made the military arrangements, and I was happy to think that during the first days of the new reign we should be under the same roof and able to converse privately upon all these great events.

Before long, a number of court carriages, with the king's at their head, set out for Saint-Cloud. We drove at full speed, when suddenly one of the horses of the king's carriage fell down, and naturally delayed the whole progress. This incident, of no importance in itself, impressed me not a little; but on principle I put aside any idea of presentiment, and was careful not to communicate to anybody the slight shock which this had given me.

Chance had allotted me a room which was immediately above that of the king. I believe that Charles X. had provisionally chosen this apartment, on the ground-floor, because it gave on to a little private garden concealed from view. I was quite ignorant of the distribution of this part of the *château*, and when, after arranging my room, I looked out from my window, I quickly withdrew my head on seeing the king walking alone around that small grass-plot. I shall never forget his attitude, which expressed sorrow and profound anxiety. His head bent, his eyes fixed to the ground, he seemed already weary of the weight upon his shoulders. I forbade my maid to give way to any of the acts of curiosity which might be prompted by the near presence of the king, and I went downstairs to join the princess.

Chapter 10

Death of Oudinot

The month of May 1825 was fixed for the coronation, which was to take place at Rheims. At the commencement of that month, Madame, Duchesse de Berry, told me that she was going to start beforehand, and that she would give us a few days at Jeand'heurs and Bar. The marshal and I hurried on in advance to prepare a suitable reception for her in our two houses. Part of the marshal's children, all of mine (who were then very little), the staff of the Royal and National Guards and several of our friends joined us to assist us in our various cares. The witty Alissan de Chazet also offered us his aid in composing an occasional play in which everyone was to take part.

Not far from the *château*, in a building forming part of the paper-works, we arranged a temporary theatre capable of holding several hundreds of people. Lamps were prepared for the illumination of the park, to which the inhabitants of Bar and the neighbourhood were invited. Provisions were laid in for the supply of the three or four different tables necessitated by the various natures of the Princess's suite. I was busily occupied with all these arrangements, when the marshal, who, with his usual temerity, had been trying to subdue a Spanish horse which no one was able to manage, fell with the beast, which rose furiously and trampled upon his body. He was carried indoors in a fainting condition. This happened on a Sunday, and on my return from attending Mass in the village with my children, I saw all my guests assembled on the steps.

One of them came forward to prepare me for the accident. The doctor of the neighbourhood had already given the first help, and soon Doctor Champion came and bled the marshal, and restored his power of breathing. Danger was thus averted; but I was yet far from easy in my mind when, two days later, I had to go and await Madame, Duchesse De Berry, at Châlons-sur-Marne, in order to attend her during the official reception prepared for her. The ordinary programme was gone through, and the next morning we set out for Jeand'heurs, accompanied by the numerous and brilliant suite which was to surround Her Royal Highness at the coronation. We found the marshal at the park-gates, with his family and his staff. My husband had made an effort worthy of his courage in rising from his sick-bed for this purpose. All the authorities and notabilities of Bar and the neighbourhood were also present. The park, adorned by its own natural beauties, and further decorated by the presence of a large number of charmingly-dressed women, offered an attractive appearance with which the princess was greatly struck. She was very natural and made a general pleasant impression.

The illumination produced an admirable effect; both when we went to the theatre and on our return, it was in all its brilliancy. The little piece, full of wit and epigram, had the additional merit of being performed by those who had been dining with Her Royal Highness, who amused herself vastly. When we returned to the brilliantly-lighted drawing-room, one of the actors sat down to the piano, and the princess danced with General de Verdière. The latter had kept on his costume as a *cantinière*, in which he had just been distinguishing himself on the boards. This man, remarkable for the excellence of his heart, his taste, and his wit, brought into everything an animation and a grace all his own.

After the country-dance, when the time to retire had at last come, he offered *Madame* his arm to lead her to her apartments. We all followed, and it was an extraordinary sight to see the tiny princess place her hand upon the enormous arm of the *cantinière* in question and mounting the large and majestic staircase of Jeand'heurs. We were all merry; for General de Verdière knew how to ally incongruity with personal distinction, and nothing ever removed the note of good breeding for which he was so eminently remarkable.

In spite of his weakness and his great fatigue, the marshal had borne better than I expected the duties imposed upon him by circumstances; and he managed to recover sufficient strength to set out for Rheims at the same time as Her Royal Highness and myself.

I occupied a small set of rooms, very high up, beneath the same roof as my princess, at the archbishop's palace, which resembled a bee-hive, so great was the concourse of members of the service of the king and of his family.

The interior of the cathedral had been disguised in a manner calculated to drive lovers of architecture to despair. But on the one hand, this had given work to a number of labourers, and on the other, it had been considered wise to revert to a certain extent to the usages and customs of the old coronations at Rheims. The king arrived twenty-four hours after us. We went, as it were *incognito*, with Madame, Duchesse de Berry, Madame la Dauphine, and both their households, and took up our places at privileged windows to watch the passing of the procession. It was magnificent; but soon a sinister rumour was spread about, which specially afflicted the Duchesse de Damas. One of the carriages of the procession was not in its place, and we heard that this was in consequence of a serious accident which had precipitated the equipage down a deep slope.

This was only too true. It was at Fismes, I believe, that the noise of the cannon frightened the sixteen horses of two of the carriages; those of the king were courageously held in and driven by the coachman, kept up their headlong course without swerving, and finally calmed down as they approached Rheims; but the next carriage, less well driven, was hurled down a terrible height, and the occupants were all more or less hurt. This accident threw a certain gloom over the rest of that day and those which followed. The youngest of the four victims, the Comte de Cossé-Brissac, the king's Lord Steward, was alone able to fulfil his functions at the ceremony; he wore a face covered with contusions and his left eye was concealed beneath a black bandage which he was not able to lay aside for several days. The Duc de Damas, the Duc d'Avaaray and the Comte Curial did not appear at all. The latter died a few months after, as the result, it was said, of his hurts.

I will not describe to you in this place the splendours of this ceremony, in the course of which Charles X. appeared in different costumes before assuming the cloak covered with *fleurs-de-lys* which he wore with infinite grace and majesty, enhanced by the brilliancy of the magnificent crown which adorned his noble brow. No, I will not here repeat these details, which you can find elsewhere; I only wish to tell you of the impression made upon me when the new king, dressed as I have described, and paying no heed to the enormous weight of his rich decorations, which must have been crushing, easily and majestically ascended the immense staircase which had been erected in the centre of the nave, and from the seat on which he took his place, opened an immense cage and set free a mass of birds which flew off in every direction beneath the magnificent arches of the cathedral. This was a symbol of the oath which ensured the liberty and well-being of the people, a graceful image which dated back to many centuries ago.

The banquet took place at about five o'clock. The princesses took no part in it; but a gallery had been erected for them in a corner of the great hall, where they were considered not to be present. Nevertheless, we were all in full court dress, covered with gold and silver, a glittering harness which we wore for some fifteen or eighteen hours in all.

A throne with two steps had been erected at one end of the immense hall. On the first step was laid a table with a single cover, and the same on the second. At the foot of this double throne stretched a table of prodigious length, destined for the great French and foreign dignitaries, the ministers, marshals, ambassadors and so forth, who were all standing in their places awaiting the entrance of the king and *M. le Dauphin*. The latter was dressed like his father in a cloak with the *fleurs-de-lys*; only his cloak was shorter, and his crown open at the top.

The king's, which was the finest I ever saw in my life, was closed by an enormous *fleur-de-lys*, composed of the finest diamonds in the world; the centre leaf contained the diamond known as the Regent. The king, with the dignity natural to him, slowly reached the throne, followed by his son; they sat down, each on his step; and then everyone sat down at the long table, and—a strange sight—in imitation of the king and the heir apparent, who dined with their crowns on their heads, all put on their hats, and ate with their heads covered.

I pass on to the year 1826, which opened under good auspices. The marshal's health was perfect; my children were growing up. Their heart and intelligence left nothing to be desired; my dear stepdaughter Stéphanie brought immense sweetness into our home. Of my two sons, one was still in command at Saumur, the other was doing well in his regiment, and had every chance of a rapid promotion. But though our personal interests were satisfactory, the marshal and I still retained a frequent, vague anxiety concerning the future of the government. Placed so near to the king and the princess, and knowing so well their loyalty and their goodwill for the prosperity of France and the general happiness, we were often alarmed at the illusions of their immediate following. Charles X.'s popularity had been only temporary. The Villèle Ministry, composed of honest men but ignorant of the manner in which to conceal what is often necessarily severe in the methods of government, frequently irritated public opinion.

To give an idea of the want of etiquette which distinguished some of the ministers, I will tell you how the Comte de Corbières, Minister of the Interior, was one day working in the king's closet (this was under Louis XVI II., but quite towards the end of his reign), and absorbed by the subject of his work, persisted in assiduously taking snuff and placing his snuff-box on the king's desk. The king watched this familiarity from the corner of his eye, but without growing angry, and soon the minister's pocket-handkerchief was placed by the side of the snuff-box.

"But, Monsieur de Corbières," said the king, at last, "you appear to be emptying your pockets."

"Perhaps so, Sire," replied the other; "but I should think that was better than filling them."

The speech was a happy one, for Corbières was a man of noted integrity.

When her mourning was over, Madame, Duchesse de Berry, who took precedence immediately after *Mme. la Dauphine*, and who, by the latter's desire, had, as mother of the future King of France, to place herself very much in view of the people, began to receive on a large scale. Sometimes there were theatrical and musical performances, sometimes balls, invitations for which were eagerly sought after. It fell to me to send out these invitations in *Madame's* name. Who will ever know the multiplicity of cares and correspondence entailed by the avidity with which invitations to these royal parties were desired? Not only did all want to be admitted to Her Royal Highness's evenings, but also to receive invitations for their relations and friends. To obtain an invitation, everyone had first to have been presented at court; only young girls were exempted from this formality.

In May, we went to Jeand'heurs. In the beginning of July, I returned alone for my service, which I was never able to neglect for long. The court was at Saint-Cloud; I went to and fro at all times of the day. At the commencement of August, I went to Dieppe with Madame, Duchesse de Berry. We returned in September, and I found the marshal on duty at Saint-Cloud, where I joined him. When his time was up, we left for Jeand'heurs, each with leave for three months, which carried us to the 25th of December.

Frequent hunting parties and a numerous gathering of friends did much to enliven this period; but I did not derive as much pleasure from it as generally, because I was suffering in health. On the government side, all seemed sooner or later to threaten, if not, as yet, the reigning dynasty, at least its security. The Villèle Ministry continued exceedingly unpopular, in spite of its averred honesty and the financial capacity of the premier.

We arrived in Paris from Jeand'heurs at the end of December. We had hardly alighted from our carriage, when we saw coming up to us the Comte Charles de Mornay, a pleasant young member of the marshal's staff, in whom my husband took a great interest.

"Well, what's the news, Mornay?" asked the marshal.

"The most important," he replied, "is that they are unbaptizing the marshals of France."

"What do you mean?"

"Count Apponyi, the new Austrian ambassador, has begun his receptions, but he refuses to admit the great dignitaries of the Empire except under their surnames, and declines to acknowledge territorial titles taken from countries which we have conquered."

"Nonsense!" replied the marshal. "That's impossible."

We talked of other things, and went to bed. The next day, while I was sitting after dinner with the marshal, who was smoking his pipe in his study, our letters were brought to us, including an invitation for the marshal and myself for the aforesaid ambassador's ball: there was no mention of the name of Reggio. I protested; but the marshal made no reply. His calmness astonished me, but all was explained when I saw him return the next morning from a walk he had taken after breakfast.

"I have just returned from the Foreign Minister's," he said. "I frightened him out of his life by telling him that I intended to call out that Austrian ambassador of his if he persisted in playing the master over us. Damas knows me, and trembling all over and very excited, he begged me to do nothing and to write nothing until he had laid the affair before the king. I agreed to wait."

All the marshals who bore Austrian titles took the matter up and complained to the king. The public showed its interest. Your father was lauded to the skies and told that, if he were recognized at the theatre, where he often went to spend an hour, he would be applauded. You can imagine that he abstained from that pleasure for some time! On the other hand, Count and Countess Apponyi tried to appease the storm which they had raised.

All did not end here, however; the opinion of Paris society was divided concerning this incident. A small minority was in favour of the Austrian ambassador, who tempted fortune by giving another ball a few days later. He had every reason to regret it; the army and notably the Gardes du Corps stayed away; the majority of notabilities followed suit; and *M. le Dauphin,* who had pronounced himself very strongly on the French side, gave his thorough approval. No Oudinot ever set foot after that in the Austrian embassy, although the ambassador declared that he had made a mistake in refusing the title of Reggio to Marshal Oudinot; but as he went on to explain that this title was taken from Reggio in Calabria and not from the Austrian Reggio (which was true), the question remained the same for the marshal and his family, for it was the principle, rather than the personal fact, with which we were concerned.

The discredit in which the ministry was held continued to increase, and reacted in a visible manner upon the feelings of the crowd towards the Royal Family. The marshal was in a better position than others to observe this, being at the head of the Paris civic militia, towards which those in power seemed to grow more and more indifferent.

"Sire," he said to Charles X., "the National Guard, which no longer regards itself as being so necessary as in the disastrous days when it alone maintained peace in Paris, is now only sustained by the confidence which it believes itself to have inspired, and which for some time earned for it Your Majesty's favour. This favour seems to be gradually diminishing; the king no longer calls the National Guard out as he used to in the past, when it was proud of being inspected by its general-in-chief, wearing its uniform, and I do not know to what lengths its discouragement would go, if it were not revived once a year by the day which places the king and his family under its exclusive care!"

To explain this speech, I must allude to a fact which dates back to the 12th of April, 1814, the day of the entry of M. le Comte d'Artois into Paris. As Lieutenant-General of the Kingdom, he had promised the National Guard, which was at that time the only force under arms, to grant it on each anniversary of that day the privilege of guarding the sovereign, in memory of the day on which it performed that glorious service. And in fact the Royal Guard outside and the Gardes du Corps inside the Tuileries, in spite of the annoyance this caused them, were obliged to surrender their posts on that day to the National Guard. Their commander-in-chief placed the sentries, gave out the pass-word, and fulfilled the duties of captain of the Guards. In a word, the king, his family and his palace were handed over for twenty-four hours to the charge of the Parisian militia.

Things went on thus till the month of April 1827, when one

morning the king said to the marshal, who had once more raised the question:

"Well, let us clear this matter up, my dear marshal. I understand that you reproach me with not calling out your troops for a long time!"

"Yes, Sire; I think you should either politely send us about our business, or else continue the marks of confidence which it seems to me we have not ceased to deserve."

"Well then, give orders for a review to be held in the Champ-de-Mars on the 29th of April."

The marshal at once instructed the officers of his staff. The chiefs of the thirteen legions of the National Guard, including the cavalry, commanded by the Duc de Fitz-James, were informed of this arrangement, of which all felt the importance.

The anniversary of the 12th of April followed shortly after the king's decision and fell two or three weeks before the great event. Never had the king shown himself more gracious towards the National Guard than he did on that 12th of April; everyone was charmed, and your father came home very satisfied with his sleepless night. For he never went to bed during the twenty-four hours of his responsibility.

Always easy-going, Madame, Duchesse de Berry excused me as often as possible from my duties in attendance; but I was very eager to be present at this review, for which the princesses prepared during some days with an increasing alarm which displayed itself in their anxious demeanour and in half-words which I caught here and there. It was quite clear that their Royal Highnesses had been prepared by some mischief-maker to expect a hostile demonstration on the part of the twenty thousand men gathered under arms on the Champ-de-Mars.

When the day came, I took my place in the *calash* following that containing the king and his family. The rising ground surrounding the Champ-de-Mars was literally covered with an evidently turbulent and excited crowd. We could not clearly distinguish the cries they uttered. There was a brilliant sunshine which drew flashes from the long rows of bayonets drawn up in line on the Champ-de-Mars. The carriages drew up beneath the balcony of the Military School. The king and *M. le Dauphin* alighted from their carriage to mount their horses. The marshal, saluting with his sword with his admirable military grace, had ridden up to receive the king, and soon the brilliant staff rode off along the ranks of the thirteen legions which stretched out far and wide in this vast open space.

Soon, cheers were heard on every side. My heart beat violently, as I gathered the various reports which officers, leaving the escort, brought now to me, now to my carriage-companion. She and I did not share the same opinion on the National Guard, and as the gentlemen were also divided, my agitation is easily explained.

"All goes well," said one; "what you hear is mainly cries of 'Long live the King!'"

Others said, "Those are seditious cries;" and this gave me the more pain because this accusation bore a certain resemblance to the triumph which consists in saying, "I told you so!"

At last the eternal review came to an end, and I saw the king, my husband and all the gold-laced band returning at a gallop. After graciously saluting the princesses, His Majesty turned his horse towards my carriage, and with an accent which I shall never forget, said:

"Well, dear duchesse, the marshal is satisfied, and so am I; on the whole it was rather good than bad."

Quite recovered, I returned to the Pavilion de Marsan, where my princess had arrived before me. She accosted me with a face of consternation; she was feverish and excited.

"Seventeen hundred and ninety-three!" she said.

Astounded at these words, which were so little in keeping with what I had just seen and heard, I was about to ask her for an explanation, when she volunteered it in these terms:

"My sister and I heard threatening words coming from the people assembled on the Champ de Mars; they were renewed as we drove off; and, as you know, the king was insulted in the ranks of the National Guard," and so on.

I endeavoured to calm this explosion; but seeing that my efforts were useless, and overcome with excitement and fatigue, I returned home, where I was soon joined by my husband. He said:

"The king, escorted by all whom you saw on horseback around him, assembled us in the yard of the Tuileries, and before alighting and going in, said, 'Well, gentlemen, there is more good than harm in all this.' His words were confirmed by the expression of his face. He dismissed us, but I went in with him to beg him urgently for leave to draw up and submit to him an order of the day to be inserted at once in the *Moniteur*. 'Justice should be done publicly, Sire,' I said, 'as the position today was public. There has been much good and little harm done, as Your Majesty admits; but this fact should be proclaimed throughout the kingdom, so that all the world may know how small was the number of those who dared to mingle a hostile voice with the loud cheers with which the king was received.' The king seemed to fall in with my views, and he said, 'Come back at nine o'clock this evening with the order you suggest.' If my advice is followed," added the marshal, "all may yet be well."

Your father and I had a long talk, and then he left me to occupy himself with the matter in hand, and the day passed without our hearing what had happened in Paris after the review was over. It seemed that after the king and the court had returned, and when the thirteen legions of the National Guard had commenced to march back, to the sound of their drums, to their respective quarters, a serious incident took place.

All Paris was out of doors; the Tuileries Gardens in particular were crammed with people. The Vicomte de Sambucy, a man most devoted to the reigning dynasty, was marching back the legion whose colonel he was from the Champ-de-Mars to the Marais, and at first led it from the Place Louis XV. towards the Rue Royale; but seeing that this street was blocked by the crowd, he was seized with the fatal idea of turning to the right and thus leading his troops into the Rue de Rivoli. The sound of the drum, joined to the general excitement of the day, brought the enormous crowd in the Tuileries Gardens to the Terrasse des Feuillants, which skirts the Ministry of Finance, occupied at that time by M. de Villèle.

By an unfortunate accident, one of the minister's servants, attracted by the noise, had gone out on the balcony. He was taken for the Minister himself; there was, some said, a certain resemblance. At sight of him a cry was heard, no one knew whence, of "Down with Villèle!" Alas, it was not the only one, and the shout was taken up to some small extent by the troop, as it marched past, and almost unanimously by the crowd in the gardens.

This demonstration brought the discontent of the president of the council to a climax. He hastened to the king, and depicted this occurrence to him as an attack coming from a troop armed in his defence which ought to involve an immediate and exemplary repression. And this in spite of his expressed opinion that the bulk of the cries issued from the people!

However this may be, this report, coming but a few moments after the king's conversation with your father, changed the whole aspect of affairs, and when in the evening the marshal, obeying his instructions, presented himself in the king's closet, he found him in a condition of extreme alarm, which was shared by all around him. The proposed order of the day, to which the marshal attached such great importance, was adjourned for no plausible reason, and your father returned home in despair, since this postponement not only destroyed the appositeness of the proposed measure, but annulled its effects. He did not, however, go so far as to foresee what was about the follow.

I spent a bad night; but fairly early in the morning, I rang for Madame Pils, who, without any preamble, exclaimed:

"*Madame la duchesse*, there is no longer a National Guard in Paris."

I thought I was dreaming when the marshal came in and told me the sad story. He was lying in bed at about midnight when Pils showed into his room a *gendarme* bringing a letter from the Minister of the Interior. I have not the original, but I remember that it was pretty nearly in these words:

> *Monsieur le Maréchal,*
> I have the honour to inform you, on behalf of the king, that the National Guard of Paris has been dissolved.
> I have the honour to be, &c.
> (Signed) Corbières.

In the morning, to the gaping surprise of the passers-by, the words "Headquarters of the National Guard" were removed from the house we occupied, and we began to think of finding a lodging elsewhere.

It would be impossible to tell you what resulted from this great event; only you must know that the government and court were greatly deceived as to the effect it produced. Some took the gloomy silence which followed the events of the 29th of April for submission; others said, as they rubbed their hands, "You see, they are delighted to be relieved from the troubles of their service."

They either did not know, or took no heed, of a significant fact; here it is. We were told that from the Porte de Saint-Denis was hung, I do not know how, a large picture representing a National Guard's uniform, with these words in large letters:

FOR SALE
A NATIONAL GUARD'S CAST-OFF UNIFORM

Followed by, in parentheses:

(MINUS THE MUSKET).

Instances were also related of insolence displayed during the review. Here is one which the marshal would quickly have punished, if the king had not prevented him in time. A grenadier left the ranks at the moment when His Majesty was passing before him, and boldly said to Charles X.:

"Down with the ministers!"

With noble coolness, the king replied:

"Sir, I have come here to receive respect, not lessons."

When, after a short retreat, the marshal returned to the Tuileries, he had made up his mind to keep a stern silence, and he followed this plan in spite of all the expressions of regret with which he was overwhelmed. These regrets referred to him personally, and not to the measure in question, upon which they seemed, on the contrary, to congratulate themselves. Alas, it was much more for the sake of the dynasty than for his own that your father deplored what had been place, and what was certainly the prelude to the Revolution.

But I was not long in a condition to follow the effects of this movement. On the 13th of May I was attacked by a congestion of the brain which made me pass a whole day for dead. The marshal, distraught, summoned all his energy in vain; the first doctors in Paris exhausted themselves to no purpose in order to bring back to me a breath of life; when M. de Caunan, who had heard me praising M. Dupuytren above all others, sent for him at his country-house at Courbevoie.

Dupuytren arrived at two o'clock in the morning, examined me, and said, "She is not dead." He forthwith set energetically to work, and without wearying you with painful and superfluous details, I will tell you that within a few hours I opened my eyes, which had been closed since the day before, and at once recognized the faces bending over me. I tried to speak to all; I thought I was articulating, but no sound came from my lips; at last I succeeded in conveying that I wished to see my children.

The violent treatment which had saved me from death had shattered my nervous system to such a degree that it was long before I recovered my normal condition. I asked for an indefinite leave to go first to Plombières and next to Jeand'heurs. The marshal was unable to go with me, and I took my daughter Louise, poor dear child, who, with the gentle care of her twelve years, did all she could for her mother. She was well seconded by Mme. Monniot, my children's devoted governess. But I did not benefit at all by my course of waters; seeing which, our excellent friend M. Gouy wrote to the marshal to come at once and take me to Jeand'heurs.

We returned to Paris at the end of the autumn. Although still languid and melancholy, I nevertheless resumed my court service, leaving out, as far as possible, all that was not absolutely essential.

It was in the course of this winter, in February, I believe, that the fall took place of the Villèle Ministry. It was an excited political winter. Nevertheless, the choice of the new ministers seemed to satisfy public opinion. M. de Martignac, who took charge of the portfolio of the Interior, gave his name to the Cabinet, which was joined by one of our friends, the Comte de La Ferronays, the nobility and loyalty of whose character were well known and transcendental. By his adhesion to the moderate system which was announced, this devoted servant of the Bourbons in exile brought a generally appreciated guarantee into the new policy. It was realized that he would never fail in his unalterable attachment to the reigning dynasty, but at the same time that his policy would be enlightened by the experience which he had acquired since his return to France.

The persistent enfeebled condition of my health during the winter of 1827 to 1828 caused me to ask for fresh leave in the spring. The month of May was spent at Jeand'heurs, where I hoped to be able to prolong my stay with you, when I received a letter from Madame, Duchesse de Berry, summoning me immediately to Saint-Cloud; this was, she told me, in order to arrange for a long tour which she was about to make through France, and which was to end in a stay at the Pyrenees, where my health would certainly recover its vigour. I pass over the following four months. You will find this period fully described, my children, in the official journal of this journey to the Pyrenees, which did, in fact, as Her Royal Highness had prophesied, restore me completely to health.

Two family sorrows followed shortly upon this period: I lost my young and charming sister-in-law de Coucy and my excellent brother-in-law de La Guérivière.

On my return from the Pyrenees, I learnt that the king had granted the marshal, for an indefinite period, the use of the fine house belonging to the crown on the Place Vendôme. Its nearness to the Tuileries and the time which this saved me doubled the value of this favour.

It was at about the same time that our dear Stéphanie was asked in marriage by M. James Hainguerlot, a wedding which realized, by forty years of happiness, the promises it had brought.

The summer of 1829 was spent, as usual, in the spot which your father loved to call his paradise, and of which he was so pleased to do the honours, not only to his family and friends, but to all who penetrated within its boundaries. I hoped not to return to Paris with my husband and children until the end of the autumn; but I suddenly received a despatch which was brought me from the post by M. Malingrey. He arrived breathless one morning with this letter, which bore the superscription of Her Royal Highness:

> Come as quickly as you can, (she said), in order to arrange for a journey which I shall soon have to undertake to meet the King of Naples, my father. He is to cross a part of France on the road to Spain, where he is taking my pretty sister Christina.

I set out at once. When I arrived at Saint-Cloud, where the court was in residence, I received my instructions at once.

"There is nothing official about the journey," said the king; "this time Madame, Duchesse de Berry, is simply indulging in a family gratification. She will stay at her own expense at hotels in the towns she stops at, and if her *incognito* is betrayed, and the authorities choose to wait upon her, they must do so without uniforms or speeches."

This suited Her Royal Highness and myself admirably, for we had hardly rested from the former journey, which, you will remember, kept us for four months in the public view. Moreover, it was a very wise resolve under the circumstances of the time, for I must tell you that the Martignac Ministry had been replaced by the Ministry of the Prince de Polignac. This step had thrown all France into excitement; dull rumours were heard in every part of the country, and a very showy demonstration had besides just attracted the public attention.

This was an almost triumphal journey made by General de La Fayette, precisely through the districts which we were to traverse. It is not well to raise altar against altar, and without seeking to throw a veil over so honest and simple action as that of going to meet her family, Madame, Duchesse de Berry, was very well advised, so shortly after her triumphs of 1828, in laying aside her royalty on this occasion.

I had only just commenced to make my arrangements, when one of my intimate friends, the Marquise de Béthisy, came to me, and told me in confidence:

"I owe it to my friendship for you to tell you something which it may be useful for you to know before you start on your journey. It would seem that the Neapolitan ambassador, who is to be one of the party, proposes to renew, in your case, the Austria-Apponyi business."

"Not really!" I exclaimed.

"Yes," continued the *marchioness*, "he relies upon that antecedent, saying that since your Reggio has been proclaimed to be the Calabrian one, there is no reason why the king, his master, should not attempt what was tried by the emperor of Austria."

No motive in the world would have induced me knowingly to abandon the title purchased by my husband at the price of his great deeds. I made an energetic protest; and anticipating the arrival of the king of Naples, I am able to state that, although the actual bearer of the name of Reggio, Prince Scilla, formed part of the court of the Italian princes whom we expected, King Francis I. ostentatiously addressed me by my title as Duchesse de Reggio.

Madame, Duchesse de Berry, was not yet informed as to the date upon which the king her father would reach the French frontier; nor did she know when the Infanta Carlota, her sister, married to Don Francis de Paula, brother to the King of Spain, would arrive in Dauphine, where the two princesses were to meet, in order to travel together towards Their Neapolitan Majesties. Taking advantage of this latitude, Her Royal Highness made several excursions. On the 15th of October, we slept at Chalon, and the next day set out for *Mâcon*. The Saone was so flooded that we saw what was almost a sea before our eyes. On alighting at a fine hotel on the quay, Her Royal Highness was informed that her *incognito*, which had been so well observed till then, had been betrayed. The authorities were eager for receptions, and offered all kinds of entertainments; but *Madame* escaped by means of kind words, and only consented to witness from her balcony a display of fireworks prepared by the soldiers of the 24th.

We here received news of the *infanta*; she was to arrive at Vienne at the same time as ourselves or shortly after, which decided Her Royal Highness not to stop at Lyons. We did not find the *infanta* at Vienne, and we pursued our road to Tain, where the two sisters alighted from their carriages at the same time, and embraced each other tenderly.

We returned to sleep at Valence, at the Hôtel de la Poste. I spent most of the time at dinner in observing the royal couple who had joined us (I see I had forgotten to tell you that the *infant* accompanied his wife). The princess, who had been long married (she was only fourteen when she married the *infant*), exercised, it was said, great influence over King Ferdinand VII., her brother-in-law; she was considered to have much influence upon the council, and to her efforts was attributed his marriage with the Princess Christina, her own sister.

For as you know, these two princesses were only sisters to Madame, Duchesse de Berry, on their father's side.

Dona Carlota was already the mother of a number of children. Her enormous stoutness deprived her of all appearance of youth. She was very gracious to me, but her tone of voice was positive and decided.

We returned to Lyons on the 20th, and alighted at the Hôtel de l'Europe, where they have enormous rooms and a very good table. Madame, Duchesse de Berry, occupied herself greatly with the *toilette* of the princess her sister. She had foreseen ever since leaving Paris that this would be necessary: and when everyone was ready, we set out in town carriages to visit the shops and manufactories, and to buy as much as possible. Then we went to the hospital, a huge and splendid edifice built by Soufflot, the architect of Saint-Géneviève in Paris. On the next day, Her Royal Highness, still retaining her so-called *incognito*, and accompanied by the authorities disguised in mufti, continued her exploration of all the curiosities of Lyons.

On leaving, we stopped at the *château* of General Guyot, near a place called the "Passage," because a Carthaginian buckler was found there a hundred years ago, and led to suppose that Hannibal must have crossed the Alps not far from there. General Guyot, who had gone through all the great wars with my husband, and who spoke of him to me as he is always spoken of, offered Her Royal Highness a splendid hospitality. Room was found for both the Spanish and French suites in this beautiful house. The luxury which was displayed was hardly calculated to prepare us for the serious undertaking of the morrow, which was no less than to sleep at the Grande-Chartreuse, which we proposed to visit at a time of year when no traveller dreams of going there.

An incredible tumult reigned in the village of Saint-Laurent-du-Pont, where our mules and guides were awaiting us, and where the arrival of two princesses and an *infant* had caused an unwonted agitation. The crowd pushed and fought; and the mayor, like all mayors or nearly all mayors, had lost his head. Each clamoured for his steed; soon Madame, Duchesse de Berry, was seated on hers; but when the turn came of the *infanta*, it was quite another thing. I heard her shouting in Spanish to General Audenarde, the commander of the department, some vehement words of which I do not know the meaning, but which seemed peremptory to him, for he made respectful signs of assent. I since learnt that she was explaining to him that she could not get into the armchair saddle which had been prepared for her. It was only too true.

Meanwhile the caravan was kept waiting, and I saw the time pass with alarm, especially when I looked at the dark defile into which we were about to plunge. The general then took a great resolve; at his request the mayor supplied an armchair; two vigorous *douaniers* pushed sticks under the seat; they raised up the *infanta*, and thus carried her out of the village. It was then only that she decided to remount her mule, which this time she straddled without any difficulty.

Night fell, the cold became keen, and soon we reached a layer of snow which threw up the imposing blackness of the rocks and gigantic pine trees, among which the rough road has, with great difficulty, been traced. At last I distinguished a dark and enormous mass before us; it was the Chartreuse.

Soon a feeble light appeared. It was Dom Bruno, the superior, who came to admit the princes. He received them with a remarkable mingling of Christian humility and of aristocratic good-breeding. The suite remained in a large house outside the monastery. None but the princes and their immediate following had the right to penetrate into the quarter of the monks. We were even told that the princesses would not have been admitted if one of them had not been mother to the heir to the throne of France.

Guided by Dom Bruno, we entered an immense hall whose white walls and great chimney, in which blazed a splendid fire, gladdened all of us. Four cells, situated at the four corners of this room, were pointed out to us, one for my princess, the second for the Spanish couple, the third for me, and the fourth for Mme. de Bouillé. A corner was also found for our maids; and while the superior replied with respect and dignity to the questions which everyone addressed to him, Brother Jean-Marie, the minister and master of ceremonies of the house, took pains to make every one comfortable. Soon he came to tell us that supper was served.

I had had the good fortune to inspire him with confidence, and all he said came through me. We followed him, accompanied by the superior, and we walked long without passing through half of the corridor, whose vastness was made evident to us by means of a little light which had been placed at its further end. At last a door opened and admitted us to a well-warmed and lighted room, in the midst of which a table was laid with supper, which naturally included no meat.

The superior withdrew, and the two-fold duty of doing the honours and of waiting at table fell to Brother Jean-Marie, who acquitted himself marvellously of his task. Whenever he experienced a momentary doubt, he would come and tap me gently on the shoulder, and ask, "Is this the right time to hand that dish?" He anxiously followed the effect produced by the cooking of the monastery. He must have been satisfied; for if it had not been thought good, we should have pretended that it was.

At the end of the meal I saw him return in triumph: he had brought a chocolate pudding! He whispered in my ear, "I think it's a success!" It was the cream of the repast, and met with all desirable triumph; and in all my life I shall never forget the happy air of this good monk, who, himself vowed to eternal privations, enjoyed this exceptional dainty through our palates.

At dessert Dom Bruno came and joined us, to take us to the common room, where the great fire was still burning, and where a table had been brought, with pens, ink and paper, and a solitary book, the life of the founder, St. Bruno.

Some of us wrote, others turned over the pages of this volume; nothing was heard in the room but the whistling of the wind and the crackling of the fire. None of us was eager to speak, for we awaited the signal for *matins*, at which we were secretly to assist. The bells were heard at eleven o'clock.

"Come," said the Reverend Father, returning to the room, "but walk quietly, I beg of you, because none of our Brothers must know what is happening here."

We followed him along that unexampled corridor, upon which each cell has its outlet.

"Let us hurry," added Dom Bruno: "we must be installed in the darkest part of the chapel before the second bell, which will toll presently, brings all the community there."

We hastened our steps as much as possible, and hardly breathed, so as not to disturb this eternal silence. We reached the chapel at last, and our group took up its position, under the Reverend Father's direction, in a corner which was so dark that it was impossible that we should be perceived, for two candles only were lit upon the altar, while all the rest of the building was in darkness. A side-door opened in the choir; the Carthusians entered one by one, with slow steps, carrying each a dark lantern, which only lit up him who carried it. Their white gowns, with a hood pulled down over the face, and the silence, which was only broken by the bell, have left me an undying remembrance.

When each Father had taken his place in his stall (there were twenty-six of them), commenced a grave and solemn chant, which lasted about half-an-hour, during which time we did not make a movement; and this could have been prolonged, so magnetized were we by this imposing scene, if the superior, who always has the liberty of his actions, and who alone can depart when he pleases from the established rule, had not left his stall to come to us and bring us back to the great hall, before the monks regained their cells.

I, for my part, brought back from the church not only an icy feeling of cold, which soon vanished before the great fire, but a deep moral emotion, which was increased by several details which I obtained from Dom Bruno. For instance, it was during their first sleep that the monks, old and young, were awakened by the stroke of the first *matins* which we had just heard. They returned to sleep, only to be summoned again, before daybreak, to the same chapel, where the exercise was continued; and in spite of the severity of their other duties, Dom Bruno told us that these interruptions of their night's rest were what cost them most in their life. They spend their days in the most complete isolation; what is called their cell consists of two rooms, one in which they sleep, the other in which they work, either intellectually or with their hands, for some of them do carpenters' or joiners' work.

Leading out of these two rooms, each has a small garden closed in with a wall; they only meet in church, and never speak to one another except during their walks, which take place once or twice a week. They then walk two by two, but the choice of a companion is never left to them; they are changed about so that they shall not develop any habits or special friendships. Their food, although they never eat meat, is nevertheless much more substantial than that of the Trappists, for instance; thus they eat fish, eggs, and so on. Their meals are brought to them and put down outside in a revolving cupboard, which they turn round to take what has been brought them and to return the empty dish. The Carthusian Order does not exact so rigorous an abstinence as many of the others; thus, when a new monk arrives, they carefully examine what comes back on the dish; if he returns it quite empty, his portion is increased the next day, because all appetites are not uniform.

I was much impressed by all I had seen and heard, and before letting the worthy superior go, I asked him, with a certain apprehension, what we others, we worldly people, might hope for, when we compared our lives with those of these penitent saints.

"Reassure yourself, *Madame*," he said, "with the thought that we have voluntarily chosen the trials which we endure here, while those which are sent you, in the world in which you live, are imposed upon you by the will of God. You have not chosen them, and yet sometimes they must have seemed very hard to you to bear. Accept them submissively, and you will reach the same point as ourselves."

Thereupon he bowed to us and wished us a goodnight, while Brother Jean-Marie, pushing hospitality to its last limits, busied himself, with surprising activity, in warming our beds.

We commenced the next day, I think, by attending Low-Mass, recited by one of the Fathers, but by daylight it was not necessary to conceal our presence in the church. We were next taken to visit an uninhabited cell, so as to give us an idea of it: you have already read my description of it. We were then shown over the kitchen and the refectory, where all take a meal together on Sundays, with orders not to exchange a word. We ended with the library, a magnificent room decorated with many pictures all representing scenes from the life of St. Bruno.

The descent on mule-back was still more fatiguing than the ascent. Personally, I was worn out by the time I reached the carriage, which brought us to Grenoble at ten o'clock in the evening. We were set down at the Marquis de Vaulserre's, who had placed his whole house, with its furniture, silver, linen, and so forth, at the entire disposal of Her Royal Highness. We needed the whole of the 26th to rest ourselves.

On the 30th, M. le Duc, Mme. la Duchesse d'Orléans, M. le Duc de Chartres, and the Princesse Louise, his sister, who had arrived on the evening of the 29th, came to pay a visit to Madame, Duchesse de Berry, and to the *infants*. It was arranged to do the round of the public institutions together. The military ones, especially, are very important. The princes and princesses stayed to dinner. M. le Duc de Blacas, the King of France's ambassador, had arrived at the same time, to bring His Majesty's compliments to the King of Naples; I applied to him at once, to know how far I was bound by the laws of hospitality in regard to the Neapolitan ladies who were to accompany the Queen of Naples.

"The first place belongs to you," he replied; "never fail to take it."

During the whole of this meeting, the Duc de Blacas showed himself very French, and eminently gracious, especially in what concerned myself.

The King, Queen and Court of Naples and the young Queen of Spain were expected on the 31st. The princesses, daughters and sister to the King of Naples, wished to go and meet him unattended. It was decided that we should await the return of the whole party at the *prefect's*, where Their Majesties were to sleep. We were at our posts between three and four o'clock when they arrived. After retiring for a little while to their apartments, the king and queen, followed by all the princesses, entered the drawing-room, where we were waiting. Madame, Duchesse de Berry, taking me by the hand, presented me to the king her father and the queen her stepmother.

They withdrew again, and then the time came for dinner; suddenly the door opened, and the King of Naples, followed by his family, entered and came up to me.

"Madame la Duchesse de Reggio," he said, "I am happy to have this opportunity of telling you that I know of your devotion to my daughter, the Duchesse de Berry, and that I appreciate it highly."

These kind words on the part of the sovereign moved me deeply; I had, moreover, made it a labour of love to contribute to the success of a reception offered to a king of the Bourbon family visiting the states of a Bourbon on the throne of France.

Here is a short description of the appearance of the Neapolitan Court. The king, very energetic in his movements, was shattered with a violent attack of rheumatism. The queen his wife, sister to Ferdinand VII., to whom she was about to marry her daughter, wore an expression of great kindness. She was still nursing her twelfth child, the Count of Trapani. The queen-elect was twenty-four years of age and extremely pretty. She maintained a great reserve before the king her father, who wielded with authority his two-fold sceptre as king and father of his family. Next came the *infant*. Among the officers and ladies attached to the Court of Naples, I will mention Prince Scilla and the Duchesses of San Martino and San Valantino.

The return journey commenced; it was strewn with great receptions and fetes. There was a recrudescence of zeal and of loud cheering at the sight of Madame, Duchesse de Berry, since she had left Dauphiné; but it was to her personally that this enthusiasm was directed. However, the King of Naples replied to all the speeches which were addressed to him personally; but the text of his replies did not contain great variety, for, to tell the truth, he harped upon the fact that he was being thanked for being "the father of his daughter."

We parted from the Neapolitan princes on the Spanish frontier.

The journey was over! I cannot describe to you my delight at rejoining my husband, my children, and at last enjoying comparative repose. . . . For the winter of 1829 to 1830 did not put an end to my occupations: on the contrary!

What most painfully struck your father and myself was the imminence of an ever-increasing danger that threatened the reigning dynasty. The blindness of its friends seemed to lend a fatal assistance to the various parties that opposed it. One of the great features of the period which we had now reached was the preparations which were being made for the Algerian campaign. The Polignac Ministry had brought General de Bourmont to the War Office. No sooner was he in office than he saw a prospect of immediate war for the government in which he was to play so active a part, and he demanded and at once obtained the command-in-chief of the landed forces. He and his four sons had determined to die or distinguish themselves. In the meanwhile the seals of the War Office were held by the Comte de Champagny. Strange and deplorable results of party spirit! In a nation generally so sympathetically inclined for war, this particular war, from the first rumours concerning it, excited loud disapproval. The masses had clearly resolved to blame the actions of the ministry before weighing their motives. Nevertheless, the preparations were hurried forward, and by the spring of 1830 we were prepared to hurl our land and sea forces against that nest of pirates.

When I returned to Paris, Madame, Duchesse de Berry, was greatly busied with the approaching arrival of the King and Queen of Naples. They were to be received as Bourbons and sovereigns, in other words, with all possible display. I confess that I was alarmed for the foreign princes at the thought of the want of sympathy which they would possibly be shown by the crowd. The Revolution was already seething, particularly in Paris. I should have wished that this court, which it was our pleasure and our honour to receive in a suitable fashion, might be spared the sight of the troubles that underran our capital.

At the beginning of May, Madame, Duchesse de Berry, obtained leave from the king to go as far as Blois to meet the king her father. With us in the carriage was the prince of Salerno, brother to Francis I., and much younger than he. He was gay and spirited, and in his earlier visits to Paris, his manners had been greatly liked. We slept at Blois, where the ordinary receptions took place. We next stopped at Châteaudun. Our third halting-place was the Château de Rambouillet, where *M. le Dauphin* and *Mme. la Dauphine* had come to await

Their Neapolitan Majesties, who returned with them and took up their quarters in the Palais-Bourbon.

Towards the end of April was held a grand review in the Champ-de-Mars, which the marshal commanded. It was the last outing of that fine Royal Guard. It was the sovereign's farewell to the picked troops who, before three months were past, were to fight at their posts of honour in the streets of Paris. My children, you must retain a vague recollection of that memorable morning. Was it a presentiment which imbued your father with the desire that you should be present, young as you were, at this review, the last which Marshal Oudinot held at the head of an army? And you, my grandchildren, would have felt an indescribable emotion if you had ever seen the warlike attitude which distinguished the marshal when, passing before the king on horseback, he saluted with his sword with a chivalrous grace which I have never seen except in him.

On the 1st of May, my husband handed over the command of the Royal Guard to his colleague Marshal Marmont, his successor for the ensuing quarter, and left to prepare to preside over the electoral college at Verdun, spending at Jeand'heurs the time that elapsed before its meetings.

The august visitors were no sooner installed in Paris than we were all busied in showing them all that was to be seen and in entertaining them in every possible manner. There was play at the king's, receptions at *Madame's*, performances in all the theatres. The King of Naples wished particularly to attend a performance at the Gymnase, which, if you remember, was under *Madame's* immediate protection. We also went to Compiègne, where splendid hunting-parties were given which delighted the Court of Naples. Charles X. was an admirable horseman, and followed the hounds as a young man might have done.

Madame, Duchesse de Berry, had asked and obtained an unusual favour to which she attached immense price. This was to receive her son for the first time at Rosny—Rosny, her joy, where during the course of each year, she spent days of delight which she strove to make as rustic as possible. She had once brought her daughter with her; but as to M. le Duc de Bordeaux, for whom they would have set a regiment marching, or what you will, she had not as yet dared hope to receive him here. The opportunity was a good one, since the King and Queen of Naples were preparing to stay at Rosny. By a still more special favour, the King of France declared that he too would be of the party. The whole family of M. le Duc and Mme. la Duchesse d'Orléans was also invited to this gathering, the preparations and details of which, as you may imagine, required infinite care.

On their return to Paris, the courts of France and Naples were invited by M. le Duc and Mme. la Duchesse d'Orléans to a magnificent ball. As an exceptional fact, it was intimated that the King of France would be present. Naturally all the guests, even the Court of Naples, arrived at the Palais-Royal before the king was expected. It was in the middle of June. All Paris was out of doors, and naturally turned towards the spot where the ball was being given, a spot always so crowded, and this time offering an infrequent and curious spectacle. Never were the police precautions more neglected than on this occasion; it was with unexampled difficulty that we were able to penetrate through the stream of people who, if they showed no hostility, neither gave any sign of pleasure. An eager curiosity was all that we were able to distinguish in the crowd.

Upon our arrival, we found the family of M. le Duc d'Orléans in a state of extreme agitation and alarm at the news they had heard of this compact crowd which the king would have to pass through. They had eyes for no one, not even the Court of Naples, and it was clear that the arrival of the King of France absorbed all their thoughts. He appeared at last; received all the masters of the palace with his habitual grace and serenity; and in order to reach the place prepared for him, crossed all those magnificent rooms filled with the elegance of Paris. In the hope of catching sight of some of the fete, the crowd, which was numerous everywhere, had with redoubled ardour come to pack itself in the gardens of the Palais-Royal, which were brilliantly lighted. One saw nothing but heads, touching each other, without any interval. How many thousands can there have been? I do not know, but we were able to form an idea of this agglomeration when the king, agreeing to the proposal of M le Duc d'Orléans, walked round the outer galleries, followed by all the princes and princesses.

The king, in uniform, wearing his blue riband and all his orders, walked easily, and looked out with his customary benevolence upon the immense populace which thronged beneath him. There rose shouts, but it was impossible to distinguish their true meaning. I have retained the impression that amid a display of great curiosity and of perhaps a little affection, the crowd seemed to solicit something from the king. To my belief, it was a change of ministry.

When this promenade along the outer galleries was finished, the king stepped inside to watch the commencement of the official quadrilles; but no sooner had the crowd lost him from sight, than loud cries issued from its midst. A flame sprang up suddenly; it came from all the chairs in the Palais-Royal garden, which had been heaped up to make room, and which took fire without its ever being discovered who was guilty of the outrage. I remember that the Comte de Rumily, *aide-de-camp* to M. le Duc d'Orléans, was as one distraught, and said to me:

"Ah! now we shall be accused of not taking all possible precautions, whereas there is not one of which we did not ourselves make certain."

I do not know whose fault it was. The public accused the *Prefect* of Police of inactivity, but it was generally believed that, in so far as the blaze was concerned, this had been caused by a discarded cigar-end. In any case, the sight was a very exciting one, but there were no serious accidents reported as the result of the fire. The departure of the king, through the same crowd, was effected without difficulty, and the ball was continued with great spirit.

This was the end of the official pleasures of my poor princess . . . She danced till daybreak, and I remember that a fine sunrise lighted my drive home.

I had come to the end of my strength, and I begged for a leave of some weeks in order to join my husband at Jeand'heurs, secretly resolved to return for the opening of the chambers, which marked the moment when would burst out, not a radical revolution—we were far from believing that—but an inevitable struggle. I wished to be present at this, and I went home to recover the necessary strength. As I have said, my husband, who had been appointed by the king chairman of the electoral college of Verdun, had left at the commencement of May, and I remember that during the visit to Rosny, the king, enquiring after the marshal, asked me:

"What shall we obtain from the elections?"

"None but opposition members, Sire!"

"Pooh! out of four returned, won't there be one on the ministerial side?"

"He does not think so, Sire."

The king did not seem convinced; nothing would move him from his sense of security. Not only did he deceive himself, but he was deceived by those about him. I heard him say about this time that, to satisfy his conscience as a sovereign, he read the papers of the most opposite shades, in order to be informed of the opinion of the masses.

"Well then," he added, "when you come to learn the number of subscribers, you see, for instance, that the *Gazette de France* has six times as many as the *Constitionnel*."

The exact contrary was the case. Who could thus have deceived the good king over a material calculation which it was not possible for him to verify for himself?

At the end of the first fortnight in June, I announced to the marshal my approaching arrival at Jeand'heurs. I wanted to see him again before his departure for Verdun. I was quietly making my preparations and my farewell calls in Paris. One morning I had forbidden my door in the Place Vendôme, when I saw Marshal Marmont, Duc de Raguse, arrive, who had insisted upon seeing me. He had, if you remember, taken up his three-monthly service as major-general on the 1st of May. He had just come from Saint-Cloud, where the king was already in residence for the summer.

"They tell me you are going back to Oudinot," he said. "Tell him again what I have told him so often, that he is the luckiest of men and I the most unlucky. I have found a new proof of this in the events of the day; your husband has passed on to me the baton of command for the precise quarter during which the government is about to take the most dangerous and fatal measures, and during my command of the Royal Guard I shall have to give military support to resolutions which I deplore as much for the dynasty as for the country. Ah, if I escape the almost certain hazard which I look upon as immediate, I shall ask for a long leave, and let all these questions be fought out without me, while I remove far from France the fatality which has always pursued me."

I listened to Marshal Marmont sadly, although I endeavoured to refute his sombre predictions.

"No," he resumed, "I can hardly be deceived since I have been at Saint-Cloud, in a position to observe all that goes on about the king; I cannot doubt that a *coup d'état* is on the point of bursting forth."

Thereupon he left me, and I only saw him once more, when I was myself at Saint-Cloud on the eve of my departure. There I dined with the Comte de Cossé-Brissac, one of our best friends, together with a large number of other guests, including the Duc de Mortemart, who sat beside me. He had just returned on leave from St. Petersburg, where he was our ambassador.

"What is all this that is happening here, *Madame la duchesse?*" he asked. "I feel as though I had fallen from the clouds; all I see and hear makes me dread a *coup d'état* as dangerous as it is ill-placed."

This language of men devoted to France and to the king proved to me more and more that a crisis was inevitable; but I only expected it for the meeting of the chambers in September, and I hurried as much as possible to join my husband and make the most of the short leave which we would be able to enjoy together. As I curtsied to the king that day at Saint-Cloud, I little thought that it was the last time I should see him or any of his august family. Madame, Duchesse de Berry, had stayed in Paris in order to be with the Court of Naples till the last. I took leave of her at the Pavilion de Marsan.

I left with my daughters on the 25th of June. We had scarcely passed the first relays when my carriage broke. It was only a slight accident, and it was being repaired, when a loud noise was heard behind us. My carriage was drawn to the side of the road, in order to leave the middle of the road to a number of equipages with six horses apiece. The servants wore the livery of M. le Duc d'Orléans, who with his family and suite was conducting the Court of Naples to his place at Rency. My children and I, who had alighted while our carriage was being repaired, recognized every face. All passed before us like an arrow from the bow. It was the last picture we carried away in our recollection.

Shortly after my arrival we were able to celebrate the capture of Algiers. It was a great triumph for our military and naval forces; we rejoiced at it with all our hearts, and I still feel indignation at the spirit of opposition which had permeated through the masses and prevented them from rejoicing, like true Frenchmen, at so great a triumph.

The general uneasiness penetrated even into our country life. At last we reached the 27th of July. The marshal—I can still see him—was playing picquet with the Marquis de Montmort; the rest of the company and I were on the step of the great courtyard when we saw an express trotting up from M. de Caunan, who had lately been appointed *Prefect* of the Meuse. He brought a message announcing the Orders in Council. . . .

Several voices exclaimed, "Ah, there will be firing!"

"Perhaps not," replied the marshal, who, with an apparent calmness with which he was endowed, especially for great occasions, always endeavoured to preserve the coolness of others; "we must wait and see."

As far as he was concerned, he was in a very lawful position, under the guarantee of an official order of the king, who had sent him to the Meuse as president of an electoral college; and during the period of the terrible days that ensued, he was obliged to say to himself, "I am at my post, and my sovereign knows where to find me, so as to send me to my command at Metz if necessary; and I cannot and must not attempt to hasten to another field to which I have not yet been summoned, and thus risk crossing with useful orders which might be addressed to me here." He was able to, and did, say to himself, "In case a new revolution is threatened, they would not repeat the mistake they committed in 1815, when they neglected to send me my orders in time to that military post of incontestable importance; I am within twenty-five leagues of it, and they know that; let us not spoil anything as the result of an intemperate zeal which might lead me aside from the useful and lawful road in which I am at present. In any case," said the marshal to me, "you, my dear, who are in a special position, and particularly attached to the person of your princess: if circumstances become difficult for her, you will go to her at once."

I must remind you that at this time we were still reduced to the slow service of the ordinary post. We were not on the line of the aerial telegraphs, and communications underwent a delay of which you have no idea nowadays; and in spite of our eager impatience, which dated from the first news of the orders, we were necessarily between twenty-four and thirty-six hours behind events. At last the news of the 28th July, which did not reach us until the 29th or 30th, determined my personal departure. The marshal sent with me his first *aide-de-camp*, the Comte de Bourcet, and I started with the two-fold object of returning to my post at the moment of danger and of obtaining orders and directions for the marshal from the king.

The details which decided my departure were such that it was with extreme emotion that I left my husband and children behind me. . . . I knew not how far I should be able to travel, nor what I should find when I arrived. They were fighting in the streets of Paris, that was all that seemed to be certain. In this conviction, it was decided that if I could come within sight of the capital, in order to know whether it was possible to cross the barricades with which it was filled, I should first turn aside and go to Stains, which is two leagues on our side of it, and then go to my post, employing every possible chance of reaching it.

All the public services were suspended; there were no diligences on the road, which we travelled as fast as possible. At one place where we stopped, we heard that the population of Paris had triumphed over the army, and especially over the Royal Guard, and had loaded the guns with human bodies, including that of Marshal Marmont. . . . In spite of the horror of this information, in which I refused to believe, you will understand nevertheless that my impressions grew gloomier as we approached the capital. At Epernay we were asked for our passports. A company of National Guards, more than hostile and almost brutal, surrounded us with their bayonets. I had assumed one of my Christian names for the purpose of this passport, which had been given me at Bar. M. de Bourcet, who had cut off his *mustachios*, declared himself to be a merchant, and at last we were allowed to pass, after being looked upon with great suspicion.

At last we reached Stains, and I immediately despatched M. de Bourcet to Paris. We had learnt the worst of the events that had taken place. I had read Louis-Philippe's proclamation, which contained the following words: "The Charter will at last be a truth," &c. This document had followed upon the successive abdications of the king and *M. le Dauphin*, both of which were signed in favour of M. le Duc de Bordeaux, whose minority was entrusted to M. le Duc d'Orléans, appointed Regent of the Kingdom by Charles X. The prince's proclamation was silent as to this fact, and I learnt, moreover, that the whole Royal Family had been obliged to leave Saint-Cloud and to flee before the triumphant revolution.

Whither had it fled? How did the present stand? How the future? All this succession of events had been communicated to me in one breath during my stoppage at Stains by an old relation of M. Hainguerlot, who occupied the estate. Need I depict to you my anguish while waiting for fresh details? Every minute seemed a century, and yet everyone did all in his power to assist me.

General Pajol had at once assumed a prominent position in the provisional government, and his wife—your sister, my children—was the first person who came to see me. Laying aside the triumph of her opinion, which had been consistently opposed to the Restoration since the Hundred Days, she saw before her nothing but my personal lot, of which she understood all the duties and difficulties. Placing herself entirely at my disposal, she returned to Paris, at my request, to beg her husband to procure me, by means of his new powers, the means of joining the royal family, whose whereabouts were at that time still unknown. On the other hand arrived M. and Mme. de Vatry, with their pockets full of banknotes, which they placed at my disposition in case I was to set out at once for some unknown place of exile. The precautions I had taken saved me from the necessity of accepting their great kindness.

M. de Bourcet returned heart-broken and distraught at the things he had seen in Paris. Kind M. de Xaintrailles, another of my husband's *aides-de-camp,* had also hastened to offer me his services. I was filled with gratitude, but my fevered mind, wandering from your father to you, my children, and from you to the royal family, did not know where to find rest. Dear Mme. de Vatry herself served me with an improvised supper which she had cooked with her own hands in the kitchen. I threw myself for a few hours on my bed, and awoke on the morning of the 2nd of August more broken than ever, to await my news from Paris. Mme. Pajol returned with the reply of the provisional government, which was presided over by Marshal Gérard. It was to the effect that no human power could at that moment assure my safe journey through a popular rising which was that very day directing its steps from Paris to the Château de Rambouillet, where the king and his family had taken refuge.

In this extremity there was, I thought, but one step for me to take: to return to my husband, explain the situation to him, and take his orders before joining an emigration which was bound to be the result of recent events. Then, if he gave me liberty of action, I could place my children, who were still very young, in a place of safety, and as quickly as possible join in her exile the princess with whom I had lived when she was on the steps of the throne.

With this intention I addressed the following letter to Her Royal Highness:

Stains, 9 August 1830.

Madame,

At the first news of the terrible troubles in Paris, I set out to come and join you. I was able to come as far as here, whence I hoped to reach Saint-Cloud. Your Royal Highness had just left. ... No one is able to tell me exactly where you are. In my deep sorrow, not wishing to set foot in Paris, I am returning to the only spot of ground which belongs to me. If I there find my husband and my children, if God, whom I implore for them and for you, *Madame,* allows me to meet them again, I will await your orders in that spot, prepared at the first summons that reaches me from Your Royal Highness, to share your prison or your exile, if such is to be your lot.

Adieu, Madame. Believe that my torn heart is always faithful to you. I am, &c.

After writing this letter, I handed it to M. Morel, for whom I had sent to Stains; he faithfully carried out his instructions. I had left my letter open, and again through General Pajol's intermediary, I applied to the provisional government to protect my messenger, and assist him in reaching his destination with all possible speed; but General Pajol was unable to see to this in person, because he had placed himself at the head of the popular movement which was directed upon Rambouillet, with the object of hastening the royal family's departure from France. I have always believed that the intention both of General Pajol and of Colonel Jacqueminot, who accompanied him, was to restrain this populace which it was impossible to hold back, and to oppose with all their might any attempts which should go beyond threats. Nevertheless, it was a melancholy command for these two brilliant soldiers to hold.

They were joined at Rambouillet by commissaries of the so-called government of the moment, who preceded the mob and warned the king, who consented to admit them to his presence. It was Marshal Maison and M. Odilon Barrot in particular who acted as spokesmen. And dear it cost them!

The king could still have defended himself with the troops which had accompanied him so far, but his sorrow at the blood which had already been spilt, and the fear of causing still more to flow, decided him to take the road of exile at once. . . .

You know the rest. . . .

Nothing particular interfered with our return journey, although there was considerable traffic along the road. We observed in particular a number of men walking singly and dressed in blue blouses; almost all of these seemed to be new, and we soon guessed that they must be soldiers of the Guard which had been dissolved by the force of events and which was quickly disbanded. Thus it was for doing their duty that these brave troops were obliged to conceal their uniforms before Frenchmen and brothers!

Victor, who had obtained leave to go to the Pyrenees with his wife, hastened back to his command at Saumur, not to recognize the new government, because he sent in his resignation at once, but to keep order within the Cavalry School until he should be replaced.

I reached Jeand'heurs at the same time as Marshal Molitor, who had arrived from his seat to arrange with my husband as to what was to be done. I described all I had seen and heard, but I was not yet able to tell anything of what had happened at Rambouillet since I had left

Stains.

One important fact had at last become known to all: this was the conditional abdication, of which I have spoken above, of Charles X. in favour of the *Dauphin* his son, and of the latter in favour of the Duc de Bordeaux, placing the government in the hands of M. le Duc d'Orléans as regent during the minority of the child. This document was deposited in the State archives, and must be there still; but M. le Duc d'Orléans, while accepting the regency, kept silence as to the rest. The chambers were convoked, and the two marshals had no doubt but that the hereditary rights of M. le Duc de Bordeaux would be, if not recognized, at least discussed; and it was with this thought that they both left Jeand'heurs, on the 5th of August, to take their places in the House of Peers, and put the weight of their votes and opinions in the balance in favour of M. le Duc de Bordeaux.

I will not enter into the details which, to my husband's great grief, obliged him to recognize the only power which, in this alarming crisis, offered to save France from a stormy republic, with all its terrible consequences. He realized in the end that he owed the support of his person and of his lofty military position to his country. But though this decision satisfied his conscience, it grievously afflicted his heart. I on my side bent beneath the weight of so many emotions, and waited from hour to hour for the decision which Madame, Duchesse de Berry, would take with respect to myself. I had heard particulars of the departure from Rambouillet, and I knew that they were making for Normandy, and that M. Morel had been able to leave and follow the same road; but where would it lead the royal family and my messenger?

A long week was spent in this uncertainty, when at last arrived, not M. Morel in person, as I expected, but a letter from him, informing me that he had succeeded in joining Madame, Duchesse de Berry, in Calvados, and sending me Her Royal Highness's reply, of which this is a copy:

> Vire (Calvados), 11 August.
>
> I have received your note, dear duchesse, and it was like you to send it. As we do not know where we shall go after stopping at Cherbourg, I advise you to stay quietly at Jeand'heurs; so soon as I have arrived anywhere, I will write to you.
>
> I have sent M. Nichols to Paris to arrange my affairs and pay my debts, so that everyone may be satisfied under these circum-

stances. He will come to an arrangement with Sassenay, Morel, Cuchetet, Mme. de Noailles, as regards the different services and the money.

He has an unlimited power of attorney.

My children are well; I, sad at leaving this beautiful France, which I regarded as my country. Pray for us and make your children pray: I embrace them. As for yourself, believe that, in misfortune as in prosperity, you have no better friend than

C.

MM. de Mesnard and de Brissac, Mmes. de Bouillé and Charette send you their kind regards.

She told me to wait at Jeand'heurs and to stay there quietly; I naturally accepted the former recommendation; as to the latter, it did not lie with me to submit to it. The marshal's position in Paris, the general condition of the kingdom, the thoughts with which the august exiles inspired me, were not these enough to bring sadness to my days and sleeplessness to my nights? I waited, but not without renewing my instances to *Madame* to be allowed to rejoin her, when I knew she was settled in Edinburgh. She did not accept my offer, and our relations were suspended until the day when I heard she was imprisoned at Blaye.

The Revolution of 1830, like that of 1815, brought about a fresh change in my husband's position and fortune. The marshal had stayed in Paris, where all was in a ferment, with his son Auguste, who, deprived of his commission in the Hussars of the Guard, beheld, while in the flower of his age, his chances of promotion shattered for the second time. By an anomaly upon which history will pronounce its judgment, the Revolution of July, not content with deposing the king and his successors, acted with nameless inconsistency, and wished to penalize the ministers, who were always responsible, under a constitutional charter, for what it blamed the sovereign himself for.

But logically it must be one thing or the other, and so soon as the throne was upset, the responsibility of the ministry disappeared with it. And yet they were violently preparing to impeach that ministry. The marshal stayed in Paris with the intention of bringing the weight of his opinion and of his exertions to bear in favour of impartiality.

The exasperation of the public was directed mainly against the head of the late Cabinet, the Prince Jules de Polignac. If the latter had erred in judgment, he had sufficient heart to believe in its existence in others; and amidst the cries of death which threatened his head, he conceived the noble thought of confiding his defence to his principal antagonist, M. de Martignac, the head of the preceding Cabinet. His appeal did not fall upon deaf ears; and that noble heart, whose beats were numbered, knowingly, and at the risk of what remained of his life, accepted this great task. He never fell below the level of the situation, and the last accents of this ever powerful and persuasive voice left an eternal remembrance of the man M. de Martignac was. He did not survive his advocacy many months.

Thenceforward we spent the three winter months at Bar, the town to which I was so attached, while each spring found us once more at Jeand'heurs. The cholera which broke out in 1832 crushed our family by the death of my stepdaughter, the Comtesse Pajol, that exceptionally gifted creature, who was carried away in the prime of life. The pestilence committed ravages everywhere, and especially in Lorraine.

For some time I had been greatly agitated by the war in the Vendee attempted by Madame, Duchesse de Berry. I had followed her destinies with my heart; I knew that she had left the king and the royal family in Edinburgh to go to Italy, where she had spent almost the whole of the year 1831. I had for some time been ignorant of *Madame's* movements, when, in the spring of 1832, the news spread of her arrival in Provence, followed soon after by her march to the Vendee. I beheld a mother's devotion in this bold resolve, but I did not for a moment believe in its success.

I suffered agonies, therefore, during the period of this hazardous enterprise. My fears were vague, but they were realized in the early part of November, when we received, with all its heart-rending details, the news of Her Royal Highness's arrest, and heard that she had first been imprisoned in Nantes Castle, and next sent, by sea, to a citadel at Blaye!

Nantes! where two years before I had seen her, so to speak, carried shoulder high in triumph! Blaye! where in the same year she had been received with transports!

You can well imagine that my first movement was to demand the place in attendance on her, in her state prison, which I had formerly the right to occupy at the Tuileries. This is the letter which I at once wrote to the august prisoner:

Madame,

Since the news of your arrest, I have but one thought, that of sharing your captivity. I would have endeavoured to do so at once, had I not been told that, before all, Your Royal Highness's permission was necessary. I ask this from your old kindness for me.

I have the honour to be, &c.

Jeand'heurs, 11 November 1832.

To this letter, which I left unsealed, I added another. Relying upon the promise which Queen Marie Amélie, immediately after she was called to share her husband's throne, had made me declare to her, *to use her authority upon every occasion when I should stand in need of it*, I addressed the following letter to her:

Madame,

I come to beg of your kindness a favour upon which I set the highest value: it is that you will be so good as to read and cause to be conveyed to Madame, Duchesse de Berry, the enclosed letter; and if the offer which it contains is accepted, I shall also have to beg Your Majesty's assistance so that the gates of the prison may be opened to me.

If my request is bold, I implore you to forgive me; but, under the circumstances, I could think of nothing but to turn to Your Majesty, of whose kindness to me I am so well assured.

Persuaded as I am that no one will see any political intention in the step I am taking, I feel, from the confidence with which I am moved, that I shall not have reason to regret my impulse.

I have the honour to be, &c.

Jeand'heurs, 11 November 1832.

I enclosed both these letters to General Oudinot, and asked him to obtain an audience of the queen at once. This was immediately granted him, and he found her in tears.

"I was prepared," said she, "for this step on your stepmother's part, and I wish with all my heart that she may reach my niece. It does not depend wholly upon me; it must be brought before the Ministers in Council; but you can rely upon my wishes and my goodwill."

My letters were brought before the council and discussed. An express was sent to Blaye, and the following reply reached me, unsealed, by care of the President of the Council, Marshal Soult:

Château de Blaye, 23 November 1832.

You cannot doubt, my dear *duchesse*, how touched I was at receiving your letter, which was sent me enclosed in a very charming note from the Marquis Oudinot, whom I beg you to thank for me. I do not accept your offer; the sacrifice would be too great. I know how much your family needs your care, and I should never forgive myself for depriving them of it I shall be very glad to have news of you and yours.

Do not doubt, my dear *duchesse*, my gratitude and my friendship.

My health is not good, but I have courage and patience.

(Signed) Marie-Caroline.

M. de Mesnard begs to be remembered to you."

To this I replied as follows:

Bar-le-Duc, 1 December 1832.

On reading your generous refusal, inspired by my family feeling and duties, I thought that I ought to have the honour to renew my application, assuring you, *Madame*, that I should consider nothing too much to surround you with the care which my duty and my respect command me; for it is especially in a circumstance of this kind that it behoves me to give you a proof of the attachment with which your former kindness has inspired me."

The above words, my children, are copied from the draft in your father's handwriting; I made so little alteration in the sense of his words that I prefer to give his text rather than mine. But meanwhile the marshal was suddenly seized with an illness so serious that it made us dread cholera, which was still so near us! General Oudinot, his wife and his son arrived at once; prompt care delivered us from our mortal fears, and we arrived at Bar, so as, in this bad season of the year, to be more within reach of assistance. It was only from there that, on the 14th of December, I despatched my second letter to Madame, Duchesse de Berry, enclosing it to Marshal Soult, with the following lines:

Monsieur le maréchal,

My husband's serious and painful illness has taken up all my thought and time, and has prevented me until today from sending my reply to the letter of Madame, Duchesse de Berry. I am now easier in my mind, and my first care, *Monsieur le maréchal*, is once more to beg you to be so good as to forward my renewed application to Blaye.

If in the first instance I applied to the queen, this was not to deny your competency, *Monsieur la maréchal*, but so as to have a powerful chance of success the more; I knew that this affair would subsequently follow its usual course and fall beneath your influence, which I was far from doubting.

General Oudinot has not failed to tell me of your kind disposition towards me. The reason I am not confiding this letter to him to deliver to you is that he is detained here on account of his father's health.

Here is the marshal's reply:

Paris, 20 December 1832.

Madame la maréchale,

I learnt with much regret from the letter which you did me the honour to write to me on the 14th of this month that M. le Maréchal Duc de Reggio was ill and in great pain; but I have since heard the good news of his recovery to health. I beg you to assure him of my sympathy.

Your letter enclosed one for Madame, Duchesse de Berry. I have the honour to inform you that I have forwarded it to M. le Colonel Chousserie, principal governor of the Citadel of Blaye, who will deliver it.

Accept, *Madame la maréchale*, &c,

(Signed) Marshal Duc de Dalmatie.

I received no answer to my letter of the 1st of December, and it was a great shock to me when in the course of the winter of 1832 to 1833 I read, in the *Moniteur*, an official declaration of Madame, Duchesse de Berry, dated from Blaye, and announcing that Her, Royal Highness had contracted a second marriage during her stay in Italy in 1831. It was not until later that the princess declared that she had married Count di Lucchesi-Palli, whose name had not appeared in her first announcement. She doubtless had political motives for suppressing this name which she alone was able to appreciate; but all her friends regretted this omission, which was not easily explained in the eyes of the public. The authentic proofs of this union are incontestable; but *Madame* did not think fit to supply them until later.

The first child born of this second marriage was a daughter. It was born at Blaye, a short while before the liberation of Her Royal Highness, who took ship with the child. Count di Lucchesi had come to meet his wife. They sailed to Italy, and it was long before we heard any details concerning the new mode of life which her Royal Highness had adopted. We only knew that she had been very fraternally received by King Ferdinand, her brother.

After all these events, I secluded myself more than ever in my life at Jeand'heurs. We come to June 1835. Auguste's letters, more and more exciting and more and more honourable in all that concerned his difficult duties as chief of a corps, kept us in a feverish alternation, when suddenly he announced to us, as a sort of deliverance for him, that he was at last about to march against Abd-el-Kader, who was defying the French army in the province of Oran.

> General Trézel, (said Auguste in his letter), takes an enormous responsibility upon himself in attacking the *emir* under our present conditions; but as that question is not for me to decide, I only know one thing, and that is that we are at last going to fight the enemy.

Here, my children, it needs all my courage to relate a catastrophe which rent all our hearts. So acute were the young colonel's presentiments on the eve of his departure for this campaign, that he made his will. Alas, he was but too right in what he foresaw; and the ill-calculated engagement would have become disastrous for our arms, if Auguste's regiment (the 2nd Chasseurs d'Afrique), which formed the advance-guard, had not thrown itself into the post of danger.

"Forwards!" cried the colonel. "For the honour of the regiment! Forwards!"

He was the first, and the first to fall, struck with a bullet in the forehead.

Your father was kept in Paris by the sittings of the House. His heart was pierced through and through. There are certain feelings that cannot be expressed. One day, when we were having a low mass said in the chapel of Jeand'heurs for this brave soul, the marshal's sobs revealed his presence at this ceremony, of which we had not told him, so as to spare his sorrow. Soon there arrived from Africa Auguste's trunks, with his bloodstained arms. What a life was ours at Jeand'heurs after this misfortune! What a terrible loss, this young man, with his brilliant future, who had always been the glory and the charm of his family!

In August 1837 my daughter Louise was asked in marriage by

the young Comte Ludovic de Vesins. His name had appealed to me from the beginning because it had been borne by a friend of my father's, who had been imprisoned with him under the Revolution; and he himself was endowed with every gift. First introduced to us by the Comte de Courchamp, he one morning announced to us the approaching arrival of his father, whom all of you, my children and grandchildren, have known and honoured. The worthy and saintly Abbé de Vesins had married Mlle, de Faramond when only twenty years of age, and had been left a widower with five children. He had embraced the ecclesiastical state eighteen months before he was called upon to bless the union of his eldest son with my daughter. The nuptial ceremony was celebrated at Jeand'heurs on the 4th of October.

Shortly afterwards, the marshal, called to the House of Peers, went to Paris, after installing us at Bar-le-Duc for the winter. But *man proposes and God disposes.* Faithful to an old remembrance of which he made a duty, your father attended an anniversary service which was celebrated for Queen Hortense. The cold was severe, and your father brought back a serious illness from church. At first the grave nature of the attack was concealed from me; but General Oudinot, with his kind friendliness, revealed the truth to me. I called for my post-horses, and for the first time for seven years found myself upon the road to Paris, which I was now about to enter under such sorrowful circumstances. I travelled with Caroline; the young Vesins couple followed in their own carriage; they stayed with the Marquis and Marquise Oudinot in the Rue de Bourgogne, where they were expected, while I joined my husband at the Hôtel de Bruxelles in the Rue Richelieu.

I found him much more changed than I expected; and in fact he had suffered much more than either he or others had admitted to me.

The marshal told me that he had received exceptional proofs of sympathy in this circumstance; and in particular a letter from Prince Louis-Napoleon, of which the following is a copy:

Gottlieb (I think), 14th February 1838.

Marshal,

I had charged Mme. Salvage to thank you on my behalf for your kindness in taking part in the last honours shown to my mother: I did not wish myself to trouble you with my thanks; but as I have just learnt that soon after the funeral ceremony in the Rue de Rueil you were taken ill, I hasten to express to you my regret. Men who, like yourself, have contributed to shed lustre upon the Empire, are always sure of exciting in me a vivid sympathy; and it is therefore with feelings of gratitude and of real interest that I write to you today to express my wishes for your prompt recovery.

Receive, *Monsieur le marshal,* the assurance of my high esteem and of my distinguished sentiments.

(Signed) Napoleon Louis.

On the other side, the reigning family displayed a pressing solicitude throughout the marshal's illness.

To return to the recent past, I have always thought that the Duc d'Orléans saw the dangers multiply around the Elder Branch with the feeling that, there being no possibility of averting them, his own dynasty would doubtless one day profit by them. I have not a word to say in justification of this point of view. I say that when he was appointed Regent of the Kingdom by Charles X., he should have done everything in his power to protect the royal orphan; and I will go further and say that even the impossibility which he foresaw of this reign ever taking place should not have stopped him, and that in principle he was bound to fulfil his trust.

When I found your father, who was then seventy-one years of age, ill and alone in an hotel, I took the firm resolve to leave him thenceforward as seldom as possible, and this great anxiety on my part kept me in Paris and brought me back whenever the marshal returned there himself, whatever the effort might cost me.

My husband was ordered to take the waters at Bourbonne, and the season we spent there did something to divert our sadness. On his return the marshal was able to resume his habits of activity. A second season was ordered.

About this time, my eldest son had entered as a sub-lieutenant in the 16th Light Horse. Like his father, he was first garrisoned at Perpignan, and it was touching, when he obtained his first leave, to hear the father questioning the son about the situation of places which the lapse of half a century had not effaced from his memory.

Charles was next sent to Clermont-Ferrand, where a serious riot had broken out, against which the regiment was obliged to take up arms. After doing his duty and firing on a French population, my son was so affected by this that he came to beseech his father to allow him to change into Africa.

"In my time," the marshal said, at first, "one remained with one's corps."

"In your time," replied the young man, "there was fighting to be done everywhere. Now, there is no fighting except in Africa."

The marshal smiled, made no further opposition, and Charles entered the *Zouaves*. Brave lad, what a reputation he acquired amongst his comrades! They nicknamed him "*Brave de nuit!*"

It was after my Vesins children had come to live with us that Caroline's marriage was arranged with the excellent and loyal Joseph Perron, whose father had achieved a glorious career in the Indies. We confidently entrusted the fate of our angelic child to this worthy man, who had no other fault than that he refused to allow one to recognise the qualities with which he was endowed.

To the advantages of his personal alliance was joined that of the alliance of all his sisters with the noblest names in France, the Montesquieus, the La Rochefoucaulds, the Nansoutys, and so on, families with which my husband and I were already on an excellent footing. The marriage was performed with every Parisian pomp and circumstance in the rooms of the palace of the Legion of Honour, of which the marshal had just been appointed Grand Chancellor, and the religious ceremony was celebrated in the chapel of the House of Peers by Mgr. de Vesins, [1] who had come up from Agen to pronounce the nuptial benediction.

In September 1845, the marshal agreed to exchange his post as Grand Chancellor of the Legion of Honour for that of Governor of the Invalides. He had always preferred this post to any other as a finish to his career. It was well suited to him, I agree. But I, alas, beheld in it the last stage. . . .

Enriched with a fine little boy, who was born at the Hôtel des Invalides to the sound of cannon, my Vesins children returned to the south. From that moment the marshal's health began to cause me great anxiety; and this continued during the whole course of 1845 and 1846. I recalled my children from the south. They arrived in February 1847. We set out for Jeand'heurs, where we were all united. But no more ease or happiness!

The summer was spent in an indescribable agony; a fixed idea drove the marshal towards the Invalides. He did not wish to delay, he said, in returning to his post. It was there that he received the last suc-

1 The Abbé de Vesins had been raised to the See of Agen.—A. T. de M.

cours of religion. . . .

Here my narrative must cease. God has given me the strength to live after my husband's death, but He has refused me the will to describe it.

Chapter 11
Conclusion

Oudinot's last cares, consecrated to the army to which he had belonged for sixty years, were devoted to the organizing of a review; but he had scarcely had the leisure to contemplate under arms those brave warriors, who had followed him under the tricolour into the deepest recesses of Europe, and whose hair was now whitening around that of their old leader.

His body, carved with scars, from which his country had been able to draw, as from a generous reservoir, an extraordinary sum total of services, was kept up wholly by a soul of iron, which on one battle evening had depicted itself in a typical phrase, a real appropriate epigraph for this soldier's life.

The emperor congratulated the marshal upon his courage, and added:

"And yet there always comes a moment when the bravest man is afraid for at least once in his life."

"Sire," replied Oudinot, "I have never had time for that."

Years slowly accomplished what the bullets had been unable to do. On the 13th of September, the veteran breathed his last, in his eighty-first year, fortified with all the rites of religion.

The joy was refused him of seeing all his family united by his bedside to embrace him: he had given his four sons to France. The three survivors and his grandson[1] were at that time in Algeria. They came home for the funeral, which took place with great state on the 5th of October in the church of Saint-Louis des Invalides, beneath the shadow of the enemy's flags which seemed gathered there to do

1. Charles Oudinot, afterwards Duc de Reggio. He married Mlle, de Castelbajac, daughter of General Marquis de Castelbajac and of Mlle, de La Rochefoucauld, and became the father of the present head of the family.

honour to his grave.

Thus, in this year 1847, three of the marshal's children were at the same time facing the enemy. One can judge from this, and still better from the biographical notes published below,[2] of the energy displayed time after time until our own day by the members of the Oudinot family, which has sacrificed to the country two lives cut down in the flower of youth. If the traditions of courage and devotion, which are common, for that matter, among the descendants of several soldiers of the Revolution and the Empire, have been implanted with especial strength in the breast of the house in which we are interested, it is not only the memory of the marshal which has caused them to take such deep and manifold root. The amiable and graceful companion who illumined with her somewhat grave smile the second half of Oudinot's life has much to do with the budding of these determined characters.

To men who number among their near ones an eager, decided woman, prompt and bold in resolution as was the Duchesse de Reggio, timidity is an impossible thing. She offered a fine example, this young bride of twenty, who, upon the receipt of alarming news, left the kindness of her family and the comfort of her home to fly to the aid of her wounded dear one, and to snatch him from death by facing an endless journey through the heart of a country ravaged by war, and this in spite of the fatigue, in spite of the cold, in spite of the danger of falling into the hands of the Cossacks in the desolation of those vast snowy steppes. Noble conduct, a proof at once of a loving and virile heart!

The snowflakes gathered under that distant sky had left as it were a halo around the duchess's head. Later when, at the commencement of the Restoration, she entered, brilliant and adorned, into some drawing-room or other, cannot you hear the murmur rising behind her footsteps and the words whispered of "That is she! that is the young married woman who took part in the retreat from Russia!" and all heads bent forward to see her? She thus enjoyed a little triumph which had been bought at such great cost, and she fully felt the strange delight which sometimes makes us relish the memory of our cruellest trials.

This lustre apparently contributed, together with the duchess's personal charm, the distinction of her birth and the renown of the name she bore, to attract the attention of the new powers when these

2. *Vide* Appendix 3.

strove to draw towards themselves the notabilities of the preceding government. Appointed to a lofty post, she performed its delicate functions with tact. Her supple mind adroitly unravelled the complicated threads of frequently difficult situations; she moved among the personages at court without hurting any susceptibilities; and she was cleverly able to preserve an attitude full of respect both for the independent tendencies of her husband and for the absolute ideas of the sovereigns to whom she had attached herself both from sentiment and obligation.

Then, when political events and a long widowhood gave her leisure, she studiously occupied it in retracing for her children the different phases of her chequered existence. The book into which this grew, almost without her knowing it, is written in an easy, natural, unpretentious style. It bears witness to an open intelligence, a well-balanced judgment, together with a kind heart and one full of pity for human suffering. In spite of its generally restrained tone, emotion makes its way through and spreads over the more pathetic passages, such as the retreat from Moscow and the death of the Duc de Berry.

Surprise will be great at not finding these souvenirs seasoned with the satirical remarks against one's neighbour which form the ordinary relish of this class of work. Was it that the eccentricities, the absurdities and the weaknesses of men escaped the penetration of the Duchesse de Reggio; and are we to believe that so many people can have passed for so long a period before her eyes without her raising their mask and discerning the hidden sides of their nature? Surely no; but at the risk of having it believed that her perspicacity was not always aroused, she would never consent to reveal secrets which did not belong to her, and she expressed herself concerning others with great reserve. Who knows whether this scrupulous discretion did not constitute her principal merit at court and the secret of her success? Lovers of scandal, close this book! Its charm is not that of malice.

This happy disposition for benevolence was repeated in the *salon* which the Duchesse de Reggio held at Bar-le-Duc during the latter years of her life: an original and unique *salon*, to which our hostesses have not shown themselves very anxious to provide a counterpart: there was no scandal talked there! The visitors were none the less entertained. The attraction came from the gracious and simple lady who offered to all a cordial welcome, without distinction of political parties; who put everyone at his ease; who knew so much and told so well, without spitefulness; who had preserved the elegant manners of the eighteenth century; and the time spent in whose company was a lesson in urbanity.

She thus led a peaceful existence in the religious practices which she had cherished all her life, in the midst of a district filled with the glory of the name of which she was so proud. The poor worshipped her, and when, in the month of May 1868, she, who had been known far around for her charity and her sympathy, gently breathed her last, all mourned "the good duchess."

Appendix

1

SERVICES:

of M. Oudinot, Nicholas Charles, Duc de Reggio, born 25 April 1767, at Bar-sur-Ornain, Department of the Meuse, son of Nicolas Oudinot and Marie Anne Adam, married, first, 15 September 1789, to Mdlle. Charlotte Derlin, and secondly, 19 January 1812, to Mdlle. Marie Charlotte Eugénie Julienne de Coucy.

Location of services and in what capacity employed.	Rank.	Date of Nomination.	Length of actual service.		
			Years.	Months.	Days.
Médoc Regiment (infantry)	Private	2 June 1784 to May 1787[1]	2	11	
3rd Battalion of the Meuse	2nd Lieut.-Colonel	6 September 1791	2	2	
4th Demi-Brigade (formerly Regiment de Picardie)	Colonel, with field rank of Brigadier	5 November 1793		7	9
Nominated by the Representatives attached to the Armies of the Rhine and Moselle	General of Brigade	14 June 1794	1		
The appointment officially ratified	,,	13 June 1795	3	10	
Employed with the Army of the Danube	General of Division	12 April 1799		7	26
With the Army of Italy	,,	8 December 1799	1	7	16
Inspector-General of Infantry	,,	24 July 1801		4	24
Inspector-General of Cavalry	,,	18 December 1801	1	8	12
In command of 1st Division at the Camp of Bruges	,,	30 August 1803	1	5	5
Commander-in-Chief of the Grenadiers of the Reserve	,,	5 February 1805	2	10	
Entrusted with the chief command at Danzig	,,	December 1807	1	3	

[1] A break occurs here of four years and four months.

Location of services and in what capacity employed.	Rank.	Date of Nomination.	Length of actual service.		
			Years.	Months.	Days.
Commander-in-Chief of the 2nd Corps of the Army of Germany	General of D v sion.	March 1809		4	7
	Marshal of the Empire	12 July 1809		11	23
Commander-in-Chief of the Army of the North (Holland)	,,	5 January 1810	1	6	4
Commander-in-Chief of the 2nd Corps of Observation on the Elbe	,,	9 January 1812		2	
Commander-in-Chief of the 2nd Corps of the Grande Armée	,,	March 1812	1	2	21
Commander-in-Chief of the 12th Corps of the Grande Armée	,,	31 May 1813		8	8
Commander-in-Chief of the 7th Corps of the Grande Armée	,,	8 February 1814		3	12
Commander-in-Chief of the Royal Corps of the Grenadier and Chasseurs of France (formerly the Imperial Guard)	Marshal of France	20 May 1814		1	1
Governor of the 3rd Military Division	,,	21 June 1814	1	2	17
Major-General of the Royal Guard	,,	8 September 1815		1	
Commander-in-Chief of the National Guard of the Department of the Seine	,,	October 1815		3	2
Reappointed Governor of 3rd Military Division	,,	10 January 1816		11	13
Inspector-General of the National Guard of the Department of the Seine	,,	23 December 1816	6	1	19
Commander-in-Chief of the 1st Corps of the Army of the Pyrenees	,,	12 February 1823	7	6	
Out of employment because of disbandment of Royal Guard	,,	11 August 1830	8	9	6
Grand Chancellor of the Legion of Honour	,,	17 May 1839	3	5	4
Governor of the Hôtel des Invalides	,,	21 October 1842	4	10	23
Died in Paris	,,	13 September 1847			
			58	11	12

Extracts from various despatches of the Grande Armée

Campaign of Austerlitz.

Combat of Wertingen. 3rd Despatch, 18 Vendémiaire Year XIV(10 October 1805).—The emperor referring to the grenadiers of Oudinot's division: "It is impossible to see a finer body of men, more anxious to measure themselves with the enemy, more full of honour and of that military ardour which promises the greatest results."

23rd Despatch, 23 Brumaire Year XIV (14 November 1805).—The emperor also expresses his satisfaction with the grenadiers of Oudinot, who, during the fight at Austerlitz, repulsed from strong and difficult ground the Russo-Austrian troops, with a loss of 1500 prisoners, including 600 Russians.

30th Bulletin, Battle of Austerlitz, 2 December 1805.—The emperor and his entire staff formed the reserve with the ten battalions of the Guard and General Oudinot's ten grenadier battalions. With this reserve the emperor was prepared to rush wherever there was need; one may call such a reserve worth an army.

Campaign of Friedland.

24th Despatch, 21 February 1807.—At Ostrolenka, the dauntless General Oudinot commanded the left on two lines; at the head of his cavalry he charged successfully home, and cut to bits the enemy's rear-guard.

30th Despatch, 16 May 1807.—From the crumbling ramparts of Dantzig the enemy had watched the whole affair. With consternation he saw all hope of rescue fade away. General Oudinot with his own hand slew three Russians.

79th Despatch, 17 June 1807, Battle of Friedland.—Friedland was stormed and its streets strewn with corpses. The centre at this moment joined action: the attempt on the extreme right of the French army having failed, the enemy essayed such another effort towards the centre. It was received, as might have been expected, by the brave divisions of Oudinot and Verdier.

Campaign of Wagram.

30th Despatch, 30 July 1809, Battle of Wagram.—The village of Wagram was taken on the 6th, between ten and eleven in the forenoon, and the glory belongs entirely to Marshal Oudinot and his

Corps.

5th Despatch, 4 May 1809.—On the 1st May, General Oudinot made 1500 prisoners during the action at Ried.

10th Despatch, 23 May 1809.—The emperor has given the command of the 2nd Corps to the Comte Oudinot, a general tried in a hundred combats, wherein he shewed that his daring equalled his knowledge.

Campaign of Russia.

24 November 1812, the Duc de Reggio encountered Lambert's Division at four leagues from Borisow, attacked it, beat it, made 2000 prisoners, took six guns, 500 baggage-waggons of the army of Volhynie, and forced the enemy back upon the right of the Beresina.

Details of the Campaigns

Years	Campaigns
1792 1793 Year II. „ III. „ IV. „ V. „ VI. „ VII. „ VIII. „ IX.	Armies of the Moselle, the Rhine, England, and Italy.
„ XII. „ XIII.	In Camp at Bruges.
Year XIV. 1806 1807 1808	Grande Armée.
1809	Germany.
1810	Army of the North (Holland).
1812 1813 1814	Grande Armée.
1823	Army of the Pyrenees.

Wounds and Deeds of Gallantry

Received a shot in the head in the affair at Hagenau, *Frimaire* Year II.

Had a leg broken at Trèves, where he was in command, *Thermidor* Year II (August 1794).

Wounded by five sabre strokes in a night attack at Neckerau, *Vendémiaire* Year III (October 1795).

Wounded by a ball in the thigh, three sabre strokes on the arms and one on the neck, at the affair of Neuborg, *Fructidor* Year IV (1796).

Wounded by a ball in the breast at the affair of Wurenlos, at the left of the intrenched camp at Zurich, 16 *Prairial* Year VII (1799).

Wounded by a ball in the shoulder-blade at the affair of Schwitz, 27 *Thermidor* Year VII (14 August 1799).

Sword of honour and cannon given by Bonaparte, First Consul, after the Battle of Monzembemo, in December 1800 (the cannon had been taken from the Austrians by General Oudinot).

Had a ball through his thigh at the Battle of Hollabrünn, 16 November 1805.

Wounded by a ball in the left arm at the Battle of Essling in 1809.

Wounded in the head at the Battle of Wagram in 1809.

Wounded by grape-shot during the fight at Polotsk, 17 August 1812.

Wounded by a ball in the side at the Beresina, November 1812.

Wounded by a ball in the breast at the combat of Arcis-sur-Aube, 21 March 1814.

Titles and Dignities

Member of the Corps Législatif, representing the Department of the Meuse, 8 *Frimaire,* Year XII (1804).

Burgess of Neuchâtel, 1806.

Count of the Empire, 25 July 1808.

Duc de Reggio, 15 August 1809.

Minister of State and Peer of France, 1 May 1814.

French Decorations

Knight of the Legion of Honour, 11 December 1803.

Grand Officer, 14 June 1804.

Grand Cross, 6 March 1805.

Knight of St. Louis, 1 June 1814.

Commander, 24 September 1814.

Grand Cross, 3 May 18 16.

Knight of the Order of the Holy Ghost, 1820.

Foreign Decorations

Italy.—Knight of the Order of the Iron Crown, 1805.

Saxony.—Commander of the Military Order of St. Henry.

Bavaria.—Grand Cross of the Military Order of Max-Joseph, 25 June 1813.

Netherlands.—Grand Cross of the Military Order of William, May 1815.

Prussia.—Grand Cross of the Orders of the Red Eagle and the Black Eagle, 1817.

Russia.—Knight of the First Class, Grand Cross of the Order of Saint Vladimir, 25 February 1824.

Spain.—Grand Cordon of the Spanish Order of Charles III., 27 May 1824.

2

Letters of Condolence

From the President of the Council and from Reigning Sovereigns

Oudinot's memory was honoured not only by France, but also by the sovereigns of the foreign nations which he had administered or combated. These either rendered homage to an unexpected benefactor, or bowed respectfully, as in the days of chivalry, before the mortal remains of a loyal adversary. The family of the deceased received a large number of letters of condolence.

Letter From M. Guizot,

President of the Council of Ministers.

Madame la maréchale,

I must express to you my regret at not having been able to be present this morning at your illustrious husband's funeral.

I was absolutely obliged to go to Saint-Cloud to wait upon the king, who arrived yesterday. I should have taken a sad pleasure in showing honour to the memory of a man of such glorious and upright character; and I should be happy if I could find some occasion of proving to you, *Madame la maréchale*, the respect with which I have the honour to be

Your very humble and obedient servant,

(Signed) Guizot.

Tuesday, 5 October 1847.

The following letters are addressed to General Victor Oudinot:

Letter From Charles Albert King of Sardinia

Monsieur le marquis,

You did justice to my feelings when you thought that I should take a very sympathetic interest in the sad loss of Marshal the Duc de Reggio. It would be impossible for me to bear him more affection, more gratitude, or to admire him more than I did. I join our profound regrets to yours, *monsieur le général,* and I heartily wish that circumstances may bring you to Turin and enable me to assure you better than in writing of all my friendship.

(Signed) Charles Albert.

Turin, 10 October 1847.

Letter from William King of the Netherlands

Monsieur le marquis,

I have received the letter, dated 28 September last, in which you inform me of the death of your noble and honoured father, Marshal Oudinot, Duc de Reggio.

In thanking you for this communication I am pleased to do justice to the military talents and the personal valour of the deceased, and to join my voice to the chorus which proclaims his noble qualities. I hope that this appreciation will contribute to calm the regrets which this death occasions you, and that it will give you the assurance of the distinguished sentiments with which I am, *monsieur le marquis*,

Your affectionate

(Signed) William.

The Hague, 18 October 1847.

LETTER FROM LOUIS KING OF BAVARIA

Monsieur le marquis, Lieutenant-General Oudinot,

I have received the letter which you were so good as to write to me on the 28th of September to inform me of the decease of Marshal the Duc de Reggio, your father. You will have no doubt, monsieur le general, of the feelings with which I share the loss which you have just experienced. This loss meets with no less sympathy in the Bavarian army, which has so often fought under the marshal's orders; and I have always preserved the recollection of the feelings of personal esteem which the late king my father had devoted to him, and of which he had given him proofs.

I was therefore touched by the attention of your letter, which gives me at the same time the opportunity of assuring you, *monsieur le marquis*, of the sentiments of esteem with which I am

Your affectionate

(Signed) Louis.

Munich, 18 October 1847.

LETTER FROM FREDERIC WILLIAM KING OF PRUSSIA

Monsieur le Duc,

I have always borne a sincere attachment for Marshal the Duc de Reggio, your father; and the news of his death, which you announced to me in your letter of the 28th of last month, afflicted me sadly. The interest which I took in all that concerns him does not cease with his death, but passes to his family. I sympathize deeply with you, *monsieur*, in the loss you have sustained. Your late father succeeded in winning the general esteem in this country under most critical circumstances, and in a time of unexampled irritation against the sovereign whom he then served. This, in my opinion, is one of his finest titles to glory, and one which does most honour to his memory. The marshal's conduct at Berlin, as you know, was never forgotten by the late king my father, and I have inherited his sentiments.

Preserving these memories in my heart, I beg you to accept my sincere regrets, together with the renewed assurance of my perfect esteem and of my good will. With which I pray God, *monsieur le duc,* to have you in His holy and worthy keeping.

Your affectionate

(Signed) Frederic William.

Sans-Souci, 30 October 1847.

Letter from Nicholas Czar of Russia

I have received, general, the letter which you addressed to me to inform me of the death of the venerable Marshal Oudinot, your father. The loss of a man whose name stood out among the first in an epoch so fertile in great captains must needs be strongly felt by all those who render homage to talent and to military glory. This is the impression which, on this account, it was bound to produce on me. The marshal's fine actions and loyal character had earned for him, at the time, the esteem and affection of my late brother, the Emperor Alexander; and I know that the marks of honour which he received from him had always left a grateful remembrance in his heart.

This is for me a reason the more to regret him and to sympathize with the affliction which his death causes to his country and his family. I therefore greatly appreciate your attention in informing me of this event. I regard it as a proof that you consider the sentiments which your father bore to my brother and myself to form part of your inheritance. This persuasion causes me doubly to regret not having been able some time ago, as I hoped, to make your personal acquaintance; and I am pleased to take this opportunity of telling you so, while assuring you here of my sincere esteem.

(Signed) Nicholas.

St Petersburg, 18 October 1847.

3

The Soldiers

In the Oudinot Family.

The military tradition inaugurated by Oudinot was preserved in his family; his descendants have formed a numerous sequence of officers.

The reader has seen above in the *Souvenirs of the Duchesse de Reggio,* details on Victor and Auguste Oudinot, the marshal's two sons by his first wife.

Victor Oudinot (1791 + 1863) took part in the campaigns of Wagram, Spain, Portugal, Russia, Leipzig, France, Algeria (1835)—it was in this year that he obtained the rank of lieutenant-general—and finally of Italy (1849), where he commanded in chief. He made a very energetic protest against the *coup d'état* of the 2 *Decembre.*

After the Roman expedition, General Victor Oudinot received from the Comte de Chambord the following letter:

LETTER FROM THE COMTE DE CHAMBORD

To the Duc de Reggio.

Cousin, [1]

As a Frenchman, as the eldest son of the church, I could not fail to show my appreciation of the great feat of arms which you have just accomplished. Rome restored to its legitimate sovereign, the city of the Apostles brought back to its obedience to him who has inherited their divine mission: these are illustrious recollections which will always remain attached to French arms. I experienced a keen feeling of joy on beholding our soldiers add this fresh glory to so many other glories which are the patrimony of us all; I am no less happy to think that it is you who have fulfilled this fair and lofty mission, that it is to you that the honour belongs and the gratitude is due. Your sword has shown itself worthy of your noble father, the warrior of Zurich, Friedland and Wagram. Although the gates of my country are still closed to me, and my position deprives me of the happiness of distributing justly acquired national rewards to valour and to services rendered, I nevertheless feel the need of giving you here the proof of my personal satisfaction, which I know that you value.

I renew, cousin, the assurance of all my esteem and of my sincere and constant affection.

(Signed) Henry.

15 September 1849.

It will be remembered that Auguste Oudinot, the marshal's second son, died a glorious death in Algeria, at the Battle of la Macta (1835).

Two daughters of the marshal's first marriage married, one General Comte Pajol, the other General Comte de Lorencez, who both served

1. All French dukes are addressed by the king as cousin.—A. T. de M.

during the wars of the Republic and the Empire.

Pajol (1772 + 1844), one of the most brilliant cavalry officers of his time, distinguished himself particularly at Hohenlinden, at Eckmühl, in Russia, at Leipzig, at Montereau, and during the Waterloo campaign. Lorencez (1772 + 1827) took part in the Battle of Wagram and in the Peninsula, and was so grievously wounded at Bautzen that he was never afterwards able to mount his horse.

By his marriage with Eugénie de Coucy, the marshal had two sons, Colonel Charles Oudinot (10 March 1819 + 10 December 1858), who has already been mentioned, and General Henry Oudinot (3 February 1822 + 28 July 1891), who took a brilliant part in the principal campaigns of our time. Both of them distinguished themselves in 1849 under the orders of their elder brother, General Oudinot, Duc de Reggio, commander-in-chief of the expedition which resulted in the Restoration of the Holy See.

The military spirit perpetuated itself down to Marshal Oudinot's grandchildren. Two of General Pajol's sons were, the first, Charles Pajol (7 August 1812 + April 1891), a general of division; the second, Eugène Pajol (13 November 1817 + 18 April 1885), a general of brigade.

General de Lorencez left a son, Charles Ferdinand (23 May 1814 +23 April 1892), who became a general of division. It was he who, in 1862, ventured intrepidly with a handful of men into the heart of Mexico and directed the first attack against Puebla.

Lieutenant Antoine de Levezou de Vesins, grandson of Marshal Oudinot and Eugénie de Coucy, was killed at the Battle of Gravelotte on the 16th of August 1870. Although seriously wounded, he refused to leave the battlefield, and wished to spend his last strength in fighting for his country. A second wound struck him mortally; he then had himself turned so as to expire with his face to the enemy. He was hardly twenty-five years of age.

ALSO FROM LEONAUR

AVAILABLE IN SOFTCOVER OR HARDCOVER WITH DUST JACKET

IRON TIMES WITH THE GUARDS *by An O. E. (G. P. A. Fildes)*—The Experiences of an Officer of the Coldstream Guards on the Western Front During the First World War.

THE GREAT WAR IN THE MIDDLE EAST: 1 *by W. T. Massey*—The Desert Campaigns & How Jerusalem Was Won---two classic accounts in one volume.

THE GREAT WAR IN THE MIDDLE EAST: 2 *by W. T. Massey*—Allenby's Final Triumph.

SMITH-DORRIEN *by Horace Smith-Dorrien*—Isandlwhana to the Great War.

1914 *by Sir John French*—The Early Campaigns of the Great War by the British Commander.

CAVALRY AT WATERLOO *by Sir Evelyn Wood*—British Mounted Troops During the Campaign of 1815.

THE SUBALTERN *by George Robert Gleig*—The Experiences of an Officer of the 85th Light Infantry During the Peninsular War.

DIGGERS AT WAR *by R. Hugh Knyvett & G. P. Cuttriss*—"Over There" With the Australians by R. Hugh Knyvett and Over the Top With the Third Australian Division by G. P. Cuttriss. Accounts of Australians During the Great War in the Middle East, at Gallipoli and on the Western Front.

THE LIGHT INFANTRY OFFICER *by John H. Cooke*—The Experiences of an Officer of the 43rd Light Infantry in America During the War of 1812.

THE CAMELIERS *by Oliver Hogue*—A Classic Account of the Australians of the Imperial Camel Corps During the First World War in the Middle East.

RED DUST *by Donald Black*—A Classic Account of Australian Light Horsemen in Palestine During the First World War.

NAPOLEON AT BAY, 1814 *by F. Loraine Petre*—The Campaigns to the Fall of the First Empire.

NAPOLEON AND THE CAMPAIGN OF 1806 *by Colonel Vachée*—The Napoleonic Method of Organisation and Command to the Battles of Jena & Auerstädt.

THE COMPLETE ADVENTURES IN THE CONNAUGHT RANGERS *by William Grattan*—The 88th Regiment during the Napoleonic Wars by a Serving Officer.

AVAILABLE ONLINE AT **www.leonaur.com**
AND FROM ALL GOOD BOOK STORES

07/09

www.ingramcontent.com/pod-product-compliance
Lightning Source LLC
LaVergne TN
LVHW091640100826
845152LV00006B/103/J

* 9 7 8 0 8 5 7 0 6 6 9 1 6 *